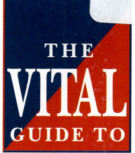

THE VITAL GUIDE TO

MILITARY AIRCRAFT

SECOND EDITION
FULLY REVISED, EXPANDED AND UPDATED

EDITOR: ROBERT HEWSON

Airlife
England

Aermacchi MB-339

From the experience gained by nearly 800 of its successful MB-326 jet trainers, Aermacchi went on to develop a more modern replacement, the **MB-339**. This retained the MB-326's licence-built (by Piaggio) Viper 632-43 turbojet and the basic airframe aft of the rear cockpit, but introduced a pressurised cockpit in a revised, deeper forward fuselage, an extended canopy with improved all-round view, a larger fin and more advanced avionics. Two prototypes preceded Italian air force (AMI) orders for 100 production **MB-339A** trainers, with the first making its maiden flight on 12 August 1976.

The MB-339 entered AMI service in August 1979. Variants for Italy included 19 **MB-339PAN**s for the 'Frecce Tricolori' aerobatic team and eight specially-equipped **MB-339RM**s for radio calibration duties. Export customers for the MB-339A included the Argentine navy (10), Dubai air wing (5), and the air forces of Ghana (2), Malaysia (13), Nigeria (12), and Peru (16). Italy has now instigated a mid-life update of its remaining MB-339As, which were boosted by a small batch of attrition replacement aircraft in 1999.

Aermacchi explored several approaches to enhancing the small trainer's light attack potential. A single-seat variant was built in 1980 as the

The upgraded MB-339CD for Italy features a revised engine and new digital cockpit systems. It can also be fitted with an in-flight refuelling probe.

No. 14 Sqn, RNZAF, was the first operator of the advanced MB-339C, which entered service in 1991. Note the 30-mm gun pod on the port wing.

M.B.339K Veltro 2, but no orders were forthcoming. This was followed by the improved **MB-339B**, which introduced the uprated 19.57-kN (4,400-lb) Viper 680 engine and enlarged wingtip tanks. This version remained as a 'one off' demonstrator, but paved the way for the **MB-339C**, which first flew in December 1985. This version introduced a digital nav/attack system and other advanced avionics. Eighteen aircraft were acquired, as **M.B.339CB**s by the Royal New Zealand Air Force.

Aermacchi is now delivering 15 upgraded **MB-339CD** (C Digital) aircraft to the Italian air force. This version will serve as a lead-in fighter trainer and adds new all-digital cockpit avionics to the basic MB-339C airframe. The first example (a converted MB-339A) made its maiden flight on 24 April 1996. Italy's MB-339CDs are powered by the Viper Mk 632-43 engine, as fitted to the MB-339A. A new Sextant mission computer and MIL-STD 1553B databus have been added, and the cockpit is equipped with a HUD, three multi-function displays and HOTAS controls. A variant of the MB-339CD, the **MB-339CE**, was sold to Eritrea in 1995, with six aircraft delivered in 1997. The definitive export version of the upgraded MB-339CD, the **MB-339FD** (Full Digital) has been ordered by Venezuela.

Specification: Aermacchi MB-339C
Powerplant: one 19.570-kN (4,400-lb) Rolls-Royce Viper Mk 680-43 turbojet
Dimensions: wing span, over tip tanks 11.22 m (36 ft 9¾ in) ; length 11.24 m (36 ft 10½ in); height 3.99 m (13 ft 1¼ in)
Weights: empty equipped 3414 kg (7,527 lb); maximum take-off 6350 kg (14,000 lb)
Performance: maximum level speed 'clean' at sea level 919 kmh (571 mph); service ceiling 14020 m (46,000 ft); standard range 1965 km (1,221 miles); combat radius 472 km (293 miles) 'hi-lo-hi' profile with four 500-lb bombs
Armament: maximum load of 1814 kg (4,000 lb) on six underwing hardpoints

Aero L-39, L-59 and L-159 ALCA

The Aero **L-39 Albatros** was developed in close co-operation with the USSR as the successor to Aero's L-29 Delfin. It became the Warsaw Pact's standard jet trainer, and has been built in greater numbers than all its Western rivals combined. Powered by an Ivchenko (now Progress) AI-25 turbofan, the L-39 used a conventional configuration with modular construction – using only three major sub-assemblies. The L-39 first flew on 4 November 1968 and it entered Czech service in 1974.

More than 2,800 L-39s have been produced, including the **L-39C** unarmed trainer, **L-39V** target tug, **L-39ZO** weapons trainer with four underwing pylons, and the **L-39ZA** ground attack and reconnaissance aircraft, fitted with a 23-mm Gsh-23 twin barrelled underfuselage cannon.

Large numbers of these 'first-generation aircraft' remain in service in Russia and the other CIS republics. Other users include Afghanistan, Algeria, Bangladesh, Bulgaria, Cambodia, Congo, Cuba, Czech Republic, Egypt, Ethiopia, Ghana, Hungary, Iraq, Libya, Lithuania, Nicaragua, Nigeria, North Korea, Romania, Slovakia, Syria, Ukraine Uganda, and Vietnam.

An improved version of the multi-role L-39ZA, the **L-39ZA/ART**, was acquired by Thailand between 1993-97. The 50 aircraft delivered to date serve as lead-in trainers but also have a target-towing capability. They have been fitted with a revised avionics fit, with systems supplied by Israel's Elbit.

This aircraft is one of the 12 L-59Ts delivered to the Tunisian air force in 1995. The L-59 is outwardly similar to the L-39ZA and L-39MS.

In the early 1990s Aero integrated a new weapons delivery and navigation system to produce the **L-39M Super Albatros**. This had a host of new avionics and was powered by the uprated PS/ZMK DV-2 engine. Eight were acquired by the Czech air force as the **L-39MS**. The export version became the **L-59**. The first customer was Egypt – ordering 48 aircraft as **L-59E**s. In 1995, 12 similar aircraft were supplied to Tunisia, as the **L-59T Fennec**.

In May 1993 Aero flew the prototype **L-139 Albatros 2000**, a modernised version powered by a US-built Garrett TFE731-4 turbofan. This paved the way for the current **L-159 ALCA** (Advanced Light Combat Aircraft), which is now in production for the Czech air force. The ALCA comes in both single-seat (**L-159A**) and two-seat (**L-159B**) versions. All ALCAs are equipped with a Fiar Grifo-L radar, a much-modernised cockpit with an FV-3000 wide-angle HUD, twin multi-function colour displays, HOTAS controls, an Allied Signal F124-GA-100 turbofan, Sky Guardian 200 RWR and an expanded warload of NATO-standard weapons.

The Czech air force has adopted the L-159 ALCA as its new standard combat aircraft and has ordered 72 aircraft. This is a two-seat L-159B.

Specification: Aero L-159 ALCA
Powerplant: one 6,300-lb (28-kN) AlliedSignal F124-GA-100 turbofan
Dimensions: wing span 9.54 m (31 ft 3½ in) including tip tanks; length 12.73 m (41 ft 9¼ in); height 4.77 m (15 ft 7¾ in)
Weights: empty equipped 4160 kg (9,171 lb); maximum take-off 8000 kg (17,637 lb)
Performance: maximum level speed 936 kmh (581 mph); service ceiling 13200 m (43,300 ft); maximum mission radius (L 159A) with two 500-lb bombs 705 km (438 miles)
Armament: centreline point for podded 23-mm GSh-23 twin-barrelled cannon with 180 rounds, and up to 2340 kg (5,159 lb) of stores on all seven hardpoints

Agusta A 129 Mangusta

The Agusta **A 129 Mangusta** (Mongoose) was conceived to meet a 1972 Italian army requirement for a modern anti-armour helicopter. It was the first combat helicopter to incorporate a fully computerised, integrated mission system to minimise crew workload. The A 129 features a conventional gunship layout with stepped tandem cockpits (pilot to rear and gunner in front), stub wings for weapons carriage, fixed, crashworthy undercarriage and a slim fuselage for minimum visual signature. Composite materials account for 45 per cent of the fuselage weight.

The first of five prototype A 129s, powered by two Piaggio-built Rolls-Royce Gem Mk 2-1004D turboshafts, made its maiden flight on 11 September 1983. The first five production Mangustas entered Italian Army Aviation (AVES) service in October 1990. The first 15 'Batch One' production-standard aircraft were fitted with the daytime-only Hughes M65 sight for the helicopter's primary anti-tank weapon, the BGM-71 TOW missile. Deliveries were completed in 1994 and were followed by the 30 aircraft of Batch Two, which were all delivered by 1996. The improved Batch Two A 129s were fitted with the Saab HeliTOW sight and all A 129s have since been upgraded with this system.

The A 129 in Italian service today does not yet have a built-in gun. Standard armament includes the TOW missile, 70-mm and 81-mm rockets and gun pods.

The A 129 Multirulo has the new M197 cannon and the five-bladed rotor of the A 129 International, but retains the Mangusta's Gem engines.

Italy deployed its Mangustas on UN-led peacekeeping operations in Somalia between 1992 and 1994. This combat experience led to a revision of the AVES requirement for the A 129. Instead of a dedicated anti-tank helicopter, the service decided it now needed a more flexible multi-role combat helicopter. As a result, Agusta is offering a new version of the A 129 that brings together a range of improvements that have been separately developed for the Mangusta in recent years.

For the export market Agusta is now offering the **A 129 International**. This aircraft has an all-new five-bladed rotor, AlliedSignal LHTEC CTS800-2 turboshafts, a completely modernised cockpit with a new mission computer and multi-function displays, a nose-mounted M197 20-mm cannon and provision for Stinger air-to-air missiles. A new FLIR/EO targeting system will be fitted and the A 129 International can be armed with laser-guided AGM-114 Hellfire missiles – just such an aircraft offered to the Australian Army was dubbed the **A 129 Scorpion**. The Italian army will acquire 15 new-build A 129s to a similar standard, but retaining the original Gem engine of the basic Mangusta. These aircraft will be known as the **A 129 Multirulo**, or the **Da Combattimento** (combat).

Specification: Agusta A 129 Mangusta
Powerplant: two 615-kW (825-hp) Rolls-Royce Gem 2 Mk 1004D turboshafts
Dimensions: main rotor diameter 11.90 m (39 ft 0.5 in); wing span 3.20 m (10 ft 6 in); length overall 14.29 m (46 ft 10.5 in); height overall 3.35 m (11 ft 0 in)
Weights: empty equipped 2529 kg (5,575 lb); maximum take-off 4100 kg (9,039 lb)
Performance: max level speed at sea level 250 kmh (155 mph); hovering ceiling 3140 m (10,300 ft) in ground effect, and 1890 m (6,200 ft) out of ground effect; combat radius 100 km (62 miles) for a 90-minute patrol
Armament: up to 1200 kg (2,645 lb) of stores on four stub-wing pylons

AIDC F-CK-1 Ching-Kuo

This line up of Ching Kuo fighters is seen at Ching Chuan Kang AB, home of the 3rd Tactical Fighter Wing. The wing was the lead unit to receive the IDF.

Taiwan's ambitious programme to develop the advanced **Indigenous Defence Fighter** (IDF) to replace its fleet of F-5s and F-104s began in 1982 after a US arms embargo was imposed to appease mainland China. However, no restrictions were placed on technical assistance, and US companies collaborated closely with AIDC to develop the new airframe (General Dynamics), radar (Westinghouse), engine (Garrett) and other systems.

The resulting **Ching Kuo** fighter (named in honour of a Taiwanese president, in 1988) is of conventional all-metal construction and configuration, bearing a passing resemblance to an F-16/F-18 hybrid with wing/fuselage blending. Elliptical intakes are located below long leading-edge root extensions (LERXes). The pressurised cockpit is fitted with a sidestick controller (like the F-16), a wide-angle HUD and two multi-function displays. The GD-53 Golden Dragon multi-mode radar is derived from Lockheed Martin's AN/APG-67V, with elements of the Northrop Grumman (formerly Westinghouse) AN/APG-66 also. Power is supplied by two ITEC TFE1042-70 turbofans, licence-built versions of the Garret (AlliedSignal) F125.

The first of three single-seat prototypes made its maiden flight on 28 May 1989, followed by the first two-seat prototype in July 1990. The first of 10 pre-production aircraft was rolled out on 9 March 1992 and introduced new enlarged engine intakes and a small ventral fin, following the loss of one of the prototypes in development flying. Deliveries to the Republic of China Air Force began nearly one year earlier than scheduled with the public unveiling of the first squadron in February 1993.

Several indigenously-developed weapons have been fielded for the Ching Kuo, including the Tien Chien (sky sword) 1 IR dogfight missile, and the Tien Chien 2 medium-range air-to-air missile. The Ching Kuo can also carry the Hsiung Feng 2 (male bee) anti-ship missile.

The single-seat version of the Ching Kuo has received the ROCAF designation **F-CK-1A**, while the **F-CK-1B** is the combat-capable two-seater. Due to the cost of the project (and the renewed availability of F-16s to Taiwan), the ROCAF requirement for 250 aircraft was cut back to 130 – of which 28 were F-CK-1Bs. The last two Ching Kuos were handed over in January 2000 and Taiwan currently has six squadrons (two wings) equipped with the type. AIDC is now working on a simplified version of the Ching Kuo as a lead-in fighter trainer for export. A prototype is expected to fly in 2002.

The Ching Kuo carries the indigenously-developed Sky Sword I IR-guided short-rangeAAMs and Sky Sword II radar-guided medium range AAMs.

Specification: AIDC F-CK-1A Ching Kuo
Powerplant: two 42.08-kN (9,460-lb) ITEC (AlliedSignal/AIDC) TFE1042-70 turbofans
Dimensions: wing span over wingtip missile rails 9.46 m (31 ft ½ in); length, including probe 14.21 m (46 ft 7½ in)
Weights: operating empty 6486 kg (14,300 lb); maximum take-off 12247 kg (27,000 lb)
Performance: maximum level speed 1296 kmh (805 mph); service ceiling 16460 m (54,000 ft);
Armament: one internal 20-mm M61A1 cannon mounted beneath the port LERX; six hardpoints (two underfuselage, one under each wing and one wingtip missile rail) for a maximum of 3,901-kg (8,600-lb) of stores

AMX International AMX

Development of the **AMX** started in April 1978 when Aeritalia (now Alenia) and Aermacchi combined their resources to meet an Italian air force (AMI) requirement for a multi-purpose strike/reconnaissance aircraft. The programme received extra impetus in 1980 when Brazil's EMBRAER joined the two Italian companies. A common specification called for good short-field performance, high subsonic operating speeds and advanced nav/attack systems for low-level day/night missions in poor visibility. This resulted in a conventional aircraft with a relatively compact airframe and moderately-swept high-mounted wings, and powered by a single Rolls-Royce Spey turbofan. Seven single-seat prototypes were built and the first of these made its maiden flight on 15 May 1984. Design work on a two-seat version, the **AMX-T**, began in 1986. The first AMX production batch included 21 aircraft for Italy and nine for Brazil. The first production-standard AMX was rolled out at Turin on 29 March 1988, and flew on 11 May.

In 1988 a second production contract for 84 AMXs was placed, following on from the initial batch of 30. This second order comprised 59 for Italy (including six AMX-Ts) and 25 for Brazil (with three AMX-Ts). The first deliveries to the Italian air

The upgraded and modernised AMX-ATA is based on the two-seat AMX-T airframe, but adds a new radar, avionics and digital cockpit systems.

This Força Aérea Brasileira A-1 (AMX) is carrying a pair of MAA-1 Piranha air-to-air missiles on its wingtip launchers.

force took place in April 1989, while Brazil took delivery of its first aircraft in October 1989. In Brazilian service the AMX is known as the **A-1**. The first of three AMX-T trainer prototypes flew on 14 March 1990. The first production-standard AMX-T was delivered to Brazil in May 1992, while the first Italian aircraft was handed over in 1994. In Brazilian service the AMX-T is designated **TA-1**.

Italy has acquired a total of 136 aircraft (110 AMXs, 26 AMX-Ts) and the final delivery was made in 1997. Brazil has ordered a total of 79 aircraft (65 A-1s, 14 TA-1s) and deliveries from EMBRAER are almost complete. The main difference between the Brazilian A-1 and Italian AMXs is that the former are armed with two 30-mm cannon, in place of the latter's single 20-mm gun. Some of the single-seat A-1s have been converted to **RA-1** reconnaissance aircraft.

In September 1999 Venezuela ordered 24 improved **AMX-ATA** (Advanced Trainer and Attack) aircraft, which will have a new digital cockpit, new radar and avionics derived from the EMBRAER ALX programme. Both Italy and Brazil are now looking at applying similar upgrades to their existing aircraft – particularly in the light of the AMX's impressive combat debut during Operation Allied Force.

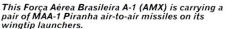

Specification: AMX International AMX
Powerplant: one 49.1-kN (11,030-lb st) licence-built Rolls-Royce Spey Mk 807 turbofan
Dimensions: wing span 9.97 m (32 ft 8½ in), over wingtip AAMs; length 13.23 m (43 ft 5 in); height 4.55 m (14 ft 11¾ in)
Weights: operating empty 6730 kg (14,837 lb); maximum take-off 13000 kg (28,660 lb)
Performance: max level speed Mach 0.86; service ceiling 13000 m (42,650 ft); combat radius 889 km (553 miles) on a hi-lo-hi attack mission with a 907-kg (2,000-lb) warload
Armament: one internal M61A1 20-mm Vulcan cannon (Italy) and two 30-mm DEFA 554 cannon (Brazil); seven stores stations for up to 3800 kg (8,377 lb) of ordnance

Antonov An-12 (Shaanxi Y-8)

Designed by the Ukrainian-based Antonov Bureau, the four-engined Antonov **An-12** (allocated the NATO code-name **'Cub'**), was the standard military airlifter of the Soviet Union and its allies from the early 1960s onwards. Roughly equivalent to the C-130 Hercules, the An-12 was a high-wing, rear-loading freighter, which was also adapted to a wide range of other specialist roles. Unlike the Hercules many versions were armed with a rear gun turret at the base of the fin. The prototype An-12 made its maiden flight on 16 December 1957. Approximately 1,265 aircraft were built at factories in Irkutsk, Tashkent and Voronezh by the early 1970s.

The first major production variant was the **An-12A** (1961) which had more fuel and more powerful engines than the An-12. In 1963 this was replaced by the **An-12B** (1963), now fitted with an independent APU. Aircraft with extra underfloor fuel tanks were designated **An-12APs** or **An-12BPs**. A wealth of special missions conversions began to appear during early 1970s. These included the **An-12PS 'Cub-B'** Elint aircraft, the **An-12B-VKP Zebra** airborne command post and the **An-12RKR** NBC reconnaissance aircraft.

The definitive transport version, the **An-12BK**, appeared in 1967 to replace the An-12B. These aircraft were exported to a number of friendly air forces, including India which used its An-12BKs as makeshift bombers during the war with Pakistan in 1971. **The An-12PP 'Cub-C'** was another specialised EW variant, with a large extended tailcone and a

Dwindling numbers of military An-12s survive in Russian service, with many aircraft now in the hands of commercial cargo airlines.

comprehensive jamming fit. The similar-looking **An-12BK-PPS 'Cub-D'** was another airborne jammer, this time fitted with a number of large scabbed-on Sirena jamming pods. Other An-12s are modified for tasks such as weather research (**An-12BKTs Tsyklon**) and ejection-seat development (**An-12LL**).

The An-12 was exported to 14 countries; Algeria, Bulgaria, China, Cuba, Czechoslovakia, Egypt, Ghana, Guinea, India, Indonesia, Iraq, Poland, Yemen and Yugoslavia. Many of these aircraft have now been retired, but a few hundred are still in service.

The An-12 is alive and well in China, were it is built as the **Shaanxi Y-8** (based on the An-12BK airframe). The Y-8 is an unlicensed copy of the An-12. It is currently in production, with a range of new variants still under development. The first Y-8 flew on 25 December 1975 and somewhere between 70 and 100 have been built. This includes the improved **Y-8A** military transport, the civil **Y-8B**, the pressurised **Y-8C** freighter, the export **Y-8D** with Western-supplied avionics, the **Y-8E** drone-launching platform, the **Y-8F** livestock carrier and **Y-8X** maritime-patrol aircraft.

Chinese-built Y-8s, like this Y-8B, have been fitted with a distinctive, extended glass nose, the same as that found on China's H-6 (Tu-16) bombers.

Specification: Antonov An-12BP 'Cub-A'
Powerplant: four 2983-kW (4,000-hp)ZMDB Progress (Ivchenko) AI-20K turboprops
Dimensions: span 38.00 m (124 ft 8 in); length 33.10 m (108 ft 7.25 in); height 10.53 m (34 ft 6.5 in)
Weights: empty 28000 kg (61,728 lb); maximum take-off 61000 kg (134,480 lb); maximum payload 20000 kg (44,092 lb)
Performance: maximum level speed 777 kmh (482 mph); maximum rate of climb at sea level 600 m (1,969 ft) per minute; service ceiling 10200 m (33,465 ft); range 5700 km (3,542 miles) with maximum fuel or 3600 km (2,237 miles) with maximum payload

Antonov An-24, An-26, An-32 (Xian Y-7)

The twin-turboprop Antonov **An-24** (NATO code-name **'Coke'**) made its maiden flight on 20 December 1959, and was aimed at an Aeroflot requirement to replace piston-engined Il-14s and Il-12s. Its robustness, strength and performance appealed to military customers, and approximately 1,200 were built by the time production finished in 1978. The major production **An-24V** variant has seating for 28-40, a side freight door and a convertible cabin.

Although derived from the An-24, the **An-26** ('**Curl-A'**) is a new design with a fully-pressurised cargo hold, uprated engines and a new rear-loading ramp to facilitate loading from trucks. All An-26s are fitted with an RU-19 turbojet in the rear of the starboard engine nacelle. As well as acting as an APU, this can be used as a take-off booster.

A small number of An-26s have been converted as Elint/Sigint/EW platforms. These bear the NATO reporting name **'Curl-B'**, and have a profusion of swept blade antennas above and below the cabin. Some An-26s delivered to Angola and Mozambique were fitted with exterior bomb-racks along the fuselage.

Along with Russia, Ukraine and most CIS states, current An-26 operators include Afghanistan, Benin, Bangladesh, Bulgaria, Cape Verde, China, Cuba,

The An-26s formerly operated by the Czechoslovakian air force are now spilt between the Czech and Slovakian air forces (seen here).

Libya has a small number of An-26 transports. The rear ramp of the 'Curl' slides down and then forward along tracks, to lie directly under the fuselage.

Congo, Czech Republic, Germany, Ethiopia, Guinea Bissau, Hungary, Iraq, Laos, Libya, Madagascar, Mali, Mongolia, Mozambique, Nicaragua, Poland, Romania, Russia, Serbia, Slovakia, Vietnam, Yemen and Zambia.

The **An-32 'Cline'** replaced the An-26 in production, and offers dramatically improved take-off performance, ceiling and payload, especially under 'hot-and-high' conditions. The cabin can accommodate up to 50 passengers, 42 paratroops, or 24 stretcher patients and three attendants. The basic production aircraft are fitted with 3812-kW (5,112-hp) AI-20D turboprops. These are mounted above the wing in very deep nacelles to give greater clearance for the increased-diameter propellers. The **An-32B** offers uprated engines and Antonov has also developed a water-bomber version (fitted with external water tanks), the **An-32P Firekiller**, In addition to the air forces of Russia, Ukraine and some CIS states, the An-32 has attracted several military customers including Afghanistan, Bangladesh, Cuba, India, Mongolia and Peru and Tanzania.

China builds its own military transport version of the An-26 as the **Xian Y-7H-500** – while also building a family of other Y-7 airliner variants based on the civil-standard An-24 airframe.

Specification: Antonov An-26B 'Curl-A'
Powerplant: two 2103-kW (2,820-hp) ZMDB Progress (Ivchenko) AI-24VT turboprops, and one 7.85-kN (1,765-lb) Soyuz (Tumanskii) RU-19A-300 turbojet
Dimensions: wing span 29.20 m (95 ft 9.5 in); length 23.80 m (78 ft 1 in); height 8.58 m (28 ft 1.5 in)
Weights: empty 15400 kg (33,957 lb); maximum take-off 24400 kg (53,790 lb); maximum payload 5500 kg (12,125 lb)
Performance: maximum level speed 540 kmh; (336 mph); range 2550 km (1,585 miles) with maximum fuel or 1100 km (683 miles) with maximum payload

Atlas Cheetah

During the 1980s South Africa embarked on an extremely ambitious, and extremely secret, transformation of its Dassault Mirage IIIs into a highly-modified and improved family of combat aircraft. The international arms embargo against the Apartheid regime made the acquisition of any new aircraft impossible, at a time when South Africa felt it was facing an increasing threat from neighbouring, hostile African nations. The state-owned firm of Atlas Aviation, with considerable help from Israel's IAI, began to adapt the modified airframe and the improved avionics suite of the IAI Kfir to the South African Air Force's own aircraft, to produce the **Cheetah** – in several distinct versions.

The most important of these was the two-seat **Cheetah D** attack aircraft, based on the Mirage IIIDZ airframe (though a few single-seat Mirage IIIEZs were also converted). Atlas modified approximately 16 aircraft to Cheetah D standard. They resemble the IAI Kfir TC-7, with their distinctive extended cranked noses and canard foreplanes. The nose houses an Elta EL/M-2001B ranging radar and the Cheetah Ds are fitted with refuelling probes. The first converted aircraft was rolled out in 1986 and entered service almost immediately.

Cheetah D development paralleled the single-seat **Cheetah E** conversions, based on the SAAF's Mirage IIIEZ fighters. The Cheetah E had much the same systems fit as the Cheetah D (including an advanced RWR, EW jamming suite and chaff/flare

The Cheetah C is now the sole air superiority fighter in SAAF service, but the aircraft also has a formidable attack capability.

dispensers, and bore a strong resemblance to the Israeli Kfir C7. Both the Cheetah E and Cheetah D were fitted with a new, reprofiled wing with a 'dog-tooth' leading edge. Sixteen Cheetah Es were built, but they were retired in the early 1990s when a radically superior Cheetah fighter was introduced.

This was the **Cheetah C**, which entered service in January 1993. Until then not a single fact about the programme had emerged – this secrecy was doubtless due to the fact that the 38 aircraft used in the Cheetah C conversions were acquired from a source outside South Africa (almost certainly Israel). The Cheetah C was a major step forward because it was fitted with an Elta EL/M-2001 multi-mode radar, and was powered by the more powerful Atar 09K50 engine. The Cheetah C is also stretched, with a plug measuring approximately 58 cm (23 in) inserted between the cockpit and engine intakes. The new radar allows the Cheetah C to be armed with the Kentron R-Darter BVR missile, as well as the agile, IR-guided U-Darter dogfight missile, used in conjunction with a helmet-mounted sight.

The Cheetah D has a dual training and attack role. Today all South Africa's Cheetahs are operated by No. 2 Sqn, based at AFB Louis Trichardt.

Specification: Atlas Cheetah C
Powerplant: one SNECMA Atar 09K50 turbojet rated at 49.03 kN (11,023 lb st) dry and 70.82 kN (15,873 lb st) with afterburning
Dimensions: wing span 8.22 m (26 ft 11½ in); canard foreplane span 3.73 m (12 ft 3 in); length including probe 15.65 m (51 ft 4¼ in); height 4.5 m (14 ft 11 in)
Performance: maximum level speed 'clean' at 12000 m (39,370 ft), 2338 kmh (1,453 mph); maximum cruising speed at 11000 m (36,090 ft) 956 kmh (594 mph); service ceiling 17000 m (55,775 ft)
Armament: two internal DEFA 30-mm cannon plus up to 4000 kg (8,818 lb) of ordnance

Avioane IAR-99 Soim

Romania has a long tradition of aeronautical achievement, and it succeeded in maintaining an independent aviation industry through the stagnant years of Communist control – which ended with the 1989 'revolution'. In 1975 the Institutul de Aviatie (INAv) began work on what would become the first aircraft to be designed and built completely 'in country', the **IAR-99** basic jet trainer. The project was formally launched in 1979, with the ambitious aim of replacing the Aero L-39 Albatros in Eastern European service. IAR-99 production was conducted by Avioane Craiova, Romania's only builder of fixed-wing military aircraft, which was founded (as IAv Craiova) in February 1972.

The IAR 99 is a conventionally-configured low-wing, single-engined trainer with a tandem seat layout. For attack training it can be equipped with a ventral GSh-23 23-mm gun pod, and has four underwing hardpoints. The prototype first flew on 1 December 1985 and two flying development aircraft were built. The first IAR-99 was equipped with a mix of UK and French-supplied avionics, but the political climate forced a change to less-sophisticated Eastern systems from the second aircraft onwards.

The IAR 99 proved to be an extremely reliable and user-friendly aircraft, with excellent handling

Romania's existing fleet of base-line IAR 99 trainers may be upgraded to IAR 99 Soim standard, once procurement of the new aircraft is complete.

This is Avioane's IAR 99 Soim demonstrator aircraft, a capable, cost-effective trainer which makes maximum use of new technology.

qualities. Deliveries of an initial batch of 20 began to the Romanian air force in 1988. Beginning in 1990, Avioane tried to develop a series of improved aircraft with Western avionics. An IAR 99 fitted with Honeywell avionics first flew on 22 August 1990, while a second demonstrator fitted with Collins systems flew on 7 November 1991. Avioane next collaborated with IAI on another upgraded version. This received the new designation **IAR-109 Swift** and made its maiden flight on 2 December 1993 – but only a single example was built.

Since 1996 Avioane has been developing the significantly enhanced **IAR 99 Soim** (falcon), in conjunction with Elbit. This version incorporates many of the advanced avionics systems applied to the Romanian MiG-21 Lancer upgrade, developed for the air force by Aerostar and Elbit, at Bacau. These include a MIL-STD 1553B databus, Elbit modular multi-role computer, Flight Visions HUD, two cockpit colour MFDs, GPS/INS, integrated Elbit chaff/flare dispenser and the Elbit DASH helmet-mounted display system. In 1998 the Romanian air force ordered 24 Soims for delivery by 2004 (with a view to then upgrading its existing IAR 99s also), and Avioane is actively offering the type on the export market.

Specification: Avioane IAR 99 Soim
Powerplant: one (17.79-kN) 4,000-lb Rolls-Royce (licence-built by Turbomecanica) Viper 632-41M Viper turbojet
Dimensions: wing span 9.85 m (32 ft 3 in); length 11 m (36 ft 1 in); height 3.87 m (12 ft 9 in)
Weights: take-off, clean 4390 kg (9,680 lb); maximum take-off 5572 kg (12,285 lb); maximum payload 1000 kg (2,200 lb)
Performance: maximum level speed 940 kmh (585 mph); service ceiling 12903 m (42,322 ft); maximum mission radius 1100 km (683 miles)
Armament: centreline point for podded 23-mm GSh-23 twin-barrelled cannon with 180 rounds, and up to 250 kg (550 lb) of stores on each of four underwing hardpoints

Beech (Raytheon) King Air

The Beech **Super King Air** family of six- to 10-seat, twin-turboprop business aircraft evolved from the **King Air 90** and **King Air 100** to the **Model 200 Super King Air**, which first flew on 27 October 1972 (the 'Super' title was dropped from all King Airs in 1996). The Model 200 was an enlarged, more powerful derivative, with a T-tail, increased wing span, extra fuel and improved pressurisation.

The Model 200 was rapidly adopted by all US armed services, primarily as utility aircraft/light transports, under the designation **C-12**. Variants include the **C-12A** (Model A200 for the US Army, USAF and Greece); **UC-12B** (Model A200C with cargo door for USMC and USN; **TC-12B** (USN crew trainers converted from C-12B); **C-12C** (with uprated PT6A-41 engines for US Army, later US Customs Service); **C-12D** (Model A200CT for US Army, USAF); **C-12E** (USAF C-12As refitted with PT6A-42s); **C-12F** (Operational Support Aircraft similar to B200C for USAF, US Army and National Guard); **UC-12F** (USN equivalent of PT6A-42-powered C-12F); **UC-12M** (C-12F equivalent for USN); **C-12R** (B200C for US Army). The designation **C-12J** has been applied to a version of the Beech Model 1900 operated by the USAF and Army, while the **C-12S** is a Model 350 operated by the US Army.

Other military operators of the (Super) King Air include Argentina, Bolivia, Canada, Chile, Colombia Ecuador, Egypt, Greece, Guatemala, Guyana, Indonesia, Ireland, Israel, Ivory Coast, Jamaica,

All of the US Army's Guardrail-configured RC-12s, like this RC-12N, are festooned with antennas for their communications intercept and jamming role.

Japan (Model 350, local designation **LR-2**), Mexico, Morocco, Pakistan, Spain, Sri Lanka, Sweden (local designation **Tp 101**), Thailand, Turkey and Venezuela. A radar-equipped maritime **B200T** patrol version serves with Algeria, Peru and Uruguay.

The US Army operates battlefield signals intelligence (Sigint) **RC-12s**, under the Guardrail programme. Current versions include the **RC-12D Improved Guardrail V** (Model A200CT, fitted with AN/USD-9 remote-controlled communications intercept system, associated antenna and wingtip pods); **RC-12G** (increased weight version based on RC-12D); **RC-12H Guardrail Common Sensor (System -3)**, increased weight version based on RC-12D; **RC-12K Guardrail Commons Sensor (System 4),** developed from RC-12H, also delivered to Israel; **RC-12N Guardrail Commons Sensor (System 1),** developed from RC-12K with new mission fit; **RC-12P Guardrail Commons Sensor (System 2),** developed from RC-12N; **RC-12Q Direct Satellite Relay** (relay platform for RC-12P).The US Navy also operates two **RC-12M RANSAC** range patrol aircraft.

Sweden is one of many nations that operates the versatile Model 200 Super King Air as a utility transport, or for priority cargoes.

Specification: Beech RC-12K
Powerplant: two 820-kW (1,100-shp) Pratt & Whitney Canada PT6A-41 turboprops
Dimensions: wing span 17.63 m (57 ft 10 in) over ESM pods; length 13.34 m (43 ft 9 in); height 4.57 m (15 ft 0 in)
Weights: empty 3327 kg (7,334 lb); maximum take-off 7348 kg (16,200 lb); maximum payload more than 1043 kg (2,300 lb)
Performance: maximum level speed at 4265 m (14,000 ft) 481 kmh (299 mph); maximum cruising speed at 9145 m (30,000 ft) 438 kmh (272 mph); service ceiling 9420 m (30,900 ft); take-off distance to 15 m (50 ft) 869 m (2,850 ft); range at maximum cruising speed 2935 km (1,824 miles)

Bell Model 205, 212 and 412

Derived from the Bell **Model 204/UH-1 Iroquois**, the improved **Model 205** was first flown in August 1961. Retaining the existing T53 turboshaft, it introduced a larger-diameter main rotor, additional fuel capacity and a lengthened fuselage. Over 2,000 **UH-1D**s were built for the US Army, followed by the similar **UH-1H**, which introduced the uprated T53-L-13 engine. A total of 2,008 UH-1Ds and 3,573 UH-1Hs were built for the US Army alone, and the type was exported to over 50 countries.

With several thousand Model 205/UH-1Hs still in service, a number of companies offer modernisation and upgrade programmes. Bell Helicopter has developed the **Huey II** upgrade, which adds the uprated T53-703 engine and a new transmission system. The Huey II has been ordered by Colombia and more sales in South America are likely. Other UH-1 conversions include the Global Helicopter **Huey 800**, which completely replaces the T53 with an LHTEC T800-800 engine and UNC Helicopter's **UH-1/T700**, which adds the GE T700 engine.

The **Model 212** 'Twin Huey' is a twin-turbine UH-1H, fitted with two PT6T-3 turboshafts driving a single shaft. Announced in May 1968, the 212 was launched with a Canadian order for 50 **CH-135** aircraft. The USAF, USN and USMC acquired it as the **UH-1N**.

In British service the Model 412 is known as the Griffin HT.Mk 1. The type serves with the tri-service Defence Helicopter Flying School.

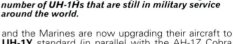

This Turkish army UH-1H is typical of the huge number of UH-1Hs that are still in military service around the world.

and the Marines are now upgrading their aircraft to **UH-1Y** standard (in parallel with the AH-1Z Cobra upgrade). The UH-1Y will be fitted with an all-new four-bladed composite rotor system and new cockpit systems. Italy's Agusta has built the Bell 212 under licence as the **AB 212**, and also developed a range of special missions versions. The most important of these is the shore-/ship-based anti-submarine variant, the **AB 212ASW**.

In 1978 Bell introduced the **Model 412**. Essentially similar to the Model 212 it featured an entirely new four-bladed main rotor system. The Model 412 has been built by Agusta as the **AB 412** and by Indonesia's IPTN as the **NB 412**. Developed versions include the **Model 412SP** (Special Performance) with extra fuel and increased maximum take-off weight; **Model 412HP**, with uprated transmission; and the **Model 412EP** (Enhanced Performance) powered by a refined PT6T-3D engine and fitted with a three-axis digital flight control system. This is now the standard production model. In 1992 Canada ordered 100 aircraft, based on the Model 412EP, as the **CH-148 Griffon**.

Since 1986 all Bell helicopter production has been undertaken in Mirabel, Quebec, by Bell Helicopter Textron Canada.

SPECIFICATION: Bell 412EP

Powerplant: two 1342-kW (1,800-hp) Pratt & Whitney Canada PT6T-3D Turbo Twin-Pac turboshafts

Dimensions: main rotor diameter 14.02 m (46 ft); height, tail rotor turning 4.57 m (15 ft); length, rotors turning 17.12 m (56 ft 2 in)

Weights: empty, standard 3079 kg (6,789 lb); maximum take-off 5397 kg (11,900 lb); maximum external hook load 2041 kg (4,500 lb)

Performance: max cruising speed, at sea level 226 kmh (140 mph); hovering ceiling, in ground effect 3110 m (10,200 ft) and 1585 m (5,200 ft) out of ground effect; maximum range, with no reserves 745 km (463 miles)

Bell OH-58D Kiowa (Model 406)

Armed combat scout helicopter

In March 1968 Bell's **Model 206A JetRanger** five-seat light helicopter was ordered into production for the US Army as the **OH-58A Kiowa** for the light observation role. Deliveries began on 23 May 1969, and over five years a total of 2,200 was procured. Export customers comprised Australia (56 licence-built **Kalkadoon**s), Austria (12 **OH-58B**s) and Canada (74 **COH-58A**s).From 1978, 585 OH-58As were converted to improved **OH-58C** standard with a flat glass canopy, an uprated engine with infra-red suppression and improved avionics.

In 1981, the Bell **Model 406** proposal was selected as the winner of the US Army Helicopter Improvement Program (AHIP) competition. This new version, known as the **OH-58D**, introduced a mast-mounted sight (housing a TV and IR sensor with a laser designator/rangefinder), a four-bladed main rotor, defensive systems (including an IR jammer and laser-warning system) specialised mission avionics and new cockpit displays.

Initial plans to upgrade 592 US Army OH-58As to OH-58D standard have been revised several times and the current total stands at 424. The first OH-58D conversions began in 1983. In 1987, 15 specially-armed OH-58Ds were upgraded for Operation Prime Chance. Based aboard US Navy vessels in the Persian Gulf, they were used on clandestine missions against Iranian fast-patrol boats, that were harassing international oil tanker traffic. The decision was taken to add a permanent weapons fit to

These Kiowa Warriors are operated by the US Army's 1-7 CAV, based at Ft Hood, where they operate as advance scouts for the 1st Cavalry Division.

all US OH-58Ds, becoming known as **OH-58D(I) Kiowa Warrior**s. All of the US Army's OH-58Ds are now Kiowa Warriors, and feature with integrated weapons pylon, uprated engine and transmission, increased gross weight, RWR, IR jammer, laser warning receiver, integrated avionics and a lighter structure. Typical weapons include Hellfire missiles, 70-mm rockets and 0.50-in gun pods. Beginning in May 1991, 192 new-build Kiowa warriors were delivered to the US Army, and 25 Kiowa Warriors have also been acquired by the Taiwanese army.

All US Kiowa Warriors have been further modified to **Multi-Purpose Light Helicopter (MPLH)** standard, with squatting landing gear and quick-folding rotor blades, fins and tails for rapid redeployment by air

The **Model 406CS Combat Scout** is a lighter and simplified export derivative of the OH-58D, retaining the main rotor, tail rotor and transmission and a similar powerplant. Fifteen TOW-capable OH-58s were delivered from June 1990 onwards to Saudi Arabia as **MH-58D**s.

This Kiowa Warrior is armed with a versatile mix of weapons, including an air-to-air Stinger missile (starboard) and a Hellfire anti-tank missile (port).

Specification: OH-58D(I) Kiowa Warrior
Powerplant: one 485-kW (650-hp) Allison 250-C30R/3 (T703-AD-700) turboshaft
Dimensions: main rotor diameter 10.67 m (35 ft 0 in); length overall, rotors turning 12.58 m (42 ft 2½ in) and fuselage 10.48 m (34 ft 4¾ in); height overall 3.93 m (12 ft 10½ in)
Weights: empty 1492 kg (3,289 lb); maximum take-off 2495 kg (5,500 lb)
Performance: maximum level speed 232 kmh (144 mph); hovering ceiling more than 3660 m (12,000 ft) in ground effect and 3415 m (11,200 ft) out of ground effect; range 496 km (308 miles)
Armament: 0.50-in gun pods, 70-mm rocket pods, plus provision for Stinger AAMs and Hellfire anti-armour missiles

Bell AH-1 Cobra

Appearing in 1965 as an 'interim' armed helicopter escort, the Bell **Model 209 HueyCobra** was derived from the UH-1, retaining its powerplant, transmission and rotor, but introducing a new, slimmer fuselage with the now-standard 'gunship' configuration of stepped tandem cockpits. Bell produced some 1,100 **AH-1G**s for US Army service in Vietnam.

The US Army's Cobra fleet underwent several upgrades over its service life. In 1989 the designation **AH-1F** was adopted for the final production-standard aircraft, grouping together the changes and improvements adopted by the preceding **AH-1P**, **AH-1E** and **Modernised AH-1S** Cobras. These aircraft have a 'flat-plate' canopy, TOW sighting system nose turret, exhaust suppressor and composite main rotor blades with tapered tips. Primary armament is four BGM-71 TOW missiles and a chin-mounted M-197 20-mm cannon. Some AH-1Fs were upgraded with the NTS/C-Nite sight, in place of the earlier day-time-only M65 system.

The AH-1 has been largely replaced by the AH-64 in US service, but some are still active with ANG and Reserve units. The AH-1F was built under licence in Japan by Fuji, and Bell AH-1F/Ss have been exported to Israel, Jordan, Pakistan, South Korea, and Thailand and Turkey.

The Japan Ground Self-Defence Force acquired 80 AH-1S Cobras (equivalent to the US AH-1F) which were built under licence by Fuji.

The AH-1W SuperCobra is the US Marine Corps' standard attack helicopter. Most surviving aircraft will be upgraded to the advanced AH-1Z standard.

Bell went on to develop a twin-engined version of the AH-1, chiefly for the US Navy and Marine Corps. The first example, the **AH-1J** of 1970 led to 1977's **AH-1T** and then to the **AH-1W SuperCobra** which the the only currently active variant. A total of 194 AH-1Ws were converted for the USMC from existing AH-1T airframes, between 1986 and 1998. The **'Whisky Cobra'** is powered by two T700-GE-401 turboshafts, has a stretched fuselage and tail, and distinctive bulged cheek fairings to accommodate updated avionics. The AH-1W is the primary assault helicopter in Marine Corps service and has been exported to Taiwan (63) and Turkey (nine). Bell is now offering an affordable 'multi-role' version of the AH-1W with all guided weapons capability removed, as the MH-1W.

The US Marines plan to upgrade 180 AH-1Ws to **AH-1Z** standard, by fitting a four-bladed main rotor, uprated T700-GE-401 engines, digital cockpit systems, integrated helmet-mounted sight, AGM-114 Hellfire missiles and an all-new Lockheed Martin Target Sight System (with a laser designator). The first AH-1Z flew on 7 December 2000. Turkey plans to acquire up to 145 similar aircraft, known as **AH-1W KingCobra**s, while another version of the AH-1Z has been offered to Australia as the **ARH-1Z**.

Specification: Bell Helicopter AH-1W
Powerplant: two 1285-kW (1,723-shp) General Electric T700-GE-401 turboshafts
Dimensions: main rotor diameter 14.63 m (48 ft); length overall, rotors turning 17.68 m (58 ft) and fuselage 13.87 m (45 ft 6 in); height overall 4.44 m (14 ft 7 in)
Weights: empty 4953 kg (10,920 lb); maximum take-off 6691 kg (14,750 lb)
Performance: maximum level speed 'clean' at sea level 282 kmh (175 mph); service ceiling 4270 m (14,000 ft); range 518 km (322 miles) with standard fuel
Armament: one chin-mounted M-197 three-barrelled 20-mm cannon; maximum ordnance 790 kg (1,741 lb)

Bell-Boeing V-22 Osprey

Bell Helicopter Textron and Boeing Vertol joined forces in the early 1980s to develop a larger derivative of the XV-15 tilt-rotor demonstrator for the **Joint Services Advanced Vertical Lift Aircraft** (formerly **JVX**) programme. This effort was launched by the US Army and then transferred to the Navy in 1983. Combining the vertical lift capabilities of a helicopter with the faster forward flight efficiencies of a fixed-wing aircraft, the resulting **V-22 Osprey** (**Bell Boeing Model 901**) was awarded a full-scale development contract in May 1986. It is powered by two Allison T406 turboshafts driving three-bladed 'proprotors through interconnected drive shafts. The wingtip-mounted engines, transmissions and proprotors can tilt through 97° 30' between forward flight and steep-descent or hovering flight. The blades and wings can also be quickly folded for stowage aboard aircraft carriers.

The first of five EMD prototypes flew on 19 March 1989 and the Osprey successfully demonstrated airborne transition from helicopter to wingborne flight in September 1989. The fifth and final prototype flew on 11 June 1991.

Initial requirements called for 913 Ospreys; 552 **MV-22A** assault transports for the USMC; 231 similar variants for the US Army; 80 USAF **CV-22A**s for long-range special forces transport; and 50 **HV-22A**s for US Navy combat SAR, special warfare and fleet logistic support missions. The US Navy also foresaw a need for up to 300 **SV-22A** ASW versions.

Under current plans the US Marine Corps hopes to acquire 30 MV-22B Ospreys per year, from 2006/07 onwards, replacing elderly CH-46E helicopters.

During the 1990s plans for the Osprey changed dramatically as the programme was cut-back, cancelled, re-instated and cut back again. The USMC requirement has dropped to 360 **MV-22B**s, while the Navy plans to acquire 48 C-SAR-configured **HV-22B**s in around 2010. All plans for US Army Ospreys have been dropped and while the USAF still has a notional requirement for 50 **CV-22B**s, these aircraft may yet be cancelled.

In May 1997 assembly began of the first production-standard MV-22B. Thirty Ospreys have been ordered into low-rate initial production and deliveries began to the USMC in mid-1999. Marine Corps evaluation of the Osprey (conducted by VMMT-204) was blighted by several crashes. Two aircraft were lost on 8 April 2000 (killing 19 Marines) while a third crashed in December. The Nos 4 and 5 prototypes were involved in earlier accidents in 1991/92. While the crashes were not attributable to any inherent design flaws all Ospreys were grounded, and the future of the expensive and controversial aircraft has been called into question once more.

The V-22 has the ability to transition from vertical to horizontal flight, thanks to its revolutionary, but controversial, tilt-wing technology.

Specification: Bell/Boeing V-22 Osprey
Powerplant: two Allison T406-AD-400 turboshafts each rated at 4586 kW (6,150 shp)
Dimensions: rotor diameter, each 11.61 m (38 ft 1 in); wing span 15.52 m (50 ft 11 in) incl. nacelles; length, fuselage excl. probe 17.47 m (57 ft 4 in); height over fins 5.38 m (17 ft 7¾ in)
Weights: empty equipped 14463 kg (31,886 lb); max take-off 27442 kg (60,500 lb); max int. payload 9072 kg (20,000 lb); max ext. payload 6804 kg (15,000 lb)
Performance: maximum cruising speed 185 kmh (115 mph) in helicopter mode and 509 kmh (316 mph) in aeroplane mode; service ceiling 7925 m (26,000 ft); assault range 953 km (592 miles)

Boeing AV-8 Harrier

Having unsuccessfully pursued their individual programmes for an advanced successor to the RAF's **Harrier GR.Mk 3** and the USMC's **AV-8A Harrier**, British Aerospace (now BAE Systems) and McDonnell Douglas (now Boeing) began to work on the joint **Harrier II** design. This radically revised aircraft featured a new, larger-area carbon-fibre supercritical wing, a completely redesigned, raised cockpit, and advanced aerodynamic lift-enhancing devices including LERXes and underfuselage lift-increasing 'dams'. The new wing was first flown on 9 November 1978, fitted to the 11th AV-8A (which became the first of two prototype **YAV-8B**s). The US Marine Corps took delivery of the first production **AV-8B Harrier II**s in 1983.

From September 1989 (the 167th airframe on), all USMC AV-8Bs were made night-attack capable with the installation of a prominent FLIR housing above the nose, a colour moving map and an improved HUD. The term **AV-8B (Night Attack)** is often applied to these aircraft. For training, McDonnell Douglas developed the **TAV-8B** with a new forward fuselage, accommodating stepped tandem cockpits. Internal fuel is reduced and to offset the reduced stability caused by the longer fuselage, the vertical fin is increased in area.

*The distinctive **FLIR** (Forward-Looking Infra-Red) sensor above the nose is what gives the Night Attack AV-8B its 24-hour operational capability.*

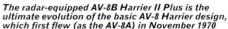

The radar-equipped AV-8B Harrier II Plus is the ultimate evolution of the basic AV-8 Harrier design, which first flew (as the AV-8A) in November 1970

In 1987 McDonnell Douglas announced plans to develop a radar-equipped version of the AV-8B, the **AV-8B Harrier II Plus**. In 1990 the US Navy authorised the development of a prototype and 24 production aircraft. The first fully-equipped true prototype flew on 22 September 1992. The Harrier II Plus is fitted with the APG-65 multi-mode radar, giving it the capability to use radar-guided missiles, such as the AIM-120 AMRAAM, for the first time.

In 1992 the USA, Spain and Italy signed an agreement covering the joint development of the Harrier II Plus. The US Marine Corps has acquired a total of 27 new-build Harrier II Pluses, and a further 72 examples converted from existing AV-8Bs. The first Harrier II Plus was delivered to the Marines in July 1993, and the first remanufactured Harrier II Plus followed in January 1996. The Spanish navy purchased 18 aircraft to supplement its existing EAV-8B Harriers, while Italy bought 16 Harrier II Pluses, and two TAV-8Bs. The last Harrier II Pluses were delivered to Spain and Italy in July and December 1999, respectively.

In May 2000 Spain signed a deal to remanufacture two of its nine EAV-8Bs to Harrier II Plus standard, and plans to bring all its Harriers to this level. The first two rebuilt aircraft will be handed over in 2003.

Specification: Boeing AV-8B Harrier II
Powerplant: one 105.87-kN (23,800-lb) Rolls-Royce F402-RR-408 turbofan
Dimensions: span 9.25 m (30 ft 4 in); length 14.12 m (46 ft 4 in); 3.55 m height (11 ft 8 in)
Weights: operating empty 6336 kg (13,968 lb); normal take-off 10410 kg (22,950 lb); maximum take-off 14061 kg (31,000 lb) for 405-m (1,330-ft) STO or 8596 kg (18,950 lb) for VTO
Performance: maximum level speed 1065 kmh (662 mph); maximum rate of climb 4485 m (14,715 ft) per minute; combat radius 167 km (103 miles)
Armament: one GAU-12A 25-mm cannon (optional) with 300 rounds; maximum ordnance 6003 kg (13,235 lb)

Boeing B-52 Stratofortress

The first **B-52 Stratofortress**es rolled off the Boeing production line in 1952, and from then until 1962 a total of 744 were built. The B-52 was the backbone of Strategic Air Command (SAC) until 1992, when the assets and tasks of SAC and TAC were merged into the newly-established Air Combat Command. Today only one version of the bomber remains in service, the **B-52H**. The USAF inventory stands at 94 aircraft, but they have a striking power out of all proportion to their number.

The B-52 is the only USAF aircraft cleared to carry all the nuclear and conventional weapons in the Air Force arsenal. The B-52 was designed as a nuclear bomber and, alongside the B-2, it is still tasked with this strategic strike mission – using free-fall nuclear bombs or cruise-missiles. Because of its immense range and heavy load-carrying ability the B-52H has now adopted a range of conventional roles, including anti-shipping attacks, mine-laying, area bombing and long-range precision stand-off attacks. B-52s fired some of the first shots of Operation Desert Storm, and flew what became the longest combat mission in aviation history, on the first night of operations in 1991. Seven **B-52G**s attacked targets in Iraq using a new version of the Air-Launched Cruise Missile, the AGM-86C, with a high-explosive warhead. This weapon gave the B-52 a completely new precision attack capability, which has now been transferred to the B-52H. The last B-52Gs were retired in March 1994.

The 'LA' tail code on this B-52H marks it one from the 2nd Bomb Wing, based at Barksdale AFB. Air Combat Command's second B-52 Wing is Minot AFB's 5th BW.

The superior conventional weapons capability of the B-52G was transferred to the B-52H under the CMUP (Conventional Mission Upgrade Program) effort. Inside the main bomb-bay the B-52 is fitted with the Common Stores Rotary Launcher which can carry four B28 nuclear bombs, eight B61 or B83 nuclear bombs or eight AGM-86B/C cruise missiles. Another 12 cruise missiles can be carried externally. Depending on the underwing pylon configuration, up to 51 750-lb bombs can be carried – 24 under the wing and 27 in the bomb-bay. The B-52H can also carry AGM-84 Harpoon anti-ship missiles, AGM-142A Have Nap stand-off attack missiles, Paveway II laser-guided bombs and Quickstrike mines.

The USAF currently has two active Bomb Wings (a total of four squadrons) and single Air Force Reserve Wing (one squadron) equipped with the B-52H. In early 2001, Boeing submitted an unsolicited proposal to the USAF to re-engine all the remaining B-52Hs. The bombers' eight TF-33 turbofans would be replaced by four more modern Rolls Royce (Allison) RB-211-535 turbofans.

This 2nd Bomb Wing B-52H is dropping a load of 750-lb M117 bombs. A B-52H can carry up to 51 M117s, totalling some 38,250-lb (17,350-kg) of high-explosive.

Specification: Boeing B-52H Stratofortress

Powerplant: eight 75.62-kN (17,000-lb) Pratt & Whitney TF33-P-3 turbofans
Dimensions: wing span 56.39 m (185 ft); length 49.05 m (160 ft 10.9 in); height 12.40 m (40 ft 8 in)
Weights: maximum take-off 229088 kg (505,000 lb)
Performance: cruising speed at high altitude 819 kmh (509 mph); penetration speed at low altitude between 652 and 676 kmh (405 and 420 mph); service ceiling 16765 m (55,000 ft); range, with one aerial refuelling, at least 13880 km (8,625 miles)
Armament: up to 22680 kg (50,000 lb) of nuclear and conventional ordnance

Boeing C-17 Globemaster III

In August 1981 McDonnell Douglas was chosen to develop the USAF's **C-X** requirement for a new heavy cargo transport, to replace the C-141 Starlifter. The new aircraft had to be capable of carrying outsize loads, such as the M1 tank and combat helicopters, while retaining a tactical operations capability, including LAPES drops and short landings into austere strips.

The design of the resulting **C-17A** adopted a classic military transport configuration with a high-mounted supercritical wing, a rear-fuselage loading ramp and undercarriage housings on each side of the fuselage. However, it incorporates such advanced features as winglets, high-performance turbofans (military versions of the Boeing 757's PW2040) and an all-digital fly-by-wire control system. Short-field performance is aided by an externally-blown flap system and thrust reversers.

The C-17 can be configured for cargo, para-troops, combat troops, hospital litter patients, or combinations of all these. For strategic airlift, it can carry 202 personnel, or 18 standard 463L pallets. Typical loads include two M2 Bradley AFVs, two 5-ton 8x8 trucks with trailers, three AH-64 Apache helicopters or six OH-58D helicopters. The C-17 can air-drop up to 102 paratroops or platform loads

The C-17 has impressive short-field capabilities, thanks to its high-performance wing (for short take-offs) and thrust-reversers (for short landings),

In USAF service the C-17 is flown by Air Mobility Command and has become an increasingly precious resource as AMC's older C-5s and C-141s wear out.

of up to 49895 kg (110,000 lb). The internal cargo loading system is fully mechanised for operation by a single loadmaster.

The C-17 endured a turbulent development period and came close to cancellation on several occasions, due largely to cost overruns and technical difficulties. Plans to acquire 210 USAF aircraft have been revised downwards to just 120. The first prototype flew on 15 September 1991, followed by the first initial production C-17A on 18 May 1992. On 5 February 1993 the aircraft was renamed as the **C-17A Globemaster III** and the first example was delivered to an operational USAF unit on 14 June 1993. On 17 January 1995, the 17th Airlift Squadron at Charleston AFB, was declared 'operationally ready for worldwide missions'. In 1997 the C-17 became a product of the Boeing Company, when McDonnell Douglas was taken over in August that year.

The C-17 won its operational spurs during Operation Joint Endeavor, supporting peacekeeping in Bosnia, and Operation Allied Force in Kosovo. Britain's Royal Air Force intends to lease four C-17s from 2001 onwards, to provide much-needed strategic airlift capability. By March 2001 the USAF had taken delivery of 73 C-17As.

Specification: Boeing C-17A Globemaster III
Powerplant: four 185.49-kN (41,700-lb) Pratt & Whitney F117-P-100 turbofans
Dimensions: span 52.20 m (171 ft 3 in) between winglet tips; length 53.04 m (174 ft in); height 16.79 m (55 ft 1 in)
Weights: operating empty 122016 kg (269,000 lb); maximum take-off 263083 kg (580,000 lb); maximum payload 78108 kg (172,200 lb)
Performance: maximum cruising speed at low altitude 648 kmh (403 mph); service ceiling 13715 m (45,000 ft); take-off field length with 75750-kg (167,000-lb) payload 2286 m (7,500 ft); landing field length 914 m (3,000 ft) with thrust reversal; range with 36286-kg (80,000-lb) payload 7630 km (4,741 miles)

Boeing C-135 family

Following successful trials of the **Boeing 367-80** transport prototype with a Boeing-designed 'flying boom' refuelling probe under the rear fuselage, the US Air Force placed an order for an initial batch of 29 **KC-135A Stratotanker** aircraft, in September 1955. These would be the first of a grand total of 732 to be built. The first KC-135A flew in August 1956 and the initial production Stratotanker was delivered to Castle AFB in June 1957. The last KC-135A was delivered to the USAF in 1965.

Two major turbofan re-engining programmes have since been undertaken. The first involved the conversion of 188 early-model aircraft to **KC-135E** standard, adding TF33 turbofans and wider-span tailplanes. The thrust reverser-equipped TF33 allowed greater safety margins, the use of shorter runways and reduced noise pollution. The KC-135E, is 14 per cent more fuel efficient than the KC-135A and can off-load 20 percent more fuel.

The Boeing-developed **KC-135R** first flew in August 1982 and is the mainstay of today's USAF tanker fleet. Over 400 these CFM56-powered conversions have been funded to date, with the first entering service in July 1984. The USAF's specialist **KC-135Q** tankers (once dedicated to the SR-71 fleet), have now been re-engined as **KC-135T** and are used for F-117 support tasks. A KC-135R can off-load 50 percent more fuel, is 25 percent more fuel efficient, costs 25 per cent less to operate and is 96 per cent quieter than a KC-135A.

France's fleet of KC-135FRs have been modified to carry underwing hose-and-drogue pods to refuel probe-equipped aircraft.

About 550 KC-135s remain in service. Boeing also built another 88 **C-135**s of various kinds for special missions. The most important of these is the **RC-135** family of reconnaissance aircraft. Current types include 15 **RC-135V** and **RC-135W** **'Rivet Joint'** aircraft, and two **RC-135U 'Combat Sent'** aircraft. These are all sophisticated electronic intelligence gathering platforms, with a range of tactical and strategic roles. There is also a single **RC-135S 'Cobra Ball'** aircraft, which uses high-powered optical systems to examine missile re-entry vehicles and satellites in low-earth orbit. All of the USAF's RC-135s are attached to the 55th Wing, based at Offutt AFB, Nebraska.

KC-135 tankers have been exported to France (14 **KC-135F**s now **KC-135FR**s) and Singapore (four KC-135Rs). Approximately 544 USAF C-135s of all types will undergo the Pacer Crag cockpit and navigation systems upgrade (Crag stands for compass radar and GPS), in addition to acquiring TCAS and GATS/GATM capability, allowing them to operate within improved future air traffic control systems.

The USAF now has a fleet of 15 RC-135V and RC-135W aircraft, which are its most important signals and electronic intelligence-gathering assets.

Specification: Boeing KC-135R Stratotanker
Powerplant: four 97.86-kN (22,000-lb) CFM International F108-CF-100 turbofans
Dimensions: wing span 39.88 m (130 ft 10 in); length 41.53 m (136 ft 3 in); height 12.70 m (41 ft 8 in)
Weights: operating empty 48220 kg (106,306 lb); maximum take-off 146284 kg (322,500 lb); internal fuel 92210 kg (203,288 lb); maximum payload 37650 kg (83,000 lb)
Performance: maximum level speed at high altitude 982 kmh (610 mph); cruising speed at 10670 m (35,000 ft) 856 kmh (532 mph); maximum rate of climb 393 m (1,290 ft) per minute; service ceiling 13715 m (45,000 ft); operational radius 4633 km (2,879 miles)

Boeing E-3 Sentry

Boeing's **E-3 Sentry** is the world's largest and most capable AWACS (airborne warning and control system) aircraft. The **EC-137D** prototype first flew on 5 February 1972, followed by the first **E-3A** on 31 October 1975. Using the airframe of a 707-320B airliner fitted with a radar 'rotodome' and an extensive crew of mission operators, the E-3 is a flying C^3I Command, Control, Communications and Intelligence) platform. E-3s are used to control the 'air battle' monitoring all airborne activity and controlling combat operations over a wide area . At the heart of the system is the AN/APY-2 Overland Downlook Radar, which is capable of tracking up to 600 low-flying aircraft. Since entering service, Sentries have been involved in combat operations in Grenada (1983), Lebanon (1983), Panama (1989) and Iraq (1991) and continuing operations in the Balkans.

Twenty-two E-3As and two EC-137Ds, collectively termed 'core' aircraft when they were standardised in the late 1970s, were upgraded to **E-3B** level with faster computers, ECM-resistant communications and additional radios and display consoles. The first E-3B was redelivered in July 1984. In 1984, 10 E-3As were modified to **E-3C** standard with a larger crew capacity, most E-3B equipment and 'Have Quick' communications equipment. All but the first 25 E-3

The large bulges which have been added to upgraded NATO and USAF (Block 30/35) E-3s house the new AN/AYR-1 'Quick Look' ESM/Elint system.

RAF Sentry AEW.Mk 1s have been consistently among the most capable E-3s, thanks to their CFM56 engines, advanced systems and excellent tactics.

airframes have inboard underwing hardpoints. E-3A 'standard' versions have been delivered to Saudia Arabia (five) and NATO (18). The USAF has 33 E-3s.

Both US and NATO aircraft have undergone recent upgrades to enhance their capabilities, and add new electronic surveillance systems. US Sentries have undergone the **Block 30/35 Modification Program**, which includes an electronic surveillance capability to detect and identify air and surface-based emitters, the JTIDS datalink, increased computer memory and GPS navigation. In addition, a five-year U.S./NATO Radar System Improvement Program (RSIP) was launched in 1999. RSIP involves major hardware and software modifications to the existing radar system.

Improved and re-engined Sentries have been delivered to the UK (seven **E-3D Sentry AEW. Mk 1**) and France (four **E-3F SDA (Système de Détection Aéroportée)**). Both versions entered service in 1991 and are powered by CFM56 turbofans. They are also fitted with IFR probes, in addition to the standard E-3 inflight-refuelling receptacle. RAF aircraft have wingtip-mounted Loral Yellow Gate ESM pods (becoming the first E-3s with this capability). CFM56 engines also power the five E-3As and eight **KE-3A** tanker aircraft, acquired by Saudi Arabia.

Specification: Boeing E-3C Sentry
Powerplant: four 93.41-kN (21,000-lb) Pratt & Whitney TF33-P-100/100A turbofans
Dimensions: wing span 44.42 m (145 ft 9 in); length 46.61 m (152 ft 11 in); height 12.73 m (41 ft 9 in)
Weights: operating empty 77996 kg (171,950 lb); maximum take-off 147420 kg (325,000 lb); internal fuel 90800 litres (23,987 US gal)
Performance: maximum level speed at high altitude 853 kmh (530 mph); operating ceiling 8840 m (29,000 ft); operational radius 1612 km (1,002 miles) for a six-hour patrol without flight refuelling; endurance more than 11 hours with flight refuelling

Boeing F-15A, F-15B, F-15C, F-15D

The McDonnell Douglas-designed **F-15 Eagle** is viewed as the world's best air superiority fighter and interceptor, particularly in the BVR (beyond visual range) air-to-air mission. It was designed for the USAF's 1968 **FX** requirement which called for a long-range air superiority fighter to replace the F-4. McDonnell won that competition and flew a prototype **F-15A** on 27 July 1972, followed by a prototype **F-15B** two-seat trainer in July 1973.

The F-15 has an advanced aerodynamic design with large lightly-loaded wings conferring high agility. It features a sophisticated avionics system and its APG-63 radar introduced a genuine look-down/shoot-down capability. Radar-guided AIM-7 AAMs form the primary armament, augmented by AIM-9 AAMs. While still in use, the AIM-7 has now been superseded by the far more capable AIM-120 AMRAAM. The USAF is also preparing to introduce the latest AIM-9X off-boresight short-range missile.

The USAF received 360 production F-15As and 58 F-15Bs from 1976. Most remaining F-15A/Bs now serve with ANG units. The only foreign F-15A/B operator is Israel, which currently operates a force of about 50 A/Bs.

The **F-15C**, an improved and updated F-15A, was the definitive production version. The two-seat **F-15D** was a similarly-improved F-15B. First flying on 26 February 1979, the F-15C introduced uprated F100 engines and provision for conformal fuel tanks (CFTs). Initial deliveries were made in September

This mix of F-15Cs (and a single F-15D) are from the two Eagle squadrons of the Kadena AFB-based 18th Wing, one of PACAF's key units.

1979 and F-15C/Ds later replaced F-15A/Bs with three wings. The F-15 Multistage Improvement Program was initiated in February 1983, with the first production MSIP F-15C produced in 1985. Improvements included an upgraded central computer, a Programmable Armament Control Set, allowing for advanced versions of the AIM-7, AIM-9, and AIM-120A missiles, and an expanded Tactical Electronic Warfare System that provides improvements to the ALR-56C radar warning receiver and ALQ-135 countermeasure set. The final 43 were fitted with a Hughes APG-70 radar.

F-15C/Ds were delivered to the USAF (408/62), Israel (18/9) and Saudi Arabia (98). The equivalent **F-15J/DJ** is Japan's principal air superiority fighter. Most of the JASDF's 213 planned Eagles have been assembled under licence by Mitsubishi.

The USAF is now fitting all its F-15A/Cs with the upgraded APG-63(V)1 radar. The first of these aircraft entered service in April 2001. During 2000, 18 special F-15Cs were fitted with the APG-63(V)2 Active Electronically Scanned Array (AESA) radar.

A yellow fin stripe marks this F-15C as an aircraft from the 2nd Fighter Squadron, 325th Fighter Wing, based at Tyndall AFB, in Florida.

Specification: Boeing F-15C Eagle
Powerplant: two 106.0-kN (23,830-lb) Pratt & Whitney F100-P-220 turbofans
Dimensions: span 13.05 m (42 ft 10 in); length 19.43 m (63 ft 9 in); height 5.63 m (18 ft 5½ in)
Weights: operating empty 12793 kg (28,600 lb); normal take-off 20244 kg (44,630 lb); maximum take-off 30844 kg (68,000 lb), with CFTs
Performance: maximum level speed more than 2655 kmh (1,650 mph); maximum rate of climb at sea level more than 15240 m (50,000 ft) per minute; service ceiling 18290 m (60,000 ft); combat radius 1967 km (1,222 miles) (interception mission)
Armament: one M61 20-mm cannon with 940 rounds; maximum ordnance 7257 kg (16,000 lb)

Boeing F-15E, F-15I Strike Eagle

The F-15 was originally intended as dual-role aircraft, incorporating air-to-ground capability and wired for the carriage of air-to-ground ordnance. This ground attack role was abandoned in 1975, but later resurrected in 1982, when the second TF-15A was modified as the privately-developed **'Strike Eagle'**. It was conceived as a replacement for the F-111. Development of the resulting **F-15E** began in February 1984 and the first production aircraft made its maiden flight on 11 December 1986.

The F-15E's primary mission is air-to-ground strike, for which it carries a wide range of weapons on two underwing pylons, underfuselage pylons and 12 bomb racks mounted directly on the CFTs. It introduces redesigned controls, a wide field of vision HUD, and three multi-purpose CRTs displaying navigation, weapons delivery and systems operations. The rear-cockpit WSO employs four multi-purpose CRT terminals for radar, weapon selection and monitoring of enemy tracking systems. The WSO also operates an AN/APG-70 synthetic aperture radar and LANTIRN navigation and targeting pods. The navigation pod incorporates its own TFR, which can be linked to the aircraft's flight control system to allow automatic coupled terrain following flight. The targeting pod allows the aircraft to self-designate LGBs. The F-15E's original F100-PW-220 turbofans were soon replaced by P&W's F100-PW-229 engine under the Improved Performance Engine competitive programme.

The F-15E is a long-range deep strike aircraft, with both conventional and nuclear weapons capability. This example is from the Lakenheath-based 48th FW.

The F-15E is arguably the best all-round combat aircraft in the world today as it combines the fighter genes of the F-15C with a precision attack capability.

The F-15E has been exported to Israel as the **F-15I Ra'am**, and to Egypt as the **F-15S**. Israel has acquired 25 F-15Is and the first two aircraft were delivered in January 1998. Israel's F-15Is are identical to USAF F-15Es, but the Saudi F-15S aircraft have been downgraded, with some air-to-air and air-to-ground capabilities deleted. The first of 72 F-15Ss made its maiden flight on 19 June 1995. Boeing has offered another version of the the F-15E, the **F-15K**, to South Korea.

The USAF took delivery of 209 F-15Es between 1987 and 1994. A follow-o batch of 17 aircraft was delivered in 2000, bringing that total up to 226 aircraft. These F-15Es were equipped with new advanced data processors, a new digital mapping system, provisions for an upgraded Programmable Armament Control System, expanded smart weapons carriage capability (to include JDAM), and an embedded Global Positioning System/Inertial Navigation System for increased accuracy. The USAF plans to upgrade all its Strike Eagles to this standard.

Specification: Boeing F-15E Eagle
Powerplant: two 129.45-kN (29,100-lb) Pratt & Whitney F100-PW-229 turbofans
Dimensions: wing span 13.05 m (42 ft 10 in); length 19.43 m (63 ft 9 in); height 5.63 m (18 ft 5.5 in)
Weights: operating empty 14379 kg (31,700 lb); maximum take-off 36741 kg (81,000 lb)
Performance: maximum level speed 'clean' at high altitude more than 2655 kmh (1,650 mph); maximum rate of climb at sea level more than 15240 m (50,000 ft) per minute; combat radius 61270 km (790 miles)
Armament: one M61A1 20-mm cannon with 940 rounds; maximum ordnance load of 11113 kg (24,500 lb)

Boeing F/A-18A, B, C, D Hornet

The **Hornet** was a more sophisticated navalised derivative of the Northrop YF-17, which was developed in its final form in partnership with McDonnell Douglas (now Boeing). The first of 11 pre-production aircraft made the Hornet's maiden flight on 18 November 1978 and production followed of 371 **F/A-18A**s. A two-seater Hornet version was initially designated **TF-18A** , before becoming the **F/A-18B**. Basically identical to the F/A-18A, provision of a second seat in tandem was accomplished at a six per cent cut in fuel capacity.

The F/A-18 was revolutionary for introducing a genuinely multi-role capability and the first truly modern fighter cockpit. The pilot has three multi-function displays and true HOTAS controls, which can switch easily from the air-to-ground role to air-to-air or defence suppression duties. The F/A-18's dogfighting capability is remarkable, advanced wing design with large slotted LERXes conferring excellent high-Alpha capability and turn performance. Similarly, the multi-mode APG-65 radar is as effective at putting bombs with high accuracy on target as it is at detecting and engaging multiple airborne targets.

The improved **F/A-18C** was first flown in September 1986. An expanded weapons capability introduced the AIM-120 AMRAAM, imaging IR AGM-65 missiles and other weapons. The F/A-18C also features an avionics upgrade with new AN/ALR-67 RHAWS, provision for the AN/ALQ-165

This VFA-82 F/A-18C is carrying a load of eight 1,000-lb Mk 83 general purpose bombs, plus two AIM-7 Sparrow and two AIM-9 Sidewinder AAMs.

airborne self-protection jammer (ASPJ) and improvements to mission computer equipment. After 137 baseline F/A-18Cs had been delivered, production switched to a night-attack capable version, featuring compatibility with Cat's Eyes PNVGs, a Hughes AN/AAR-50 TINS (Thermal Imaging Navigation Set) pod, externally-carried AN/AAS-38 targeting FLIR pod and colour MFDs.

The two-seat **F/A-18D** trainer is broadly similar to the single-seat F/A-18C. However, the US Marine Corps has developed a sophisticated two-crew combat-capable version, the **Night Attack F/A-18D** (originally known as the **F/A-18D+**). F/A-18Ds can also be fitted with the ATARS reconnaissance system, fitted in a redesigned nose.

F/A-18A/Bs were exported to Australia (57/18 **AF-18A/B**s), Canada (98/40 **CF-188A/B**s) and Spain (60/12). F/A-18C/Ds have been sold to Finland (57/7), Kuwait (32/8) and Switzerland (26/8). The last of 1,479 first-generation Hornets was delivered in late 2000, and production has now moved on to the larger, more advanced F/A-18E/F Super Hornet.

A 'aggressor' camouflage scheme marks this Hornet as an aircraft from the Naval Strike and Air Warfare Center, the unit now responsible for 'Topgun'.

Specification: Boeing F/A-18C Hornet
Powerplant: two 78.73-kN (17,700-lb) General Electric F404-GE-402 turbofans
Dimensions: wing span 12.31 m (40 ft 5 in) with tip-mounted AAMs; length 17.07 m (56 ft); height 4.66 m (15 ft 3 in)
Weights: empty 10455 kg (23,050 lb); normal take-off 16652 kg (36,710 lb) fighter mission, or 23541 kg (51,900 lb) attack mission
Performance: maximum level speed more than 1915 kmh (1,190 mph); maximum rate of climb at sea level 13715 m (45,000 ft) per minute; combat radius over 740 km (460 miles)
Armament: one M61A1 20-mm cannon with 570 rounds; maximum ordnance load 7031 kg (15,500 lb)

Boeing F/A-18E/F Super Hornet

When the US Navy was forced to cancel the General Dynamics A-12 long-range, stealthy attack aircraft, it still faced with the problem of how to replace its A-6 Intruders and early-model F/A-18 Hornets. The chosen solution was to develop an improved version of the Hornet, albeit one that would be substantially different to existing aircraft. This **Super Hornet** was first proposed in 1991 and the engineering and manufacturing development (EMD) contract was officially awarded to McDonnell Douglas in June 1992. Single-seat Super Hornets were given the designation **F/A-18E**, while the two-seat version became the **F/A-18F**.

The Super Hornet is based on the basic F/A-18C airframe, but is longer and heavier with increased wing area, larger tail surfaces and extended leading-edge extensions. Many elements, such as the engine intakes, have been redesigned to make the aircraft stealthier. The Super Hornet can carry more fuel than earlier Hornets, and has a much higher landing weight limit. The final production standard will be fitted with the AESA radar and a very advanced mission computer fit and digital cockpit.

The Super Hornet EMD contract covered seven prototypes, five F/A-18Es and two F/A-18Fs. The first Super Hornet (an E) made its maiden flight on

The F/A-18E/F has a reprofiled, deeper wing with larger control surfaces than the F/A-18C/D, and a distinctive 'dogtooth' on the wing's leading-edge.

Under current plans the F/A-18E will replace the US Navy's early-model Hornets, while the two-seat F/A-18E/F will replace the F-14 Tomcat.

29 November 1995. On 14 February 1996 the first aircraft arrived at the Naval Air Warfare Centre, Patuxent River, for a three-year test programme. The fifth and final EMD prototype made its maiden flight on 11 October 1996. Carrier trials began in mid-1996 and low-rate initial production was approved in March 1997 (the same year that Boeing took over the programme from McDonnell Douglas). By 12 January 1999 the Super Hornet test fleet had flown 4,000 hours.

During flight tests the F/A-18E/F encountered a number of unexpected problems, and suffered much criticism for poor handling and a lack of performance. With the Joint Strike Fighter facing an uncertain future, the Super Hornet is the only next-generation fighter immediately available to the US Navy, and so the rectification of any problems with the aircraft was of the highest priority.

In November 1999 the F/A-18E/F passed its critical Operational Evaluation and achieved its initial operating capability in 2000. The first active squadron is VFA-122, which was established at NAS Lemoore, in January 1999. The US Navy hopes to acquire 785 Super Hornets. Boeing is now offering a SEAD version of the F/A-18E/F to replace the EA-6B Prowler, dubbed the **F/A-18C²W** or the '**Growler**'.

Specification: Boeing F/A-18E/F Super Hornet
Powerplant: two 97.9-kN (22,000-lb) General Electric F414-GE-400 afterburning turbofans
Dimensions: wing span 13.62 m (44 ft 8½ in) with tip-mounted AAMs; length 18.31 m (60 ft 1¼ in); height 4.88 m (16 ft)
Weights: empty 13387 kg (29,574 lb); normal take-off 29927 kg (66,000 lb), attack mission
Performance: maximum level speed Mach 1.8; combat ceiling 15240 m (50,000 ft); maximum combat radius 760 km (472 miles)
Armament: one M61A1 20-mm cannon with 570 rounds; maximum ordnance load 8051 kg (17,750 lb)

Boeing T-45 Goshawk

At the beginning of the 1980s the US Navy launched its VTXTS requirement, to find a replacement for its TA-4J and T-2C carrier-capable trainers. In November 1981, a modified version of the British Aerospace (now BAE SYSTEMS) Hawk was chosen, following a fierce competition. This aircraft was selected by the US Navy as its T45TS (Training System), with McDonnell Douglas (now Boeing) becoming the prime contractor. The principal sub-contractor was British Aerospace, which built the wings, centre and rear fuselage, fin, tailplane, windscreen, canopy and flying controls. As first proposed there were to be two variants, a 'wet' **T-45A** fitted for carrier operations and a 'dry' **T-45B** restricted to land-based training. Life extension of the T-2 and TA-4J led to a decision to acquire 300 T-45As only (later reduced to 187).

In order to tailor the basic Hawk airframe to meet stringent US Navy requirements for carrier operations, the aircraft has a strengthened twin nosegear, compatible with its ship's steam catapults. The main gear is redesigned, with longer stroke oleos. Fin height and tailplane span are increased and a single ventral fin is added. The ventral airbrake is replaced by two fuselage side-mounted units. The T-45 has new full-span leading-edge slats and is fitted with an arrester hook, US Navy standard cockpit instrumentation and radios, Martin-Baker Mk 14 NACES ejection seats and a revised fuel system.

The T-45C is the latest version of the Goshawk. It is fitted with the 'Cockpit 21' system, adding two new monochrome multi-function displays for each pilot.

The T-45A was given the name **Goshawk** and work on two prototypes began in February 1986. The first T-45 made its maiden flight on 16 April 1988 and an aircraft made its first carrier landing (aboard the USS *John F. Kennedy*) on 4 December 1991. The first squadron to be equipped with T-45As was VT-21, part of Training Wing 2, based at NAS Kingsville, Texas. This unit was declared operational in October 1993. Full-rate T-45A production was authorised in 1995.

In 1994 a new advanced 'glass' cockpit fit, called 'Cockpit 21', was flown in a development aircraft for the first time. This makes the T-45 more compatible with the current generation of Navy combat aircraft and it is planned to be refitted to all earlier aircraft. Beginning in 1997 the new digital cockpit systems were fitted to all new-built T-45s (from the 87th example onwards) and these upgraded aircraft have been designated **T-45C**s. T-45Cs can be identified by the GPS antenna fitted to their spines. T-45C deliveries are scheduled to continue until 2005.

The T-45A is based on the Hawk Mk 60, but a number of important changes have been made for its demanding carrier training role.

Specification: Boeing T-45C Goshawk
Powerplant: one 26.00 kN (5,845 lb st) Rolls-Royce/Turboméca F405-RR-401 turbofan
Dimensions: wing span 9.39 m (30 ft 9¾ in); length 11.98 m (39 ft 4 in) including probe; height 4.26 m (14 ft)
Weights: empty 4460 kg (9,834 lb); maximum take-off 6387 kg (14,081 lb)
Performance: maximum level speed 'clean' at 2440 m (8,000 ft) 1006 kmh (625 mph); maximum rate of climb at sea level 2440 m (8,000 ft) per minute; service ceiling 12200 m (40,000 ft); take-off distance to 15 m (50 ft) 1100 m (3,610ft) at maximum take-off weight; ferry range on internal fuel 1532 km (952 miles)

Boeing X-32 (JSF)

The US **Joint Strike Fighter** (**JSF**) programme is an ambitious effort to develop a replacement for an entire generation of USAF, US Navy and US Marine Corps aircraft using one common 'stealthy' airframe. The JSF is earmarked to replace the F-16, F/A-18, AV-8B and other types in the US inventory, and will also be exportable to customers worldwide. The JSF has its roots in a number of studies for advanced, affordable combat aircraft that were launched in the early 1990s. These were merged into the **JAST** (**Joint Advanced Strike Technology**) programme in 1995, which later became JSF.

Three contractors – Boeing, Lockheed Martin and McDonnell Douglas – were selected by the US DoD to submit JSF designs. In November 1996 Boeing and Lockheed Martin were selected to build two demonstrator aircraft, essentially JSF prototypes, to conduct a Concept Demonstration Program. At the end of this period one single contractor would be chosen to build its winning JSF design. Boeing's CDP aircraft was given the designation **X-32**.

While the JSF concept demands a common airframe, there will be different versions for the three main US users, and two distinct variants of the basic design. The USAF and the US Navy are looking for a conventional take-off and landing

The X-32A CTOL JSF demonstrator flies alongside an F/A-18D Hornet, illustrating the substantial size of the new aircraft.

Boeing's X-32A is not a sleek or slender aircraft, but it is a very advanced aerodynamic design that incorporates much new technology.

(CTOL) capability, though Navy aircraft will have to be modified for carrier operations. The Marines need aircraft with short take-off and vertical landing (STOVL) capability to replace the Harrier, so the USMC's JSF variant will have to have a modified propulsion system for vertical lift. Britain's Fleet Air Arm (Royal Navy) has also signed up to acquire the STOVL JSF to replace its Sea Harriers.

Boeing has built two different CDP aircraft. The CTOL **X-32A** and the STOVL **X-32B**. The X-32A made its maiden flight on 18 September 2000, while the X-32B flew for the first time on 29 March 2001. Boeing's JSF design is far more unconventional than its rival, the Lockheed Martin X-35, and features a one-piece blended wing, with twin all-moving vertical tails and inset rudders. The STOVL version has two directional, ventral exhaust nozzles. The X-32's high wing layout was chosen to aid STOVL performance and the chin-mounted air intake 'droops' to allow a greater intake of engine air for STOVL flight and hovering.

A decision date on the winning JSF design has been pushed back several times, but is now planned before the end of 2001. The first operational aircraft are expected to be the Marines' STOVL variants in 2008, followed by the CTOL aircraft in 2010.

Specification: Boeing X-32A JSF (CDP)
Powerplant: one Pratt & Whitney JSF119-614 turbofan, with two-dimensional cruising nozzle
Dimensions: wing span 10.97 m (36 ft); length 13.65 m (44 ft 8 in) excluding probe; height 4.00 m (13 ft 1 in)
Weights: maximum take-off 16692 kg (36,800 lb)
Performance: maximum level speed over Mach 1.0;
Armament: one internal Bk 27 27-mm cannon
(Full specification not available)

Boeing AH-64 Apache

Hughes' **AH-64A Apache** was developed to meet a US Army requirement for an advanced attack helicopter (AAH) suitable for the all-weather day/night anti-armour role. The AH-64 is a two-seat helicopter with armoured structure, advanced crew protection systems, avionics, electro-optics, and weapon-control systems, including the TADS/PNVS (Target Acquisition and Designation System/Pilot's Night Vision Sensor). Hughes was bought by McDonnell Douglas in 1984, which became McDonnell Douglas Helicopters 1985. In 1997 McDonnell Douglas was itself taken over by Boeing.

The **YAH-64** prototype first flew on 30 September 1975. The production-standard **AH-64A** entered US Army Aviation service in April 1986 and the last of 821 AH-64As delivered to the Army was handed over on 30 April 1996. The first export customer for the AH-64A was Israel, in 1990. Subsequent customers included Saudi Arabia, the UAE, Egypt and Greece.

In January 1991 Army AH-64As flew the very first mission of Operation Desert Storm, attacking radar positions inside Iraq. The lessons learned from Desert Storm fed directly into a new and substantially improved version of the AH-64, the **AH-64D**. This aircraft is designed to use the Longbow millimetre-wave radar, which significantly increases the Apache's ability to detect, classify and identify targets at long ranges. AH-64Ds fitted with the Longbow radar (mounted above the main rotor) are known as

The first WAH-64D Longbow Apache was handed over to the UK Army Air Corps in March 2000 and deliveries will continue until 2003.

AH-64D Longbow Apaches, and are armed with a new version of the Hellfire anti-tank missile, the AGM-114L (or Longbow Hellfire). This radar-guided weapon can be fired from concealed positions and does away with the need to remain in line-of-sight contact demanded by the standard laser-guided Hellfire missile. The first of six AH-64D prototypes flew on 15 April 1992.

The US Army plans to remanufacture 501 AH-64As as Longbow Apaches. Work on the first batch of 232 aircraft began in 1995 and about 170 aircraft had been delivered by mid-2001. A second batch of 269 AH-64Ds will be delivered between 2002 and 2006. The AH-64D has been ordered by the Netherlands (30), Singapore (9) and the UK (67). The Dutch AH-64Ds will not be fitted with the Longbow radar. The UK's Apaches are being assembled by Westland, as **WAH-64D**s. Egypt and Israel are upgrading some of their existing AH-64As to AH-64D standard. The US Army also plans to replace the TADS/PNVS target sight with the next-generation Arrowhead system.

Greece was the first European customer for the Apache, and took delivery of its first AH-64As in June 1995. A total of 20 are now in service.

Specification: Boeing AH-64D Apache
Powerplant: two 342-kW (1,800-hp) General Electric T700-GE-701C turboshafts
Dimensions: main rotor diameter 14.63 m (48 ft); length overall, rotors turning 17.76 m (58 ft 3¾ in) and fuselage 14.97 m (49 ft 1.5 in); height overall 4.66 m (15 ft 3.5 in)
Weights: empty 5165 kg (11,387 lb); maximum take-off 9525 kg (21,000 lb)
Performance: maximum level speed 'clean' 293 kmh (182 mph); maximum vertical rate of climb at sea level 762 m (2,500 ft) per minute; range 428 km; 300 miles) with internal fuel
Armament: one M230 Chain Gun 30-mm cannon with 1,200 rounds, with 2841-kg (6,263-lb) or ordnance

Boeing CH-47 Chinook

The Boeing **CH-47 Chinook** (originally Boeing Vertol) is the US Army's standard medium-lift helicopter and utilises Vertol's proven twin-rotor concept with externally-mounted engines. The first of 350 **CH-47A**s was first flown on 21 September 1961 and the type entered service in August 1962. The subsequent **CH-47B** (108 built) had uprated engines and increased-diameter rotor blades. The **CH-47C** introduced greater improvements, including further uprated engines and additional fuel. A total of 270 was built, of which 182 were retrofitted with composite blades and crashworthy fuel systems. CH-47Cs were also sold to Argentina, Australia, Egypt, Greece, Iran, Libya, Morocco, Spain and the UK (RAF designation **Chinook HC.Mk 1/1B**)

The US Army standardised all its earlier Chinooks as **CH-47D**s, beginning in 1982. The CH-47D is a mix of conversions from all three former variants and some new-build machines. The full programme covers 403 aircraft for Army Aviation, re-engined with T55-L-712 turboshafts (with a greater emergency power reserve and greater battle damage resistance), a new NVG-compatible flight deck and triple cargo hooks. The CH-47D can carry up to 55 troops, or a wide variety of loads up to a maximum of 10341 kg (22,798 lb) externally or 6308 kg

In 1990 the RAF decided to upgrade its Chinook HC.Mk 1s to HC.Mk 2 (CH-47D) standard. Following their overhaul by Boeing, deliveries began in 1993.

The Royal Netherlands Air Force's Chinooks are CH-47Ds that have been fitted with the 'glass' cockpit systems of the CH-47SD.

(13,907 lb) internally. The **CH-47D International Chinook** (**Model 414**) is an export-optimised variant. US Army re-equipment with the CH-47D is now complete, the variant in service with active-duty, National Guard and Reserve units. Foreign operators include Australia, Greece, Korea, the Netherlands, Spain, Thailand, and the UK (**Chinook HC.Mk 2/2A**). In Japan Kawasaki has built CH-47Ds under licence as the **CH-47J** and has also developed the improved FLIR and radar-equipped **CH-47JA**. The latest Boeing-built version of the Chinook is the '**Super D**' or **CH-47SD**, fitted with a 'glass' EFIS cockpit, radar and enlarged fuel tanks (similar to those of the MH-47E). Customers include Singapore and Taiwan.

The US Army's 25 **MH-47E** special operations aircraft are used for covert infil/exfil work. They have a fixed IFR probe, NVG-compatible advanced cockpit displays, jam-resistant communications, a terrain-following and mapping radar and AAQ-16 FLIR. Comprehensive defences include missile-, laser- and radar-warning receivers, jammers and chaff/flare dispensers. MH-47Es are armed with M-134 0.30-in mini-guns. The UK is planning to acquire eight similarly-modified versions (based on the CH-47SD) as the **Chinook HC.Mk 3**.

Specification: Boeing CH-47D Chinook
Powerplant: two 2237-kW (3,000-hp) Textron Lycoming T55-L-712 turboshafts
Dimensions: rotor diameter, each 18.29 m (60 ft); length, rotors turning 30.14 m (98 ft 10¾ in) and fuselage 15.54 m (51 ft 0 in); height 5.77 m (18 ft 11 in) to top of rear rotor head
Weights: empty 10151 kg (22,379 lb); maximum take-off 22679 kg (50,000 lb); maximum payload 10341 kg (22,798 lb)
Performance: maximum cruising speed at optimum altitude 256 kmh (159 mph); maximum rate of climb at sea level 669 m (2,195 ft) per minute; service ceiling 6735 m (22,100 ft); operational radius between 185 and 56 km (115 and 35 miles)

Boeing/Sikorsky RAH-66 Comanche
Advanced scout helicopter

The US Army issued its **LHX** (Light Helicopter Experimental) requirement in 1982, initially calling for 5,000 helicopters to replace UH-1, AH-1, OH-6 and OH-58 scout/attack/assault aircraft. By 1990 this number had been cut back to 1,292 aircraft for the scout/attack role only. Boeing/Sikorsky's 'First Team' was awarded the contract (over the Bell/McDonnell Douglas 'Super Team') for three (later two) **YRAH-66** dem/val aircraft on 5 April 1991.

The **RAH-66 Comanche** has a five-bladed all-composite bearingless main rotor and an eight-bladed fan-in-fin shrouded tail rotor. Its largely composite airframe is designed for low observability, employing a degree of faceting and sunken-notch intakes for the two LHTEC T800 turboshafts. The undercarriage is retractable, and all weapons are housed internally, with missiles carried in bays on the fuselage sides, directly attached to the bay doors which act as pylons when they are open. A chin turret will house a 20-mm cannon, and in the extreme nose is a sensor turret for a FLIR and a laser designator. The Longbow MMW radar of the AH-64D Apache will also be fitted in a radome above the main rotor.

The Army has specified maximum avionics commonality with the USAF's F-22 and the Comanche pilot (front) and WSO each have two flat screen MFDs for presentation of tactical situation, moving map and FLIR/TV information. The pilot also has a wide field-of-view helmet-mounted display system, allied to an electro-optical night navigation and

The Comanche is lighter but only slightly smaller than the AH-64, and will back up – but not replace – the Apache in the combat role.

targeting systems. Flight control is by a triplex fly-by-wire system, with sidestick cyclic-pitch controls. The RAH-66 also features a wide array of defensive equipment, including laser-, IR- and radar-warning receivers, RF and IR jammers.

Work on the first prototype began in November 1993, and it flew on 4 January 1996. The early flight test programme was slowed by gearbox failures, but by August 1997 progress was being made once more. The second prototype was rolled out in April 1998 and made its maiden flight on 30 March 1999. One 1 June 2000 the RAH-66 was approved to enter its engineering and manufacturing development (EMD) phase. Boeing/Sikorsky will build 13 EMD RAH-66s, and the Army hopes to then acquire an interim batch of 12 aircraft between EMD and the launch of initial low-rate production, in 2006. The first EMD aircraft will fly in 2004. The US Army's 2000 Aviation Force Modernization Plan still recommends the acquisition of 1,213 Comanches, valued at nearly $34 billion. The first RAH-66s are scheduled to be operational in December 2006.

The Boeing/Sikorsky team has now rebuilt one RAH-66 with a revised empennage and tail, and also added a radome for the Longbow radar.

Specification: Boeing/Sikorsky RAH-66 Comanche (provisional)
Powerplant: two 1068-kW (1,432 shp) LHTEC T800-LHT-800 turboshafts
Dimensions: main rotor diameter 11.90 m (39 ft ½ in); length overall, rotor turning 14.28 m (46 ft 10.25 in) and fuselage 13.20 m (43 ft ¾ in) excluding gun barrel; height overall 3.39 m (11 ft 1.5 in) over stabiliser
Weights: empty 3942 kg (8,690 lb); normal take-off 4807 kg (10,597 lb)
Performance: max level speed 324 kmh (201 mph); ferry range 2334 km (1,450 miles)
Armament: one General Dynamics three-barrelled 20-mm cannon with up to 500 rounds, with 2296 kg (5,062 lb) of ordnance

BAE SYSTEMS Hawk 50, 60

The BAe (Hawker Siddeley) **Hawk T.Mk 1** trainer for the RAF first flew in August 1974. It has a low-mounted wing, stepped tandem seats and is powered by a single Adour 151-01 turbofan. It entered service in 1976, replacing Hunter and Gnat advanced trainers. The RAF's 175 Hawk T.Mk 1s were fitted with three weapons stations as standard for advanced tactical training. In 1983, 89 (including the Red Arrows' aircraft) were modified to **Hawk T.Mk 1A** standard as back-up, point-defence fighters with two AIM-9L AAMs and a centreline Aden 30-mm cannon pod. In 1989 BAe launched a re-winging programme for RAF Hawks with 72 wing sets refurbished between 1989 and 1995. In 1998 a rear-fuselage rebuild programme was authorised to extend the structural lives of RAF Hawks until 2010. This work is now being carried out by BAE SYSTEMS, the new name adopted by BAe after its merger with GEC Marconi. A single RAF Hawk T.Mk 1 has been modified to serve as the **ASTRA** (Advanced System Training Aircraft) Hawk, for variable stability handling training with the Empire Test Pilot's School.

In 1977 BAe introduced the upgraded **Hawk Series 50** export version. The Series 50 is powered by a 23.1-kN (5,200-lb) Adour 851 turbofan which

Saudi Arabia is the largest export customer for the first-generation Hawks with a fleet of 50 Hawk Mk 65/65As delivered between 1987 and 1997.

The extra power provided by the Hawk Mk 60's Adour 861 engine has made it a popular choice for Middle Eastern customers, such as Kuwait.

increased the Hawk's range and payload performance significantly. Series 50 Hawks are fitted with four underwing pylons and an improved cockpit (including a new weapons control panel). The Hawk Series 50 was sold to Finland (57 **Hawk Mk 51/51A** aircraft), Indonesia (20 **Mk 53**), and Kenya (12 **Mk 52**). The Finnish Hawks were assembled locally by Valmet.

The follow-on **Hawk Series 60** export version introduced a 25.4-kN (5,700-lb st) Mk 861 Adour engine, and an 'advanced wing' with additional leading-edge fences and revised flaps. Operating weights, range and performance were boosted compared to the Series 50 and the Series 60 aircraft had built-in provision for IR-guided air-to-air missiles (such as the AIM-9 and R.550).

Customers for the Hawk Series 60 include Abu Dhabi (16 **Mk 63/Mk 63C** aircraft), Dubai (nine **Mk 61**), Korea (20 **Mk 67**), Kuwait (12 **Mk 64**), Saudi Arabia (50 **Mk 65/Mk 65A**), Switzerland (20 **Mk 66**) and Zimbabwe (13 **Mk 60/Mk 60A**). Korea's Hawk Mk 67s are a unique 'long-nosed' version, similar to the Hawk 100, with nose-wheel steering. The Swiss Hawks were assembled locally by F&W. The related Boeing (McDonnell Douglas) **T-45** is described under a separate entry.

Specification: BAE SYSTEMS Hawk T.Mk 1
Powerplant: one 23.1-kN (5,200-lb) Rolls-Royce/Turboméca Adour Mk 871 turbofan
Dimensions: wing span 9.39 m (30 ft 9¾ in); length 10.775 m (34 ft 4¼ in); height 3.98 m (13 ft ¾ in)
Weights: empty 4400 kg (9,700 lb); maximum take-off 5700 kg (12,566 lb)
Performance: maximum level speed 'clean' 1065 kmh (661 mph); maximum rate of climb at sea level 3600 m (11,800 ft) per minute; service ceiling 13545 m (44,500 ft); combat radius 638 km (397 miles) with gun pod, two AIM-9s and four 500-lb bombs
Armament: one centreline 30-mm ADEN cannon; maximum ordnance 3000 kg (6,614 lb)

BAE SYSTEMS Hawk 100, 200

The success of the Hawk in the export market convinced British Aerospace (now BAE SYSTEMS) to develop more capable versions for advanced training and front-line combat missions. The first of these to emerge was the **Hawk Series 100**, an enhanced ground-attack version of the Hawk Series 60. While largely similar to earlier aircraft, the Hawk 100 introduced an uprated Adour Mk 871 turbofan, an increased span wing (with combat manoeuvre flaps, wingtip missile launch rails and six stores stations), a lengthened nose housing an optional FLIR and/or laser rangefinder, an advanced cockpit with HUDWAC, MFDs and HOTAS and attack-optimised avionics. A single 30-mm ADEN gun pod is an optional fitting on the fuselage centreline in place of a further stores station.

The first flight of the (converted) prototype came on 21 October 1987. The first production prototype flew on 29 February 1992. The launch customer for the Hawk 100 was Abu Dhabi, in 1989. Customers to date include Abu Dhabi (18 **Mk 102** aircraft), Indonesia (eight **Mk 109**), Malaysia (10 **Mk 108**) and Oman (four **Mk 103**).

BAE SYSTEMS has developed a follow-on version of the Hawk 100, the **Hawk LIFT** (Lead-In Fighter Trainer). This version has a three-screen digital cockpit and other improved onboard systems. The launch customer was South Africa, in 1998, with an order for 24 aircraft. Similar advanced trainers (but not true LIFT aircraft) are being acquired by Canada

The Hawk 200 provides affordable and effective combat power, in a compact package. These aircraft are Omani Hawk Mk 203s.

(18 **Mk 115**, local designation **CT-155**) and Australia (33 **Mk 127**, local designation **A27**).

The single-seat **Hawk 200** variant retains the Hawk 100's engine, combat wing and stores capability, but has a redesigned forward fuselage for a single cockpit, a Lockheed Martin AN/APG-66H radar in a reprofiled nose, and two 25-mm ADEN cannon. For self-protection the Hawk 200 is fitted with the Sky Guardian 200 radar warning system and chaff/flare dispensers. The Hawk 200 can be fitted with an air-to-air refuelling probe.

A prototype first flew on 24 April 1987, but the full mission fit was first applied to the third development aircraft, which flew on 13 February 1992. The Hawk 200 can undertake air defence, close air support, battlefield interdiction, anti-shipping and photo-reconnaissance missions. Oman became the launch customer, in 1990, but the first production-standard aircraft was delivered to Malaysia, in 1994. Hawk 200 customers include Indonesia (32 **Mk 209** aircraft), Malaysia (18 **Mk 208**) and Oman (12 **Mk 203**).

The most obvious external changes on the Hawk 100 are its extended 'chisel' nose and wingtip air-to-air missile launchers.

Specification: BAE SYSTEMS Hawk 200
Powerplant: one 26-kN (5,845-lb) Rolls-Royce/Turboméca Adour Mk 871 turbofan
Dimensions: wing span 9.39 m (30 ft 9¾ in); length 10.95 m (35 ft 11 in); height 4.13 m (13 ft 6 ¾ in)
Weights: empty 4440 kg (9,810 lb); maximum take-off 9100 kg (20.061 lb)
Performance: maximum level speed 'clean' 1065 kmh (661 mph); maximum rate of climb at sea level 3508 m (11,510 ft) per minute; service ceiling 13715 m (45,000 ft); ferry range 2528 km (1570 miles) with two drop tanks
Armament: one centreline 30-mm ADEN cannon; maximum ordnance 3000 kg (6,614 lb)

BAE SYSTEMS Harrier

During the late 1970s BAe (now BAE SYSTEMS) initiated independent development of an advanced Harrier. This was abandoned and the **Harrier GR.Mk 5** designation was used instead for a licence-built version of the McDonnell Douglas (Boeing) **AV-8B Harrier II** (*described separately*), for which British Aerospace was a sub-contractor. Two pre-series and 60 production aircraft were ordered, with the first (pre-series) flying in April 1985. Numerous detail differences from the AV-8B were specified by the RAF, with indigenous equipment such as ejection seats, self-defence systems and avionics.

Problems with several systems imposed a two-year delay on RAF service entry and the aircraft were accepted lacking major equipment items, including the new 25-mm ADEN cannon, Zeus ECM system and missile approach warning system. Initial RAF deliveries began in May 1987 and the first squadron was declared operational in November 1989. Nineteen GR.Mk 5s were completed to an interim **GR.Mk 5A** standard, with provision for **GR.Mk 7** avionics, and were delivered straight into storage to await conversion to full night-attack standard. All remaining GR.Mk 5/5As have now been converted to GR.Mk 7 standard.

The RAF's two-seat Harrier T.Mk 10s are operated by No. 20(R) squadron which handles the operational conversion task for RAF Harriers.

GR.Mk 7s deployed for operations over Iraq during Operation Warden were painted in this temporary grey finish on top of their regular camouflage.

The Harrier **GR.Mk 7** is the RAF equivalent of the **Night Attack AV-8B**. Its nose is fitted with a TV/laser target seeker/tracker of the Angle Rate Bombing Set, and a FLIR is mounted in the housing above. Two forward hemisphere antennas for the Zeus ECM system are located under the nose. The Harrier GR.Mk 7 has an NVG-compatible cockpit with a digital colour map. The RAF ordered 34 new-build GR.Mk 7s in 1988 and a converted pre-series aircraft was first flown as such in November 1989. The first production GR.Mk 7 was delivered in May 1990 and operational service began in late 1992. Along with the new-build aircraft, 41 Harrier GR.Mk 5s and 19 GR.Mk 5As were converted to GR.Mk 7 standard – between 1990 and 1994. The first GR.Mk 7 unit was No. IV Squadron, which re-equipped in September 1990. As a result of operations over Bosnia RAF Harriers have been given a useful reconnaissance capability using the Vinten GP-1 camera pod.

To augment the GR.Mk 7 force the RAF also acquired 13 two-seat **Harrier T.Mk 10** trainers, based on the same next-generation airframe, with common (fully-operational) systems to the GR.Mk 7. The T.Mk 10 prototype first flew on 7 April 1994 and the type entered service in March 1995.

Specification: BAE SYSTEMS/Boeing Harrier GR.Mk 7
Powerplant: one 96.75-kN (21,750-lb) Rolls-Royce Pegasus Mk 105 turbofan
Dimensions: wing span 9.25 m (30 ft 4 in); length 14.53 m (47 ft 8 in); height 3.55 m (11 ft 7¾ in)
Weights: operating empty 7124 kg (15,705 lb); maximum take-off 14515 kg (32,000 lb) for CTO or 8754 kg (19,300 lb) for VTO
Performance: maximum level speed 1090 kmh (677 mph); take-off run 524 m (1,720 ft); range 870 km (650 miles)
Armament: two ADEN 25-mm revolver cannon in underfuselage pods with 100 rpg; maximum ordnance 6.003 kg (13,235 lb)

BAE SYSTEMS Sea Harrier

Developed from the RAF's **Harrier GR.Mk 3**, the **Sea Harrier FRS.Mk 1** introduced a redesigned forward fuselage and nose fitted with a Ferranti Blue Fox radar, a new canopy and raised cockpit for improved view, and a 96.3-kN (21,492-lb st) Pegasus Mk 104 engine. Avionics changes included addition of an auto-pilot, a revised nav/ attack system and a new HUD. An initial order was placed in 1975 for 24 FRS.Mk 1s and a single **T.Mk 4A** trainer. The first operational squadron (No. 899 Sqn) was commissioned in April 1980 and two units (Nos 800 and 801 Sqns) were subsequently deployed during the Falklands War where they served with distinction, scoring 23 confirmed victories.

Post-Falkland attrition replacements and further orders subsequently took total RN procurement up to 57 FRS.Mk 1s and four trainers (including three **T.Mk 4N**s). Improvements included revised wing pylons for carriage of four AIM-9Ls (on twin launch rails), larger-capacity drop tanks and installation of an improved Blue Fox radar and RWR. In 1978, the Indian Navy became the second Sea Harrier operator, ordering a total of 24 **FRS.Mk 51**s and four **T.Mk 60** trainers.

A mid-life update was initiated in 1985 to refine the Sea Harrier as a more capable interceptor. BAe (now BAE SYSTEMS) converted two FRS.Mk 1s to serve as **FRS.Mk 2** prototypes, with the first flying in September 1988. Despite the addition of an extra equipment bay and a recontoured nose to house

The Royal Navy's Fleet Air Arm has two front-line Sea Harrier FA.Mk 2 squadrons, Nos. 800 and No. 801 Sqns, plus the training Squadron No 899.

the Blue Vixen multi-mode pulse-Doppler radar (giving compatibility with the AIM-120 AMRAAM), the FRS.Mk 2 is actually nearly 0.61 m (2 ft) shorter overall due to the elimination of the FRS.Mk 1's pitot probe. The cockpit introduces new multi-function CRT displays and HOTAS controls. The FRS.Mk 2 designation was changed to **F/A.Mk 2** in May 1994 and then to the current **FA.Mk 2** in 1995.

Two development aircraft were built, with the first flying on September 1988. The contract for the modification of 29 existing FRS.Mk 1s to Sea Harrier FA.Mk 2 standard was signed in December 1988, and was followed by a further four aircraft in 1994. Another 18 new-build FA.Mk 2s were also acquired, and delivered between 1995 and 1998. Seven T.Mk 4/4N trainers have been converted to **Sea Harrier T.Mk 8** standard, to meet the requirement for FA.Mk 2 training. In August 1994 No. 899 Sqn embarked four FA.Mk 2s aboard HMS *Invincible* for operations over Bosnia, and No. 801 Sqn made the first full deployment of the FA.Mk 2 in January 1995, aboard HMS *Illustrious*.

The Sea Harrier T.Mk 8 trainer is an upgraded version of the earlier T.Mk 4 fitted with some of the systems of the FA.Mk 2 – though it lacks a radar.

Specification: BAE SYSTEMS Sea Harrier FA.Mk 2
Powerplant: one 95.64-kN (21,500-lb) Rolls-Royce Pegasus Mk 106 turbofan
Dimensions: span 7.70 m (25 ft 3 in); length 14.17 m (46 ft 6 in); height 3.71 m (12 ft 2 in)
Weights: operating empty 6616 kg (14,585 lb); maximum take-off 11884 kg (26,200 lb), STO
Performance: maximum level speed 1144 kmh (711 mph); service ceiling 15545 m (51,000 ft); combat radius 750 km (460 miles) on a hi-hi-hi interception mission with four AAMs
Armament: two 30-mm ADEN cannon in under-fuselage pods, maximum ordnance 3224 kg (7108 lb)

BAE SYSTEMS Nimrod

The British Aerospace/BAe (Hawker Siddeley) **Nimrod** was developed from the Comet airliner as a replacement for the Avro Shackleton. Development began in 1964, when two Comet 4Cs were converted to serve as prototypes with tail MAD 'stinger', nose-mounted search radar and a fin-tip ESM football. A new 14.78-m (48-ft 6-in) long ventral weapons bay was added, giving a distinctive 'double-bubble' cross-section. The first Spey-powered prototype made its maiden flight on 23 May 1967. Forty six **Nimrod MR.Mk 1**s were ordered with the type entering service in October 1969.

Seven airframes were substantially modified to **Nimrod AEW.Mk 3** standard, with Marconi AEW radar housed in huge radomes at either end of the fuselage. The ill-fated project was cancelled in 1986 following radar development problems.

From 1975 the 35 remaining MR.Mk 1s were upgraded to **MR.Mk 2** configuration with a new central tactical system, Searchwater radar and new communications equipment. Operation Corporate in 1982 added IFR probes and underwing weapons pylons, resulting in the designation **MR.Mk 2P**. All aircraft now have wingtip Loral ESM pods and can carry BOZ 100 chaff dispenser pods and/or the Ariel towed radar decoy for added self-protection.

A single Nimrod MR.Mk 2P was painted in this overall grey camouflage scheme, but the scheme has not been adopted by the rest of the fleet.

The RAF's Nimrod are all based at RAF Kinloss, in Scotland, where they are divided among the four squadrons of the Kinloss Wing.

Three aircraft were ordered as **Nimrod R.Mk 1** (later **R.Mk 1P**) intelligence-gathering platforms to serve with the RAF's dedicated special reconnaissance unit, No. 51 Squadron. These aircraft have no MAD tailboom and no searchlight. Instead they have been fitted with dielectric radomes in the nose of each external wing tank and on the tailcone. The aircraft have been progressively modified since they were introduced, gaining additional antennas above and below the fuselage and wing tanks, as well as Loral wingtip ESM pods. A Nimrod MR.Mk 2 was converted to R.Mk 1 standard when one of the original R.Mk 1s crashed in 1995.

In 1996 the RAF chose to upgrade 21 existing Nimrods to **Nimrod MRA.Mk 4** (**Nimrod 2000**) standard, to meet its future maritime patrol needs. The modified Nimrods will be re-engined with four 'marinised' 68.9-kN (15,500-lb) Rolls-Royce BR710 turbofans (necessitating a rebuilt wing box and wing inner panels), fitted with an entirely new advanced mission system and expanded weapons capability. The Nimrod MRA.Mk 4 programme is expected to extend aircraft life by another 25 years, however severe engineering delays have put back the type's intended service entry date from December 2000 to March 2005.

**Specification: BAE SYSTEMS
Nimrod MR.Mk 2P**
Powerplant: four 54-kN (12,140-lb) Rolls-Royce RB.168-20 Spey Mk 250 turbofans
Dimensions: span 35 m (114 ft 10 in); length 38.63 m (126 ft 9 in); height 9.08 m (29 ft 8.5 in)
Weights: typical empty 39010 kg (86,000 lb); maximum normal take-off 80514 kg (177,500 lb);
Performance: maximum cruising speed 880 kmh (547 mph); economical cruising speed at optimum altitude 787 kmh (490 mph); typical patrol speed at low level 370 kmh (230 mph) on two engines; service ceiling 12800 m (42,000 ft); maximum endurance 15 hours
Armament: maximum ordnance 6124 kg (13,500 lb)

BAE SYSTEMS VC10

United Kingdom
Air-to-air refuelling aircraft

Modification of the civil Vickers/BAC **VC10** airliner into a transport gave the RAF useful passenger and cargo-carrying capacity. Meeting a 1960 specification for a strategic long-range transport for the RAF's Transport Command, the first military VC10s were similar to the civil Standard VC10 but were featured uprated Conway engines, the **Super VC10**'s additional fin fuel cell, rearward-facing seats, a side-loading freight door, an IFR probe and an APU in the tail cone. As the **VC10 C.Mk 1**, the aircraft incorporated seating capacity for up to 150 passengers or 76 stretcher cases and six medical attendants. The first of 14 RAF VC10s made its maiden flight in November 1965 and initial deliveries began in July 1966. No. 10 Squadron was the sole C.Mk 1 operator and undertook regular route flights from April 1967. Carrying less than half its full payload, the VC10 had a range exceeding 8047 km (5,000 miles).

In 1978 a programme was initiated to convert surplus VC10 airliners into tankers, to augment the Victor K.Mk 2 fleet. Five Standard VC10 Series 101s and four Super VC10 Series 1154s were converted to become **VC10 K.Mk 2s** and **VC10 K.Mk 3s**, respectively. These aircraft were fitted with extra fuel tanks in the cabin, three hose-and-drogue units (HDUs) – two underwing and one in the rear fuselage – and a closed-circuit television system for monitoring of refuelling operations. The K.Mk 3 also had an additional fuel tank in the fin. The first VC10

The VC10 K.Mk 2 was the first of the VC10 tanker family to be completely retired. This No. 101 Sqn aircraft is seen refuelling two Tornado F.Mk 3s.

K.Mk 2s joined No. 101 Squadron at Brize Norton in May 1984, with the first K.Mk 3s following in 1985. Four years later another five Super VC10s were converted to short-range **VC10 K.Mk 4** tanker standard. The VC10 K.Mk 4s have Mk 17 and Mk 32 in-flight refuelling pods, closed-circuit TV, air-to-air TACAN, avionics systems and the same engines as the VC10 K.Mk 3, but no cabin fuel tanks.

To augment the dedicated tanker fleet, eight of the VIP-tasked VC10 C.Mk 1 transports were upgraded to **VC10 C.Mk 1(K)** standard. Beginning in 1990, this process retained the full passenger- and freight-carrying capability, but introduced two Flight Refuelling Mk 32 underwing hose-and-drogue pods. In 1992 it was decided to convert 13 C.Mk 1s to C.Mk 1(K) configuration, with the last regular C.Mk 1 leaving service in 1995 for its rework.

The RAF is now accelerating the retirement of the VC10 fleet with the intention of replacing it, and ultimately the TriStar tanker fleet, with a contractorised air-to-air refuelling service supplied under the Future Strategic Tanker Aircraft programme.

Engaged in Eurofighter tanking trials, this VC 10 is wearing the toned-down grey scheme that has replaced the earlier hemp finish applied to the fleet.

Specification: BAE SYSTEMS (British Aerospace/BAC/Vickers) VC10 C.Mk 1K
Powerplant: four 96.97-kN (21,800-lb) Rolls-Royce Conway RCo.43 Mk 301 turbofans
Dimensions: wing span 44.55 m (146 ft 2 in); length 48.38 m (158 ft 8 in) excluding probe; height 12.04 m (39 ft 6 in)
Weights: empty 66224 kg (146,000 lb); maximum take-off 146510 kg (323,000 lb); maximum payload 26037 kg (57,400 lb)
Performance: maximum cruising speed 935 kmh (581 mph); maximum rate of climb at sea level 930 m (3,050 ft) per minute; service ceiling 12800 m (42,000 ft); range 6273 km (3,898 miles) with maximum payload

CASA Aviojet

Designed by CASA with assistance from MBB and Northrop, the **C.101 Aviojet** has been built as a trainer and light strike aircraft. The first prototype made its maiden flight on 27 June 1977. Design features include an unswept wing with fixed leading edge and slotted flaps, a single Garrett (AlliedSignal) TFE731 turbofan and a stepped cockpit with tandem ejection seats. The Spanish air force purchased two batches of 60 and 28 TFE-731-2-2J-powered **C.101EB-01** trainers, as the **E.25 Mirlo** (Blackbird). All have hardpoints, but these are not used. A nav/attack system modernisation was introduced on all C.101EBs between 1990 and 1992.

The **C.101BB** attack/trainer introduced an uprated TFE731-3-3J engine and was exported as the **C.101BB-02** to Chile. These aircraft have six underwing hardpoints and a large underfuselage bay beneath the rear cockpit, which can house a gun pack or other stores. Four **C.101BB-03**s were delivered to Honduras.

The dedicated attack variant, the **C.101CC**, first flew on 16 November 1983 and is powered by a TFE731-5-1J engine with a higher military power reserve. The C.101CC has a greater fuel load than earlier versions, though not an increased weapons payload. Jordan received 16 **C.101CC-04**s for advanced training.

The most well-known Aviojets are the aircraft that make up the Patrulla Aguila, the Spanish air force's aerobatic display team.

In the Fuerza Aérea de Chile CASA's C.101CC-02 Aviojet became the A-36 Halcón, with most aircraft built under licence by ENAER.

In May 1985 CASA flew the prototype TFE731-5-1J-engined **C.101DD** Aviojet This attack-optimised model introduced improved navigation systems, a weapon-aiming computer, and a Ferranti HUD. It also had HOTAS controls, an ALR-66 RWR and a Vinten chaff/flare dispenser, and was compatible with Maverick missiles. Intended as an improved trainer and light attack aircraft, it did not attract any orders, though CASA did offer a variant for the USAF/US Navy JPATS competition.

In Chile, the state manufacturer **ENAER** built and developed several versions of the Aviojet. Beginning in 1980 ENAER began to assemble C.101BB-02s, under the local designation **T-36**. These aircraft were fitted with a ranging radar in the nose and were used for advanced tactical training. Four were built by CASA, followed by 10 ENAER-built examples. In 1986 they were upgraded to **A-36BB** standard.

The ENAER **A-36CC Halcón** (**C.101CC-02**) was a dedicated light attack version, powered by a TFE731-5 engine. Four were built by CASA, followed by another 19 ENAER-built Halcóns ('hawk'). ENAER developed a single **A-36M** prototype as a Sea Eagle-armed maritime attack aircraft, but the programme was shelved.

Specification: CASA C.101CC Aviojet
Powerplant: one 20.91-kN (4,700-lb) Garrett TFE731-5-1J turbofan
Dimensions: span 10.60 m (34 ft 9½ in); length 12.50 m (41 ft); height 4.25 m (13 ft 11¼ in);
Weights: empty equipped 3500 kg (7,716 lb); maximum take-off 6300 kg (13,889 lb)
Performance: maximum level speed 806 kmh (501 mph); maximum rate of climb at sea level 1494 m (4,900 ft) per minute; service ceiling 12800 m (42,000 ft); combat radius 519 km (322 miles) on a lo-lo-lo interdiction mission with one cannon pod and four 250-kg (551-lb) bombs
Armament: provision for a twin Browning M3 0.50-in machine-gun pack with 220 rpg; maximum ordnance 2250 kg (4,960 lb)

CASA (Airtech) CN-235 and C-295

The **CN-235** light tactical transport was designed and developed under a joint initiative by Spain's CASA and Indonesia's IPTN. They founded the **Airtech** concern in 1980 to develop a robust aircraft that could serve both as a military transport and a regional airliner. The CN-235 has all the classic elements of a military transport, including a rear-loading ramp, high wing and rough-field landing gear. The aircraft is powered by a pair of proven General Electric CT7 turboprops, and is capable of dropping troops and supplies from its side doors and rear ramp. Military design features predominated in the CN-235 and it had little success in the commercial market. However is has become popular with air forces worldwide, fitting into a niche below the capacity and costs of the C-130 Hercules.

Two prototypes were built with CASA's example making the first flight on 11 November 1983. The initial production variant was the **CN-235 Series 10**, powered by CT-7A engines. Military variants were designated **CN-235M-10**s and aircraft were delivered to Botswana, Indonesia, Saudi Arabia, Spain (as the VIP-configured **T.19A**) and the UAE. The improved **CN-235M-100** followed, powered by uprated CT7C engines. The Series 100 introduced a major step forward in performance. IPTN-built aircraft were designated **CN-235M-110**s. Customers include Chile, Ecuador, France, Gabon, Indonesia, Ireland, Morocco, Oman, Papua New Guinea, South Africa, South Korea, Spain (**T.19B**), Turkey and the UAE.

The Irish Air Corps is unique in operating two CN-235MP maritime patrol aircraft, which monitor Irish waters and the country's EEZ responsibilities.

The **CN-235M-200** (IPTN **-220**) introduced higher operating weights and still better performance. It has been acquired by Indonesia and Malaysia.

Turkey signed a licence-production deal in 1990 to build 50 of its 52 aircraft. These were delivered between 1992 and 1998. Manufacturer **TAI** is now working on a maritime patrol version for Turkey. CASA developed its own maritime patrol version, the **CN-235MP Persuader** which is in service in Ireland. IPTN has also been working on its own maritime patrol version, the **CN-235MPA**, but its development has been slow and only a prototype has been built.

In 1997 CASA announced the independently-developed **C-295**. The C-295 is 10 ft ½ in (3.05 m) longer than the CN-235, increasing its payload by over 50 per cent. The C-295 is powered by two Pratt & Whitney Canada PW127G turboprops, and is fitted with a Sextant Topdeck EFIS cockpit. A technology demonstrator made its maiden flight on 28 November 1997 and the first production-standard C-295 flew on 22 December 1998.

In February 2000 the Spanish air force signed the launch order for nine C-295s, to enter service in 2004. The UAE has also ordered four MPA versions.

Specification: CASA (Airtech) CN-235-100
Powerplant: two 1394-kW (1870-hp) General Electric CT7-9C turboprops
Dimensions: span 25.81 m (84 ft 8 in); length 21.40 m (70 ft 2½ in); height 8.18 m (26 ft 10 in);
Weights: empty equipped 8800 kg (19,400 lb); maximum take-off 16000 kg (35273 lb)
Performance: maximum cruising speed 422 kmh (262 mph); maximum rate of climb at sea level 579 m (1,900 ft) per minute; service ceiling 6860 m (22,500 ft); maximum range 4352 km (2704 miles) with a 3550-kg (7,826-payload)
Armament: MPA versions have two hardpoints under wing. Indonesian development aircraft fitted with Exocet or Harpoon missiles

Chengdu J-7 (F-7)

China was granted a licence to manufacture the MiG-21F-13 and its Tumanskii R-11F-300 engine in 1961, as the **J-7**. A Shenyang-built prototype flew on 17 January 1966 followed by a few development aircraft, and full production began at Chengdu in June 1967. The production-standard **J-7I** entered service in small numbers and was replaced by the **J-7II**, powered by an uprated WP7B turbojet. The J-7II has become the standard production variant for the People's Liberation Army Air Force, and the baseline for a range of improved export aircraft.

Shenyang used the more advanced MiG-21MF to develop the **J-7III**. This version is powered by a WP13 engine, has day/night capability thanks to its JL-7 radar, increased fuel capacity and the characteristic enlarged spine of the MiG-21MF (compared to earlier versions). However, the J-7III has been slow to enter Chinese service and the first examples were not ready until 1992. No J-7IIIs are understood to have been exported.

Albania and Tanzania were customers for the first export version of the of the J-7I, the **F-7A**. The improved **F-7B** (J-7II) was delivered to Egypt, Iraq, Sudan and Zimbabwe. The F-7B can be armed with the MATRA R.550 Magic air-to-air missile (copied in China as the PL-7). A hybrid version has been deliv-

The J-7III would appear to be the best available version of the J-7 as it is based on the MiG-21MF design, but few aircraft have entered PLAAF service.

The F-7MG is a development of the J-7II. While it retains the familiar lines of an early-model MiG-21, it boasts an entirely new wing design.

ered to Sri Lanka as the **F-7BS**. These aircraft have the fuselage, tail and systems of the F-7B with the four-hardpoint wing of the F-7M.

Western avionics were incorporated for the first time in the **F-7M Airguard**, which was equipped with a GEC-Marconi HUDWAC, a Skyranger ranging radar, air data computer, radar altimeter, IFF and other improved systems. F-7Ms have been delivered to Bangladesh, Iran and Myanmar (Burma).

Pakistan has acquired its own version of the F-7M, the **F-7P Airguard**, which can carry four AIM-9 Sidewinder missiles and has a Martin-Baker Mk 10L ejection seat. A developed version of this aircraft, the **F-7MP**, is equipped with the Italian FIAR Grifo 7 fire-control radar and a further improved (western-sourced) avionics fit.

Shenyang has moved on to develop the export-driven **F-7MG** with an entirely new double-delta wing and WP13F engine. Pakistan is reported to be acquiring up to 100 aircraft as the **F-7PG**, while the PLAAF aerobatic team '1st August' is equipped with an equivalent version, the **J-7EB**.

China has developed a two-seat training version of the J-7, the **JJ-7** (export version **FT-7**). This aircraft has been developed by **Guizhou** and is based on the J-7II/MiG-21US.

Specification: Chengdu F-7M Airguard
Powerplant: one 59.82-kN (13,448 lb st) Liyang (LMC) Wopen-7B(BM) turbojet
Dimensions: wing span 7.15 m (23 ft 5¼ in); length 13.95 m (45 ft 9 in) excluding probe; height 4.10 m (13 ft 5¼ in)
Weights: empty 5275 kg (11,629 lb); normal take-off 7531 kg (16,603 lb)
Performance: maximum level speed 2175 kmh (1,350 mph); service ceiling 17500 m (57,420 ft); combat radius 850 km (520 miles) on a hi-hi-hi air superiority mission with two AIM-9 missiles and three 500-litre (132-US gal) drop tanks
Armament: two Type 30 30-mm cannon with 60 rpg; plus 1000 kg (2,205 lb) of ordnance

Dassault Atlantic, Atlantique

A 1957 NATO requirement for a long-range maritime patrol aircraft inspired the French-designed **Breguet Br.1150 Atlantic**. Breguet set up the pan-European SECBAT consortium with partners in Belgium, Holland, Germany and Italy to provide components for the aircraft, which was assembled at Toulouse.

The Atlantic is a twin-turboprop maritime patrol and anti-submarine aircraft, with a crew of 12. It was originally equipped with a Thomson-CSF search radar and US-supplied mission systems, similar to those of the P-2 Neptune. A 'double-bubble' fuselage provides for a 9.15-m (30-ft) long internal weapons bay underneath the main cabin floor. The prototype aircraft made its maiden flight on 21 October 1961. The Atlantic became the standard patrol aircraft for the French, German and Italian navies. It entered service in 1965 with France and German taking delivery of 40 and 20 aircraft, respectively. Another nine were delivered to the Dutch navy between 1969 and 1972 (later replaced by P-3 Orions) and Italy took delivery of 18 Atlantics between 1972 and 1974. Beyond the SECBAT partner nations, the only export sale was three former-French aircraft delivered to Pakistan in 1975-76.

Germany converted five aircraft to serve as **'Peace Peek'** intelligence-gathering platforms, using a US-supplied Sigint/Elint system. The 'Peace Peek' aircraft are outwardly very similar to the standard Atlantic, but they are fitted with distinctive

The upgraded Atlantique is now the standard maritime patrol aircraft in French service. It is most readily identified by its nose-mounted FLIR turret.

underwing antennas. In recent years Italy has upgraded its aircraft, adding a new radar and mission avionics. The upgraded aircraft have ben painted in an overall grey scheme and now carry a prominent antenna housing above the extended dorsal spine fairing.

Dassault took over Breguet in 1971 and it led the effort to develop an improved version of the original Atlantic, the **Atlantic Nouvelle Génération (ANG)**. The result of this was the Dassault **Atlantique** (or **ATL 2**) a version of the Atlantic with new avionics and some structural improvements/strengthening. The sole customer for the Atlantique is France's Aeronavale which acquired 30 aircraft (down from a planned total of 42). A prototype flew in May 1981, the first production-standard Atlantique flew in October 1988 and deliveries began in 1989. The final example was delivered in January 1998. Dassault is now offering an improved **Atlantique 3** design – with an EFIS cockpit, AE2100 turboprops and an all-new mission system – to replace the first-generation Atlantics in Italy and Germany.

Germany's Atlantics have been upgraded to carry wingtip ESM pods, and this aircraft is also carrying an underwing FLIR pod (to port)

Specification: Dassault Atlantique (ATL 2)
Powerplant: two 4549-kW (6,100-hp) Rolls-Royce Tyne RTy.20 Mk 21 turboprops
Dimensions: wing span 37.46 m (122 ft 10¼ in); length 31.71 m (104 ft); height 10.89 m (35 ft 8¾ in)
Weights: empty 25700 kg (56659 lb); normal take-off 46200 kg (101,850 lb)
Performance: maximum level speed 648 kmh (402 mph); service ceiling 9145 m (30,000 ft); operational radius 1850 km (1,150 miles) a five-hour ASW patrol, or 1110 km (690 miles) for an eight-hour patrol
Armament: 3600-kg (7,936-lb) internal ordnance, 3500-kg (7,716-lb) external ordnance on four underwing hardpoints

Dassault Mirage III, 5 and 50

The classic Dassault **Mirage III** Mach 2 delta-winged fighter was first flown in prototype form on 17 December 1956. Production of 1,422 Mirage IIIs, **Mirage 5**s and **Mirage 50**s continued until 1992. Most early **Mirage IIIC** interceptors have been withdrawn, as have most **Mirage IIIB** trainers, although a few remain in use as testbed and research aircraft.

The multi-role **Mirage IIIE** fighter (and equivalent **Mirage IIID** trainer) was flown in 1961 and intro-duced provision for an AN52 nuclear bomb. France received 183 (plus 20 equivalent IIIBE trainers) which remained in defence-suppression and conventional attack roles until late 1993. The Armée de l'Air also received 70 **Mirage IIIR**s with camera nose (including 20 **Mirage IIIRD**s with Doppler navigation). All have now been supplanted by the Mirage F1CR. Mirage IIIs are still in service in Argentina (**Mirage IIIEA** and **Mirage IIIDA**), Brazil (upgraded **Mirage IIIEB** and **Mirage IIIDB**, known locally as the **F-103E/F-103D**), Pakistan (ex-Australian **Mirage IIIO**s, ex-Lebanese **Mirage IIIBL**s and a variety of other second-hand aircraft sourced via Dassault and Switzerland (upgraded **Mirage IIIS**, **Mirage IIIRS** and **Mirage IIIDS**). Both Brazil and Switzerland have fitted their Mirages with canards.

Pakistan has a large and varied fleet of Mirage III and Mirage 5 variants, including this Mirage IIIDP trainer acquired from Dassault.

Brazil maintains a single squadron of upgraded Mirage IIIE air defence aircraft, operated by 1° Esq 'Jaguares' based at Anapólis.

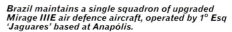

In 1966, a simplified (non-radar) attack version of the Mirage III was developed as the **Mirage 5**. The **Mirage 5D** trainer and camera-nosed **Mirage 5R** are related variants. The original simplified aircraft later became available with an ever-greater range of avionics options, including the re-introduction of lightweight radars. The **Mirage 50** first flew in April 1979 and introduced the Mirage F1's Atar 9K-50 engine endowing better field performance, faster acceleration, a larger weapon load and improved manoeuvrability.

Current operators include Argentina (Mirage 5), Chile (Mirage 5 and Mirage 50), Colombia (Mirage 5), Congo (Mirage 5), Egypt (Mirage 5), Gabon (Mirage 5), Libya (Mirage 5), Pakistan (Mirage 5), Peru (Mirage 5), the United Arab Emirates (Mirage 5) and Venezuela (Mirage 50).Argentina's aircraft are a mix of IAI-built **'Finger'** (upgraded **Mirage 5**s) and locally-upgraded **'Mara'** aircraft. Chile's Mirage 50s have been upgraded by ENAER to **Pantera** standard, while the FACh also operates upgraded former-Belgian Mirage 5 **Elkan**s. Peru's **Mirage 5P3/P4** aircraft have been upgraded with new on-board systems (such as an RWR and a laser range-finder), while Venezuela's **Mirage 50EV/DV**s have been fitted with canards.

Specification: Dassault Mirage 5
Powerplant: one 60.8-kN (13,668 lb) SNECMA Atar 9C-3 turbojet
Dimensions: span 8.22 m (26 ft 11.6 in); length 15.56 m (51 ft 0.6 in); height 4.50 m (14 ft 9 in)
Weights: empty equipped 7150 kg (15,763 lb); maximum take-off 14700 kg (32,407 lb)
Performance: maximum level speed 2338 kmh (1,453 mph); maximum rate of climb at sea level 11160 m (36,614 ft) per minute; service ceiling 18000 m (59,055 ft); combat radius 1315 km; 817 miles) of a hi-hi-hi interception mission with two AAMs and three drop tanks
Armament: two internal DEFA 552A 30-mm cannon with 125 rpg, plus up to 4000 kg (8,818 lb) of ordnance

Dassault Mirage F1

Despite its suffix, the **Mirage F1C** was the initial production version of Dassault's successor to its highly successful Mirage III/5 delta. It was developed to meet an Armée de l'Air (AA) requirement for an all-weather interceptor. Forsaking the Mirage III's delta configuration for a high-mounted wing and conventional tail surfaces, the prototype first flew on 23 December 1966. **Mirage F1C** production deliveries to the AA began in May 1973. The initial 83 aircraft were followed by 79 **Mirage F1C-200**s with fixed refuelling probes (necessitating a small fuselage plug). The AA also received 20 **Mirage F1B** tandem-seat trainers which retained their full combat capability.

Dassault converted 64 F1C-200s to serve as dedicated tactical reconnaissance platforms. These **Mirage F1CR-200**s are equipped with an infra-red linescan unit, undernose cameras and centreline pods for SLAR, LOROP or Elint equipment. They also have a modernised cockpit with a Martin-Baker Mk 10 ejection seat, new RWR and two additional underwing hardpoints for chaff/flare dispensers. The F1CR fleet is now being equipped with the PRESTO stand-off reconnaissance pod, replacing the interim DESIRE system.

The **Mirage F1CT** (T-Tactique) was a logical product of the shortfall in French ground attack capability and a surplus of air defence fighters following Mirage 2000C deliveries. From 1991, 55 Mirage F1Cs were converted to F1CT standard

France's dual-role Mirage F1CRs are tasked with reconnaissance and attack missions, and had their combat debut in 1991, during Desert Storm.

have been given expanded tactical capability with a laser rangefinder, improved RWR and chaff/flare dispensers. F1CTs are most often deployed with the French units still based in Africa. The last remaining AA F1C squadron is also based in Africa, with EC4/33 in Djibouti.

The Mirage F1 has been widely exported. F1Cs were sold to South Africa (**F1CZ**, now withdrawn), Morocco (**F1CH**), Jordan (**F1CJ**), Kuwait (**F1CK**, **F1CK2**, now withdrawn), Greece (**F1CG**) and Spain (**F1CE**). The **Mirage F1A** was a simplified version for day visual attack missions, equipped with the Aïda II ranging radar in a reprofiled nose. It was sold to Libya (**F1AD**) and South Africa (**F1AZ** fitted with a laser-ranger, now withdrawn).

The **Mirage F1E** (and corresponding **Mirage F1D** trainer) was an upgraded multi-role fighter/attack version for export, fitted with an INS, central nav/attack computer and HUD. F1Es were exported to Ecuador (**F1JA/E**), Iraq (**F1EQ**), Jordan (**F1EJ**), Libya (**F1ED**), Morocco (**F1EH** and **F1EH-200**), Qatar (**F1EDA** and **F1DDA**) and Spain (**F1EE-200**).

Between 1999 and 2001 Spain's 52 Mirage F1s received a cockpit upgrade adding new communications, self-defence and navigation systems

Specification: Dassault Mirage F1C
Powerplant: one 70.21-kN (15,785-lb) SNECMA Atar 9K-50 turbojet
Dimensions: wing span 9.32 m (30 ft 6¼ in) with wingtip AAMs; length 15.30 m (50 ft 2½ in); height 4.50 m (14 ft 9 in)
Weights: empty 7400 kg (16,314 lb); maximum take-off 16200 kg (35,715 lb)
Performance: maximum level speed 2338 kmh (1,453 mph); service ceiling 20000 m (65,615 ft); combat radius 425 km (264 miles) on a hi-lo-hi attack mission with 14 250-kg (551-lb) bombs
Armament: two internal DEFA 553 30-mm cannon with 135 rpg; maximum ordnance load of 6300 kg (13,889 lb)

Dassault Mirage 2000C, 2000-5

For the third Mirage generation, Dassault returned to the delta configuration, using negative longitudinal stability and a fly-by-wire flight control system to eliminate many of the shortcomings of a conventional delta. As such, the **Mirage 2000** has its predecessor's large internal volume and low wave drag, but has improved agility, slow-speed handling and lower landing speed. The first of five prototypes was initially flown on 10 March 1978. The first of 37 production **Mirage 2000C**s made its maiden flight on 20 November 1982 and deliveries began in April 1983, with IOC in July 1984. All early production **2000C-S2**, **-S3** aircraft had SNECMA M53-5 engines, and introduced successive improvements to the Thomson-CSF RDM radar. The **Mirage 2000C-S4** and **-S5** introduced the uprated M53-P2 powerplant and the superior RDI radar optimised for look-down/shoot-down intercepts with two MATRA Super 530D missiles. With RDM radar, Mirage 2000Cs carried Super 530F and Magic 1 missiles.

Export versions of the RDM-equipped, M53-P2-powered variant have been delivered to Abu Dhabi (**Mirage 2000EAD**, 22 aircraft), Egypt (**Mirage 2000EM**, 16), Greece (**Mirage 2000EG**, 36), India (**Mirage 2000HS Vajra**, 46) and Peru (**Mirage 2000P** 10).

Qatar's two-seat Mirage 2000-5s are known as Mirage 2000-5DDAs. These aircraft are quipped with the RDY radar, but are not combat capable.

The Mirage 2000-5F is the Armée de l'Air's version of the freshly upgraded multi-role fighter. It can carry the Mica missile – with four fitted on this aircraft.

The **Mirage 2000B** tandem two-seat trainer first flew in August 1983. It loses some internal fuel and both cannon in order to accommodate the second cockpit. Abu Dhabi's two-seat trainers are known as **Mirage 2000DAD**s, India's are **Mirage 2000TH**s and Peru's are Mirage **2000DP**s. The reconnaissance-configured **Mirage 2000R** has a radar nose and carries podded sensors: multi-camera, side-looking airborne radar, and long-range optical. Abu Dhabi has acquired eight **Mirage 2000RAD**s.

The upgraded **Mirage 2000-5** introduces an advanced five-screen cockpit display, Mica AAMs, RDY multi-mode radar, and advanced self-protection suite and additional avionics. The 2000-5 is aimed largely at the export market, and significantly improves the basic aircraft's combat capability. The French air force is also acquiring the **Mirage 2000-5F** through the conversion of 37 of its existing 2000Cs. The first converted prototype flew on 26 February 1996. The first export customer for the -5 came in 1992 when Taiwan ordered 60 **Mirage 2000-5EI**s (including 12 **2000-5DI** trainers). Deliveries began in 1997. Other orders have come from Qatar (12 **Mirage 2000-5EDA/DDA**s). Abu Dhabi (UAE) and Greece are acquiring a further improved version the **Mirage 2000-5 Mk II**, also referred to as the **Mirage 2000-9**.

Specification: Dassault Mirage 2000-5
Powerplant: one 95.12-kN (21,384-lb) SNECMA M53-P2 turbofan
Dimensions: wing span 9.13 m (29 ft 11½ in); length 14.36 m (47 ft 1¼ in); height 5.20 m (17 ft ¾ in)
Weights: empty 7500 kg (16,534 lb); maximum take-off 17000 kg (37,478 lb)
Performance: maximum level speed more than 2338 kmh (1,453 mph); maximum rate of climb at sea level 17060 m (55,971 ft) per minute; service ceiling 18000 m (59,055 ft); combat range over 1480 km (920 miles) with four 250-kg bombs
Armament: two 30-mm DEFA 554 cannon with 125 rpg; 6300-kg (13,890-lb) ordnance

Dassault Mirage 2000N, 2000D

French requirements for a Mirage IVP replacement to carry the ASMP stand-off nuclear missile resulted in Dassault receiving a contract in 1979 for two **Mirage 2000P** (Pénétration) prototypes (later designated **Mirage 2000N** (Nucléaire)). Based on the 2000B two-seat trainer, the 2000N has a strengthened airframe for low-level flight and considerable differences in avionics, including twin INSs, and Antilope 5 radar optimised for terrain following, ground mapping and navigation. It provides automatic terrain following down to 91 m (300 ft) at speeds up to 1112 kmh (691 mph). Both pilot and WSO have moving map displays. ASMP delivers a 150- or 300-kT warhead up to 80 km (50 miles) from a low-altitude launch point. Outboard, the Mirage 2000N carries a pair of large, 2000-litre (440-Imp gal) drop tanks and two self-defence MATRA Magic AAMs. Further protection is provided by the Serval RWR, Sabre electronic jammers and a Spirale chaff/flare system.

The prototype Mirage 2000N was flown on 3 March 1986. The first 30 production aircraft were built to **Mirage 2000N-K1** standard, without the Spirale countermeasures equipment. The -K1 was a dedicated nuclear strike variant, and was armed with two AN.52 free-fall bombs before the ASMP missile was ready for service. The second batch of 44 deliveries were **Mirage 2000N-K2**s, which had a dual nuclear/conventional capability, and full ASMP compatibility. France's Mirage 2000N deliveries

The two-seat Mirage 2000N is France's dedicated nuclear strike aircraft. This example is a late-production Mirage 2000N-K2.

were completed in 1993. The 2000N-K1 aircraft have since been upgraded to acquire a limited conventional attack capability.

While the Mirage 2000N is largely dedicated to nuclear strike, Dassault has also developed a similar version for conventional long-range precision attack missions. This is the Mirage 2000D, which outwardly looks almost identical to the 2000N. According to Dassault the D suffix stands for 'Diversifié' (diversified). The prototype Mirage 2000D first flew on 19 February 1991 (in fact, this aircraft was modified from the 2000N prototype). France has ordered a total of 86 Mirage 2000Ds and the final aircraft was delivered in 2001.

As with previous Mirages increasing levels of capability have been introduced during the aircraft's life. The initial production **Mirage 2000N-R1** aircraft did not have the full weapons capability of the late production standard **Mirage 2000N-R2**s. The -R2 aircraft introduced the Apache and Scalp stand-off missiles, the Samir self-protection fit, and the Atlis II laser-designation system.

The Mirage 2000D looks very similar to the 2000N, but does not have a nuclear role. This aircraft is carrying a single Apache stand-off missile.

Specification: Dassault Mirage 2000D
Powerplant: one 95.12-kN (21,384-lb) SNECMA M53-P2 turbofan
Dimensions: wing span 9.13 m (29 ft 11½ in); length 14.55 m (47 ft 9 in); height 5.15 m (16 ft 10¾ in)
Weights: empty 7600 kg (16,755 lb); maximum take-off 17000 kg (37,478 lb)
Performance: maximum level speed more than 2338 kmh (1,453 mph); maximum rate of climb at sea level 17060 m (55,971 ft) per minute; service ceiling 18000 m (59,055 ft); combat range over 1480 km (920 miles) with four 250-kg bombs
Armament: two 30-mm DEFA 554 cannon with 125 rpg; 6300-kg (13,890-lb) ordnance

Dassault Rafale

Dassault's **Avion de Combat Experimentale** (**ACX**), evolved as an early 1980s technology demonstrator for a national combat aircraft programme even before France's withdrawal from the EFA (Eurofighter) project in August 1985. The **Rafale A** ACX testbed was first flown on 4 July 1986. It established and proved the basic design, configuration and performance of the definitive Rafale, or **ACT** (**Avion de Combat Tactique**), as well as its fly-by-wire control system and mainly composite structure. Rafale is powered by a pair of SNECMA M88-2 turbofans, with the more powerful M88-3 now under development. Rafale's RBE2 multi-mode electronically-scanned radar is one of the first phased-array fighter radars to be developed in the west, and will be fully-integrated with the OSF IRST/FLIR sensor package above the nose. Rafale will also be fitted with the Spectra RF/laser/IR self-protection system.

The Armée de l'Air's generic '**Rafale D'** (discret, 'stealth') family is four per cent smaller than the prototype Rafale A, and uses 'low-observable' (stealthy) elements in its airframe. In addition to these design techniques, Dassault may also have developed a classified 'active stealth' system to further reduce the aircraft's radar-cross section.

The French navy's Rafale Ms will initially be dedicated to air defence. Here the M01 prototype is seen firing a Mica EM active radar-guided AAM.

The two-seat Rafale B has evolved into a combat-capable long-range attack aircraft, and will be numerically the most important version for France.

The **Rafale C** is the Armée de l'Air's production-standard single-seat multi-role combat version, and a prototype first flew on 19 May 1991. **Rafale M** is the Aéronavale's single-seat carrierborne fighter, modified for carrier operations with an arrester hook, a 'jump strut' nosewheel leg and no forward centreline pylon. The prototype Rafale M flew on 12 December 1991. The **Rafale B** was originally planned as a straightforward dual-control trainer, but is now being developed into a fully operational version. The first prototype flew on 30 April 1993.

Rafale's development and acquisition plans have been very badly hampered by budget restrictions. The first aircraft to enter service will be the Aeronavale's 60 Rafale Ms – the first production-standard example flew on 6 July 1999. Rafale M will be fully operational in 2002. The two-seat **Rafale BM** will enter service in 2007. The initial **Rafale M-F1** air defence aircraft will be replaced by the multi-role **Rafale M-F2** in 2004/05. Deliveries of the full-standard **Rafale M-F3** will begin in 2007, and all 60 Rafale Ms will be in service by 2012.

The Armée de l'Air is acquiring a total of 212 Rafales, with the first to be delivered in 2003. The air force is splitting its Rafales 60:40 between the fully combat-capable Rafale B and Rafale C aircraft.

Specification: Dassault Rafale C
Powerplant: two 86.98-kN (19,555-lb) SNECMA M88-2 turbofans
Dimensions: wing span 10.9 m (35 ft 9¼ in) with tip-mounted AAMs; length 15.30 m (50 ft 2½ in); height: 5.34 m (17 ft 6 ¾ in)
Weights: empty, equipped 9060 kg (19,973 lb); maximum take-off 21500 kg (47,399 lb)
Performance: maximum level speed 'clean' 2125 kmh (1,321 mph); combat radius 1055 km (655 miles) on an air-to-air mission with eight Mica missiles and four fuel tanks
Armament: one 30-mm GIAT DEFA 791B cannon in port engine intake trunking; 14 stores stations for maximum of 8000 kg (17,637 lb) of ordnance

Dassault/Dornier Alpha Jet

In July 1969 France's Dassault and Germany's Dornier agreed to jointly develop and produce a new advanced trainer. The resultant **Alpha Jet** had swept shoulder-mounted wings, two Larzac turbofans and stepped tandem cockpits. French and German equipment fits varied considerably. Because the Luftwaffe decided to continue its military pilot training in the US, its requirement for the Alpha Jet moved on to a light ground-attack replacement for its Fiat G91R/3s. This necessitated advanced nav/attack systems, including a twin-gyro INS, Doppler navigation radar, HUD, and a belly-mounted 27-mm Mauser cannon pod (instead of the 30-mm DEFA pod found on French Alphas). The initial order for 200 aircraft for each country was ultimately reduced to 175.

Alpha Jet development was finally approved in February 1972, and two prototypes were flown in France and Germany in 1973 and 1974 respectively. French production **Alpha Jet E**s (Ecole) began flying in November 1977 and service trials commenced in 1978. German production started with the first **Alpha Jet A** (Appui Tactique) flying in April 1978. In 1993 Germany retired all but 20 German Alphas (for lead-in training for Tornado crews) and a total of 50 surplus aircraft was transferred to Portugal. Initial exports were made to Belgium (33), Egypt (30 including 26 locally-assembled **Alpha Jet MS 1** trainers), Ivory Coast (12), Morocco (24), Nigeria (24), Qatar (six) and Togo (five).

An elaborate tiger scheme marks this Portuguese Alpha Jet as an aircraft of 301 Esquadra, a unit that belongs to the NATO Tiger Squadron Association.

In addition to Portugal refurbished former-Luftwaffe Alpha Jet As have been sold to Thailand and the UK. In Thailand 25 aircraft will serve as lead-in fighter trainers while 12 were acquired by Britain's Defence Evaluation and Research Agency

For lead-in fighter training and light ground-attack, Dassault launched the **Alpha Jet NGEA** (Nouvelle Génération Appui/Ecole) or **Alpha Jet MS2** programme in 1980. It featured uprated engines and new avionics including an INS, CRT HUD and laser rangefinder, plus provision for Magic AAMs. Customers included Cameroon (seven) and Egypt (15).

In the early 1990s Dassault proposed an MS2-derived **Alpha Jet 3 Advanced Training System**, or **Lancier**, with twin multi-function cockpit displays for mission training with such sensors as AGAVE or Anemone radar, FLIR, laser, video and ECM systems, plus advanced weapons. This version may form the basis for a possible upgrade now being considered for the Alpha Jet Es still in Armée de l'Air service.

The blunt-nosed Alpha Jet E is still the standard jet trainer for France's Armée de l'Air, but it will have to be upgraded to function in the Rafale era.

Specification: Dassault/Dornier Alpha Jet E

Powerplant: two 13.24-kN (2,976-lb) SNECMA/Turboméca Larzac 04-C6 turbofans
Dimensions: wing span 9.11 m (29 ft 10 ¾ in); length 11.75 m (38 ft 6½ in); height 4.19 m (13 ft 9 in)
Weights: empty equipped 3345 kg (7,374 lb); maximum take-off 8000 kg (17,637 lb)
Performance: maximum level speed 1000 kmh (621 mph); service ceiling 14630 m (48,000 ft); operational radius 361 nm (670 km; 416 miles) on a lo-lo-lo mission with two drop tanks
Armament: one ventral cannon pod (27-mm Mauser or 30-mm DEFA), four underwing stations for up to 2500 kg (5,511 lb) of stores

Denel AH-2A Rooivalk

South Africa's **Rooivalk** (red kestrel) helicopter was designed to meet a 1981 SAAF requirement for an indigenously-designed attack helicopter. The Atlas Aircraft Corporation (renamed Denel Aviation in 1996) began work on a number of technology development aircraft, including the **XH-1** weapons testbed (based on an Alouette III airframe) and the **XTP-1** (a modified Puma). Experience with these aircraft fed directly into the Rooivalk prototype, the **XH-2** (Experimental Helicopter 2), which made its maiden flight in 1990.

The Rooivalk follows the well-proven attack helicopter layout of stepped, twin-tandem seating in a narrow fuselage, with stub wings for weapons carriage, nose-mounted sensors and an undernose cannon. Drawing on South Africa's substantial combat experience from the 'Bush War' conflicts in Namibia and Angola, Atlas designed the Rooivalk as a highly-survivable aircraft able to absorb battle damage while protecting its crew and remaining operational on the battlefield.

Several elements of the Aerospatiale (Eurocopter) Puma design found their way into the Rooivalk – hardly surprising as the Puma was an important type in the SAAF inventory and many were modified and upgraded by Atlas to improved Oryx standard. The

This is the first production-standard AH-2A Rooivalk, seen carrying a load of eight ZT6 Mokopa anti-tank missiles and two 68-mm rocket pods.

Denel's Rooivalk attack helicopter has so far only entered service with one squadron (No. 16 Sqn) of the South African Air Force.

Rooivalk has the Puma's Turboméca Turmo IV engine (licence-built as the Topaz in the XDM and ADM) and the same rotor system. The Rooivalk is designed to carry up to 16 Denel ZT6 Mokopa anti-tank missiles, in addition to rocket pods and Mistral IR-guided anti-aircraft missiles. The 20-mm under-nose cannon is linked to a helmet-mounted sight.

The XH-2 prototype was refined to serve as the **XDM (Experimental Development Model)** which first flew on 11 February 1990. A second prototype was built as the **ADM (Advanced Demonstration Model)**, and it first flew in 1992. A third pre-production Rooivalk, the **EDM (Engineering Development Model)** flew on 17 November 1996. In 1996 the South African Air Force signed an order for 12 Rooivalks, with the service designation **AH-2A** (previously **CSH-2**). The first deliveries were made in January 1999, and the SAAF has a requirement for up to 36 additional aircraft.

An export version of the Rooivalk was a strong contender for the British Army's attack helicopter requirement in 1993/94 and a version dubbed the **RedHawk** was offered for Australia's Air 87 competition in 2000/01. Malaysia announced an initial deal for eight Rooivalks in 1998, but a firm order remains as yet unsigned.

Specification: Denel Rooivalk
Powerplant: two 1420-kW (1,904-hp) Turboméca Makila 1K2 turboshafts
Dimensions: rotor diameter 15.58 m (51 ft 1½ in); length 18.73 m (61 ft 5½ in), including rotors; height 5.185 m (17 ft ¼ in)
Weights: empty 5730 kg (12,632 lb); maximum take-off 8,750 kg (19,290 lb)
Performance: maximum cruising speed 278 kmh (173 mph); hovering ceiling, IGE 5850 m (19,200 ft), OGE 5455 m (17,900 ft); maximum range 1335 km (829 miles) with external tanks
Armament: one 20-mm Armscor F2 cannon with 700 rounds of ammunition, four underwing stations for up to 2032 kg (4,470 lb) of stores

EH Industries EH101

Ranking as one of Europe's most important current helicopter programmes, the **EH101** has its roots in the cancelled **Westland WG 34** design that was adopted in late 1978 to replace the Sea King. Negotiations between Westland and Agusta in November 1979 led to the establishment of European Helicopter Industries Ltd to manage the programme. In January 2001 Agusta and Westland completed a merger to become AgustaWestland.

The three-engined EH101 is powered by RTM322-01/8 turboshafts (UK aircraft), T700-GE-T6As (Italian navy) or CT7-6s (Canadian Forces). The five-bladed main rotor uses a BERP-derived high-speed tip design and an elastomeric hub. The cockpit is fitted with a Litton six-screen EFIS system.

Several other potential roles were planned from the outset, including military and civil transport and utility duties. Nine preproduction aircraft were built to develop these different configurations, with the first EH101 making its maiden flight on 9 October 1987. EHI built demonstrators for the UK and Italian naval ASW standard, the military and civil utility standard (fitted with a rear ramp) and the civil passenger carrying version (the **Heliliner**). The programme suffered several set backs when two of the pre-production aircraft crashed, in 1993 (PP2) and 1996 (PP7).

The first EH101 operator was the Tokyo police, which took delivery of its first aircraft in 1997. In October 1991 the UK ordered 44 aircraft for the

The Merlin HM.Mk 1 has a mission fit that includes a FLASH dipping sonar, AQS-903 signal processor, Orange Reaper ESM and Link 11 datalink.

Royal Navy, to be known as **Merlin HM.Mk 1**s. In July 1992 Canada ordered 35 **CH-148 Petrel** (later 28) and 15 **CH-149 Chimo** aircraft to replace its Sea King ASW and Labrador SAR helicopters respectively, but this order was cancelled in November 1993 after a change in government. Following a lengthy re-evaluation process Canada reordered 15 **CH-149 Cormorant** SAR aircraft (based on the 'civilianised' **AW320 Cormorant** design) in January 1998, and is still studying the EH101 for its ASW requirements.

In March 1995 the UK placed a second order for 22 **Merlin HC.Mk 3** aircraft for the RAF. In October 1995 the Italian navy ordered 16 aircraft (plus eight options), comprising eight **Mk 110** ASW aircraft, four **Mk 112** AEW/ASW aircraft and four **Mk 410** utility aircraft.

The first production-standard Merlin HM.Mk 1 flew on 6 December 1995 and the first naval trials squadron, No. 700M Sqn, was commissioned on 1 December 1998. The first batch of six RAF Merlin HC.Mk 3s was handed over to the newly-reformed No. 28 Sqn, at RAF Benson, on 8 March 2001.

The RAF's Merlin HC.Mk 3s replace the Westland Wessex, now largely retired, and may ultimately replace the Puma in the transport role.

Specification: EHI Merlin HM.Mk 1
Powerplant: three 1724-kW (2,312-hp) Rolls-Royce/Turboméca RTM322-01 turboshafts
Dimensions: main rotor diameter 18.59 m (61 ft); length overall, rotors turning 22.80 m (74 ft 9¾ in); height overall 6.62 m (21 ft 8¾ in) with rotors turning
Weights: operating empty 10500 kg (23,149 lb); maximum take-off 14600 kg (32,188 lb)
Performance: maximum speed 309 kmh (192 mph); service ceiling 4575 m (15,000 ft); ferry range 2093 km (1,300 miles) with auxiliary fuel; endurance 5 hours on station with maximum weapon load
Armament: maximum ordnance 960 kg (2,116 lb), comprising four torpedoes

EMBRAER Tucano, ALX

Development of the EMBRAER **EMB-312 Tucano** (Toucan) high-performance turboprop trainer started in 1978 in response to a Brazilian air force specification. First flown on 16 August 1980, the first of 133 **T-27**s for the FAB entered service in September 1983. Designed to provide a 'jet-like' flying experience, the Tucano has a single control lever governing both propeller pitch and engine throttling, ejection seats, and a staggered tandem-place cockpit. Four underwing hardpoints can carry ordnance for weapons training.

Tucanos have been exported to Argentina (30), Colombia (14), Egypt (54), France (40), Honduras (12), Iran (25), Iraq (84), Paraguay (6), Peru (30) and Venezuela (31). French Tucanos are the improved **EMB-312F** version, with an updated cockpit avionics fit. Venezuela operates an armed version of the T-27 trainer, designated **AT-27**.

The Tucano's most notable export success came in March 1985, when it won a British order for 130 aircraft to replace the RAF's Jet Provost trainers. Considerable modifications were made to tailor the basic airframe to exacting requirements, including substituting an 820-kW (1,100-shp) Garrett TPE331-12B turboprop – which significantly improved the rate of climb – and reprofiling the cockpit to provide

The Shorts Tucano T.Mk 1 became the RAF's basic trainer from 1987 onwards. All RAF training aircraft are being repainted in this overall black scheme.

The ALX (service designation T-29/AT-29) is a radical evolution of the original Tucano design. Brazil will use its aircraft to patrol the vast Amazonian region.

commonality with the BAe Hawk. EMBRAER flew a Garrett-engined prototype in Brazil in February 1986 and delivered this to Shorts in Belfast as a pattern aircraft. The resultant Shorts **Tucano T.Mk 1** retains only 20 per cent commonality with EMBRAER-built aircraft. The first production aircraft flew on 30 December 1986, and initial deliveries to the RAF took place in June 1988. Customers for the armed export Shorts Tucano include Kenya (12 **Tucano Mk 51**s) and Kuwait (16 **Tucano Mk 52**s).

EMBRAER is currently building 99 **ALX** (**T-29**) light combat aircraft for the FAB, based on the **EMB-314 Super Tucano** (previously **EMB-312H Tucano H**) design. The ALX is stretched by 1.37 m (4 ft 5¾ in) compared to the EMB-312 and fitted with a 1193-kW (1,600-hp) PT6A-68-1 turboprop. The ALX has an armoured, NVG-compatible cockpit with HUD and MFDs, five weapons hardpoints and a FLIR system (two-seat version). Embraer flew a Tucano H development aircraft in September 1991. Two EMB-314 prototypes made their maiden flights on 15 May and 14 October 1993, respectively, and they now serve as the ALX development aircraft. Brazil plans to acquire between 30 and 40 two-seat **AT-29**s to replace its AT-26 Xavante (licence-built MB.326) advanced jet trainers.

Specification: EMBRAER EMB-312 Tucano
Powerplant: one 559-kW (750-hp) Pratt & Whitney Canada PT6A-25C turboprop
Dimensions: wing span 11.14 m (36 ft 6½ in); length 9.86 m (32 ft 4¼ in); height 3.40 m (11 ft 1¾ in)
Weights: basic empty 1870 kg (4,123 lb); max take-off 3175 kg (7,000 lb), with stores
Performance: maximum level speed 448 kmh (278 mph); maximum rate of climb at sea level 680 m (2,231 ft) per minute; service ceiling 9145 m (30,000 ft); typical range 1844 km (1,145 miles) with internal fuel; endurance about 5 hours with internal fuel
Armament: four stores stations for maximum ordnance of 1000 kg (2,205 lb)

Eurocopter Dauphin, Panther (Z-9)

In the early 1970s Aerospatiale (now Eurocopter) began development of a helicopter to replace the Alouette III. The initial version, the **SA 360 Dauphin**, featured a four-bladed main rotor, fenestron tail rotor, tailwheel landing gear and accommodation for a pilot and up to nine passengers. Production aircraft were powered by a 783-kW (1,050-shp) Astazou XVIIIA. Despite the development of a military **SA 361H**, it was obvious that the Dauphin needed twin engines. The Arriel-powered **SA 365C Dauphin 2** flew for the first time on 24 January 1975. The **SA 365N** introduced a retractable tricycle undercarriage, greater use of composites in the construction and other improvements.

Aerospatiale developed the **SA 366G1** for a US Coast Guard requirement to replace its Sikorsky HH-52s. The **HH-65A Dolphin** featured many US-built components, including 507-kW (680-hp) Textron Lycoming LTS101-750A-1 engines. A total of 101 HH-65As was delivered between 1987 and 1991.

Eurocopter went on to develop the improved **AS 365N3 Dauphin** and the significantly redesigned **AS 365N4** (now renamed the **EC 155**). Eurocopter has redesignated its military Dauphin variants on several occasions, leading to a confusing list of names and numbers. Today, two baseline versions are on offer, the army/air force **AS 565UB Panther**, and the armed navalised **AS 565SB Panther**. These designations supersede a range of earlier models including the armed **AS 565AA**, the anti-

The armed AS 565SB Panther can carry four AS 15TT anti-ship missiles and is fitted with an undernose Omera ORB 32 search radar.

tank **AS 565CA**, the utility **AS 565UA**, the armed naval **AS 565SA** (later **AS 565SB**) and the naval utility/SAR **AS 565MA** (later **AS 565MB**).

Beginning in 1987 the Brazilian army took delivery of 36 AS 565AAs, becoming the major customer for the land-based military Dauphin. Interest in the naval version (originally **AS 365F**) has been stronger. In 1980 the Saudi navy ordered four SAR/surveillance-configured AS 365Fs (later AS 565MA) and 20 missile-armed attack-configured **AS 365N**s (later AS 565SA). In 1986 Ireland took delivery of five AS 365Fs for SAR and fisheries patrol. In 1988 the French navy ordered 13 **AS 565F**s for shipboard operations. In 1994 the Israeli navy ordered 20 **AS 565SA Atalef** ('bat') aircraft for a similar role.

The Dauphin is built under licence by the Harbin Aircraft Manufacturing Company (HAMC) in China, as the **Z-9 Haitun** ('dolphin'). The initial production **Z-9** variant was equivalent to the SA 365N and it was followed by the **Z-9A** (AS 365N1), the **Z-9B** (AS 365N2) and the **Z-9G** (missile-armed version for the People's Liberation Army).

The French navy's shipboard AS 565F Dauphins (now referred to as AS 565SB Panthers) are used for SAR and 'planeguard' rescue tasks at sea.

Specification: Eurocopter AS565SB Panther
Powerplant: two 635-kW (851-hp) Turboméca Arriel 2C turboshafts
Dimensions: main rotor diameter 11.94 m (39 ft 2 in); length overall, rotor turning 13.68 m (44 ft 10¼ in); height overall 3.98 m (13 ft ¾ in)
Weights: empty 2281 kg (5,028 lb); maximum take-off 4250 kg (9,370 lb)
Performance: maximum cruising speed at sea level 278 kmh (173 mph); maximum rate of climb at sea level 468 m (1,535 ft) per minute; hovering ceiling 2600 m (8,530 ft) IGE, and 2500 m (8,200 ft) OGE; radius of action 250 km (155) with four missiles
Armament: four AS 15TT anti-ship missiles

Eurocopter Gazelle

Successor to the ubiquitous Sud Alouette II, the Aérospatiale (now Eurocopter) **Gazelle** originated in a mid-1960s project by Sud Aviation. Despite using many of its predecessor's dynamic systems (including the 268-kW (360-shp) Astazou II powerplant), the **X.300** design, soon renamed **SA 341**, achieved increased speed and manoeuvrability through adoption of a more powerful turboshaft, aerodynamically-shaped cabin and covered tailboom, and advanced rotor technology. The Gazelle used a rigid main rotor head, glass-fibre blades and the revolutionary 'fenestron' or fan-in-fin tail rotor. The **SA 340** prototype flew on 12 April 1968 with non-standard conventional rotors. The revised SA 341 Gazelle incorporated the new rotor technology, and introduced a longer cabin, larger tail surfaces and a 440-kW (590-shp) Astazou III.

Six versions were launched initially: **SA 341B** (British Army **Gazelle AH.Mk 1**); **SA 341C** (Royal Navy **HT.Mk 2** trainer); **SA 341D** (RAF **HT.Mk 3** trainer); **SA 341E** (RAF **HCC.Mk 4** VIP transport) – all with the Astazou IIIN; **SA 341F** (French army – ALAT) with Astazou IIIC; and military export **SA 341H**. In the UK, Westland built 294 Gazelles, including 212 AH.Mk 1s. Generally unarmed, they carried rockets during the 1982 Falklands War,

French army (ALAT) Gazelles have always operated in the armed role. This SA 342M is seen launching a HOT wire-guided anti-tank missile.

The British Army Air Corps' Gazelle AH.Mk 1s continue to give sterling service, operating as scouts for the TOW-armed Lynx attack helicopters

while nearly 70 were fitted with target-finding magnifying sights for missile-armed Lynxes, during the late 1980s. Of 170 SA 341Fs, ALAT converted 40 to carry four HOT ATGMs as **SA 341M**s and 62 with a GIAT M621 20-mm cannon and SFOM 80 sight as the **SA 341F/Canon**. Others have acquired an Athos scouting sight.

Powered by a 640-kW (858-shp) Astazou XIVH, the **SA 342** replaced the SA 341. Foreign exports began with the military **SA 342K**, the latter soon replaced by **SA 342L**s with an improved fenestron. The ALAT equivalent is designated **SA 342M** and over 200 have been delivered since 1980, typically armed with four HOT missiles and fitted with an M397 sight.

During the 1991 Gulf War, 30 French SA 342Ms were converted to **SA 342M/Celtic** standard, fitted with two Mistral air-to-air missiles and a SFOM 80 sight. This interim model has been replaced by the definitive **SA342ML1/ATAM** anti-helicopter model. This version is armed with four Mistrals and a T2000 sight, and 36 Gazelles have been thus converted. The ALAT is also upgrading 70 of its attack-configured AS 342Ms to **AS 342M1 Viviane** standard, through the addition of the Viviane thermal-imaging sight, with a laser-rangefinder.

Specification: Eurocopter SA 341F Gazelle
Powerplant: one 440-kW (590-hp) Turboméca Astazou IIIA
Dimensions: main rotor diameter 10.50 m (34 ft 5½ in); length overall, rotor turning 11.97 m (39 ft 9 in) and fuselage 9.53 m (31 ft 3 in); height overall 3.18 m (10 ft 5.25 in
Weights: empty 920 kg (2,028 lb); maximum take-off 1800 kg (3,968 lb)
Performance: maximum cruising speed 264 kmh (164 mph); maximum rate of climb at sea level 540 m (1,770 ft) per minute; service ceiling 5000 m (16,405 ft); hovering ceiling 2850 m (9,350 ft) IGE; range 670 km (416 miles)
Armament: maximum payload 700 kg (1,540 lb)

Eurocopter Puma, Super Puma, Cougar

The Aerospatiale (now Eurocopter) Puma is a medium-lift transport helicopter, designed to a French army specification, and is in service with air arms around the globe. The basic Puma which first flew in April 1965 carries 15 fully-equipped troops or 2 tonnes of internal cargo (2.5 tonnes underslung). Initial military versions comprised: **SA 330B** for the ALAT (Aviation Légère de l'Armée de Terre), **SA 330C** for military export and **SA 330E** (RAF **Puma HC.Mk 1**). Availability of uprated Turmo IVC engines in 1974 better equipped the Puma for 'hot-and-high' operations and the French air force bought 37 of the resulting military **SA 330H** variant as **SA 330Ba**s. Glass-fibre rotors became available in 1977, uprating the H to **SA 330L** standard.

In 1978 Aerospatiale introduced the **SA 332 Super Puma**, re-engined with pair of more powerful Turbomeca Makila 1A turboshafts. The initial military version, the **AS 332B**, was no larger than the original Puma, but in 1979 the **AS 332M** (military) introduced a 76-cm (30-in) increase in cabin length.

In the late 1980s, the basic military Super Puma was split along two lines, the **AS 332 M1 Super Puma Mk I** and the **AS 332M2 Super Puma Mk II**. The Mk I was an AS 332M (stretched AS 332B) fitted with the Makila 1A1 engines. The Mk II was stretched again, by a further 0.76 m (2 ft 6 in). In 1990, the military line was reorganised once more, as the **AS 532 Cougar**. Versions included the **AS 532UC** (formerly **AS 332B1**), a short-fuselage

The reliable and well-proven Puma HC.Mk 1 (built by Westland) is the mainstay of the RAF's Support Helicopter Force.

transport; **AS 532UL** (formerly **AS 332M1**) basic transport; **AS 532AC**, armed version of the AS 532UC; **AS 532AL**, armed version of the AS 532UL. A specialised naval version of the long-fuselage **AS 332F1** was developed as the **AS 532SC**, with the Royal Saudi Navy as its launch customer. This version could be armed with Exocet anti-ship missiles. French Army Aviation has developed a version of the **AS 532UL** to carry its **Horizon** battlefield surveillance radar.

The **AS 532U2** (formerly **AS 322M2**) was the stretched, up-engined military transport version, while the **AS 532A2 Cougar Mk II** was its armed derivative. The AS 532A2 is the basic airframe used for the French air force's new **RESCO** Combat Search and Rescue helicopter.

The final (basic) Cougar variant was developed in 1997. This was the **AS 532UB Cougar 100**, a simplified 'low cost' basic transport version without the external sponsons, revised main undercarriage struts and a new systems fit. An armed version was designated the **AS 532AB**.

The Royal Saudi Navy is a customer for the armed AS 532A2 Cougar Mk II, which is currently the ultimate evolution of the Puma family.

Specification: Eurocopter AS 532A2 Cougar
Powerplant: two 1236-kW (1,657 hp) Turboméca Makila 1A2 turboshafts
Dimensions: main rotor diameter 16.20 m (53 ft 1½ in); length overall, rotors turning 19.5 m (63 ft 11 in) and fuselage 16.79 m (55 ft ½ in); height overall 4.97 m (16 ft 4 in)
Weights: empty 5012 kg (11,050 lb); maximum take-off 11340 kg (25,000 lb)
Performance: maximum cruising speed 277 kmh (172 mph); maximum rate of climb at sea level 441 m (1,447 ft) per minute; service ceiling 5180 m (17,000 ft); hovering ceiling 2690 m (8,820 ft) in ground effect and 1900 m (6,240 ft) out of ground effect; range 926 km (575 miles)

Eurocopter Squirrel, Fennec

The civil **AS 350B Ecureuil** (**Squirrel**) led to the militarised **AS 350L** which first flew in March 1985. Powered by an Arriel 1D turboshaft, the **AS 350L** later became the **AS 350L1** when powered by the 732-shp (546-kW) Arriel 1D1 turboshaft. A military version of the twin-engined **AS 355 Twin Squirrel**, the **AS 355M**, was developed in 1988/89. France was the primary customer for this version with the air force acquiring 52 aircraft. An export version was dubbed **AS 355M2**.

In January 1990 Aerospatiale (now Eurocopter) renamed the single-engined military variants as the **AS 550 Fennec** and twin-engined aircraft as the **AS 555 Fennec**. Variants included the **AS 550U2** transport, **AS 550A2** cannon-armed version, **AS 550C2** missile-armed version, **AS 550C2** naval utility version, **AS 555UN** utility transport; **AS 555AN** cannon-armed version, **AS 555MN** naval utility version, and the **AS 555SN** armed naval version. In French service the AS 355AN has been solely gun-armed, usually with the GIAT M621 20-mm cannon

The naval version of the AS 555 can be fitted with an RDR-1500 search radar under the nose and a Magnetic Anomaly Detector under the tailboom. The AS 555 can be armed with two torpedoes.

The single-engined AS 550A2 can be armed with a M621 20-mm cannon pod, and is equipped with the ESCO HeliTOW sighting system above the roof.

The Argentine navy is one customer for the radar-equipped, weapons-capable AS 555SN Fennec, which offers affordable shipboard ASW capability.

In 1990 the Danish army acquired 12 combat-capable AS 550C2s, armed with the ESCO HeliTOW system. This comprises a roof-mounted sight and four TOW missiles in twin pods on each pylon. A similar system is in service in Singapore.

A specialist training version of the civil-standard AS 350B2, the **AS 350BB**, was developed for the UK's Defence Helicopter Flying School. The School operates two versions of the aircraft, 26 **Squirrel HT.Mk 1**s and 12 NVG-capable **Squirrel HT.Mk 2**s.

In Brazil Helibrás has built over 300 Squirrels under licence as the **Esquilo**. The air force operates 16 **CH-50** transports (AS 550U2), 20 **TH-50** trainers with a secondary fire-fighting role (AS 550U2), 11 armed **CH-55**s (AS 555U2) and two VIP-dedicated **VH-55**s (AS 355F2). The navy operates 16 **UH-12**s (AS 550BA) and nine **UH-12B**s (AS 355F2). The Army flies a mix of 36 **HA-1**s (AS 550A2s). The Paraguayan air force and navy operate four AS 350B Esquilos.

In 1996 China's Change Aircraft Industries Corporation unveiled its **Z-11** helicopter, which is clearly a direct copy of the AS 350B. The Z-11 is certified in civil and military versions, and is now in service with the People's Liberation Army. Change claims that the Z-11 first flew in 1994 but few facts are known about its development.

Specification: Eurocopter AS 555 Fennec
Powerplant: two 302-kW (406-hp) Turboméca TM 319 Arrius 1A turboshafts
Dimensions: main rotor diameter 10.69 m (35 ft ¾ in); fuselage length 10.93 m (35 ft 10¾ in); height overall 3.34 m (10 ft 11½ in)
Weights: basic empty 1436 kg (3,166 lb); maximum take-off 2600 kg (5,732 lb)
Performance: maximum cruising speed at optimum altitude 222 kmh (138 mph); service ceiling 3800 m (12,460 ft); maximum rate of climb at sea level more than 384 m (1,260 ft) per minute; range 722 km (448 miles)
Armament: optional cannon, machine gun pods, one homing torpedo

Eurocopter Tiger

The Eurocopter **Model 665 Tiger/Tigre** was developed to meet a Franco-German requirement for a next-generation anti-tank helicopter (German **PAH-2** and French army **HAC**). Development began in 1984, and resumed in March 1987 (after reappraisal) in a modified form to cover a common anti-tank version for the two armies, and an armed escort version (HAP) for the French army. A development contract awarded to Eurocopter in November 1989 provides for construction of five prototypes including two in full anti-tank Tiger (Germany)/Tigre (France) configuration and one as the escort Gerfaut.

The Tiger has a slender fuselage with two seats in tandem, stepped and offset to each side of the centreline. The structure makes extensive use of composite materials, and an advanced four-bladed composite semi-rigid main rotor is fitted. Other design features include Spheriflex tail rotor and fixed tricycle undercarriage with single wheels and high energy absorption.

The original German army **PAH-2 Tiger** was a dedicated anti-tank variant, but was redesigned as a more flexible multi-role aircraft under the designation **UHT** (originally **UHU**), with a mast-mounted FLIR night-vision system for the WSO, and a nose-mounted FLIR for the pilot. The aircraft is able to carry up to eight HOT 2 or Trigat anti-armour missiles, or four HOTs and four Stinger 2 AAMs for self-defence. Germany has a requirement for 212

Pre-production aircraft PT4 was used to trial the French Tiger HAP configuration, with a roof-mounted sight and Mistral AAMs.

UHTs, and the first 80 have been ordered. The first 115 French army Tigers will be **Tiger HAP**s. Originally known as the **Gerfaut**, HAP is an escort and fire-support variant, with no mast-mounted sight, but with a roof-mounted TV, FLIR, laser rangefinder and direct-optics sensors, and with an undernose 30-mm cannon turret. France will later receive 100 dedicated anti-tank **Tiger HAC**s (renamed from the original 'Tigre'), with a UHT-type mast-mounted sight and other improvements.

The first Tiger prototype flew on 27 April 1991, at first with a mast-mounted sight, but later reconfigured with a roof-mounted sight in the Gerfaut configuration. It was once expected that the French army would receive Gerfauts in 1994 and Tigres in 1999, with the Bundeswehr receiving its first UHU Tigers in 1998. Service introduction is now scheduled for 2003. A joint French/German training centre has been established at Le Luc, in France. The Tiger was unsuccessfully offered to the British and Dutch armies. A HAP-based variant, the **Aussie Tiger,** is a contender in the Australian Air 87 competition.

The German Army Tiger UHT configuration has a mast-mounted sight. It has no undernose cannon though one may be added in the years to come.

Specification: Eurocopter PAH-2 Tiger

Powerplant: two 873-kW (1,171-hp) MTU/Turboméca/Rolls-Royce MTR 390 turboshafts
Dimensions: main rotor diameter 13.00 m (42 ft 7¾ in); fuselage length 14.00 m (45 ft 11¼ in); height overall 4.32 m (14 ft 2 in)
Weights: basic empty 3300 kg (7,275 lb); normal take-off 5800 kg (12,787 lb); maximum overload take-off 6000 kg (13,227 lb)
Performance: maximum cruising speed at optimum altitude 280 kmh (174 mph); max rate of climb at sea level more than 600 m (1,969 ft) per minute; endurance over 3 hours
Armament: (HAC) primary armament of Mistral AAMs; (HAP) GIAT AM-30781 30-mm cannon and stub wings with up to four pylons

Eurofighter Typhoon

The **Eurofighter** consortium was officially formed in June 1986 by Britain, Germany and Italy (soon joined by Spain) to produce an air superiority fighter for service from the late 1990s. This followed the issue of an outline Air Staff Target by the four partners, plus France, in 1983. The Eurofighter design drew heavily on BAe's **Experimental Aircraft Programme** (**EAP**), and a number of other technology demonstrator programmes. The twin-RB.199 EAP technology demonstrator first flew in August 1986 and amassed invaluable data before retirement in May 1991. The Eurofighter copied EAP's unstable canard delta layout, adding active digital fly-by-wire flight controls, advanced avionics, multi-function cockpit displays, carbon-fibre composite construction and extensive use of aluminium-lithium alloys and titanium.

The new ECR-90 multi-mode pulse-Doppler look-up/look-down radar was selected for development in May 1990, building on the proven and highly-regarded Blue Vixen used by the Sea Harrier. While optimised for AMRAAM use, ECR-90 also provides CW illumination for SARH AAMs. The radar is supplemented by an IRST. Integrated defensive aids comprise missile approach, laser and radar warning systems, wingtip ESM/ECM pods,

The name Eurofighter Typhoon has been adopted for export sales of the Eurofighter aircraft, outside the initial four customer nations.

chaff/flare dispensers and a towed radar decoy.

A development contract signed in late 1988 covered the building and testing of eight **EFA** prototypes (though this total was subsequently reduced to seven). In 1992, Germany demanded major cost-reductions, triggering major project reviews and leading to major delays. against threats of withdrawal. Various less capable 'New EFA' configurations were studied before Germany decided to procure a smaller number of standard aircraft, stripped of their advanced DASS, and re-christened as the Eurofighter 2000. The original requirement for 765 EFAs (250 each for the RAF and the Luftwaffe, 165 for the AMI and 100 for the Ejercito del Aire) was cut back and now stands at 620, (232 for the RAF, 180 for the Luftwaffe, 130 for Italy and 103 for Spain). The name **Typhoon** was adopted for export aircraft (and for the RAF's Eurofighters) in 1998, and strong interest in the aircraft has already been expressed by Greece and Norway.

The prototype EFA 2000 made its long-awaited first flight on 27 March 1994 from Manching, Germany, and began what was to be a successful (if occasionally troubled) flight test programme. The first production Eurofighters were rolled out during 2001, and service entry is expected in 2003.

Two of the seven Eurofighter development aircraft, the British-built DA4 (seen here) and Spain's DA6, were built in two-seat configuration.

Specification: Eurofighter
Powerplant: two 90-kN (20,250-lb) Eurojet EJ200 turbofans
Dimensions: wing span 10.50 m (34 ft 5½ in); length 14.50 m (47 ft 7 in); height 4.00 m (13 ft 1.5 in)
Weights: empty 9750 kg (21,495 lb); maximum take-off 21000 kg (46,297 lb)
Performance: maximum level speed 2125 kmh (1,321 mph); take-off run 500 m (1,640 ft) at normal take-off weight; landing run 500 m (1,640 ft) at normal landing weight; combat radius between 463 and 556 km (288 and 345 miles)
Armament: Mauser Mk 27 27-mm cannon, maximum ordnance 6500 kg (14,330 lb)

Fairchild A-10 Thunderbolt

Originally conceived as a counter-insurgency air-craft for the Vietnam War, the Fairchild **A-10A Thunderbolt II** emerged in 1972 as a dedicated close air support aircraft, with a primary anti-armour role. The A-10's operating environment dictated a highly-survivable design incorporating a large-area wing for excellent low-altitude manoeuvrability, rear-mounted engines shrouded from ground fire by either the wings or tailplane and redundant, armoured and duplicated flight controls and hydraulic systems. Titanium 'bathtubs' protect both the pilot and the ammunition tank.

The principal weapon is the AGM-65 Maverick anti-armour missile, supplemented by an enormous GAU-8/A 30-mm seven-barrelled rotary cannon. Avionics of the A-10 remained very basic for most of the aircraft's career, with no laser designator or rangefinder fitted. The pilot has a HUD, and a screen for displaying images from Maverick or other EO-guided weapons. A Pave Penny marked target seeker detects and tracks targets designated by laser. Most current aircraft have received the LASTE modification, which finally adds an autopilot and also improves gun accuracy.

The A-10 entered USAF service in 1977. At its peak deployment, a six A-10 squadrons were stationed in the UK, with more in Korea and the Continental USA. Debates raged as to the vulnerability of the A-10, and it was finally decided to gradually withdraw the type in favour of the F-16. At the

This A-10 of the Spangdahlem-based 81st FS is carrying a huge warload of Mk 82 bombs, Maverick missiles, Sidewinder AAMs and an ALQ-131 ECM pod.

same time, redundant A-10s became available to replace OV-10s in the forward air control role. Unchanged, these were redesignated **OA-10A** and redistributed to tactical air support squadrons.

For the FAC role the A-10s are armed with rocket pods for marking targets and AIM-9 AAMs for self-defence. In the twilight of its career, the A-10 proved its worth during 1991 Desert Storm opera-tions, destroying huge numbers of tanks, artillery pieces and vehicles. A modest upgrade programme is now underway, Lockheed Martin having won the contract in February 2001. The A-10 will receive a 'precision engagement capability' adding a new mission computer, new cockpit MFDs, a MIL STD 1760 databus, a new datalink, precision-weapons capability (including JDAM and WCMD), improved navigation equipment, TERPROM TRNS and new defensive aids. A re-engining programme has been proposed, but not funded. The A-10 has not been exported, although it is still possible that some 50 airframes may be sold to Turkey. The type is expected to remain in USAF service until 2028.

For its primary intended role as a tank killer on the Central European front, the A-10 was built around the massive GAU-8 30-mm cannon.

Specification: Fairchild A-10A

Powerplant: two 40.32-kN (9,065-lb) General Electric TF34-GE-100 turbofans
Dimensions: wing span 17.53 m (57 ft 6 in); 16.26 m (length 53 ft 4 in); height 4.47 m (14 ft 8 in)
Weights: basic empty 9771 kg (21,541 lb); maximum take-off 22680 kg (50,000 lb)
Performance: maximum level speed 706 kmh (439 mph); maximum rate of climb 1828 m (6,000 ft) per minute; combat radius 1000 km (620 miles) on a deep strike mission or 463 km (288 miles) on a close air support mission
Armament: one GAU-8A 30-mm cannon with 1,174 rounds; maximum ordnance load of 7258 kg (16,000 lb)

Ilyushin Il-76, Il-78, Beriev A-50

Ukraine/Russia
Transport and AEW platform

The Ilyushin **Il-76** (NATO code-name **'Candid'**) was developed as a successor to the An-12 for both Aeroflot and the Soviet air force. Larger, heavier and more powerful than the contemporary Lockheed C-141, the Il-76 uses extensive high lift devices, thrust reversers and a high flotation undercarriage to achieve much better short- and rough-field performance. The cargo hold is fully pressurised and can be quickly reconfigured by using interchangeable passenger, freight or air ambulance modules. The first prototype 'Candid-A' made its first flight on 25 March 1971 and a development squadron was in service by 1974. Series production began in 1975 and more than 850 had been built by the beginning of 1999, with production continuing 'for stock' at a trickle.

'**Candid-A**' (civil) and '**Candid-B**' (military) sub-types comprise the basic military Il-76, the civil **Il-76T** and military **Il-76M** with additional fuel tankage, and the similar **Il-76TD** and military **Il-76MD** with uprated Soloviev D-30KP-1 turbofans for improved 'hot-and-high' performance. Other military 'Candid-As' include the **Il-76 Skalpel** and **Il-76 Aibolit** mobile operating theatres, the **Il-76PP** ECM jammer (four produced, but never deployed), the **Il-76VKP** (**Il-82**) communications relay aircraft, and

Most, though not all, military transport versions of the Il-76 have a rear gun turret in the tail fairing. This is a Ukranian air force IL-76MD.

This A-50 'Mainstay' is leading a pair of Su-30 interceptors. The A-50 is a conversion of the Il-76MD airframe, conducted by Beriev.

the new stretched **Il-76MF**, with more powerful PS-90AN turbofans. This was flown in August 1995, and eight are in production. There have also been four **Il-76LL** engine testbeds, **Il-76K**, **Il-76MDK** and **Il-76MDK-2** cosmonaut training aircraft and a single **Il-76MDP** firebomber conversion. Foreign operators include India, Iran, Iraq, Libya, North Korea, Syria and Yemen.

The **Il-78M 'Midas'** is a three-point tanker fitted with three UPAZ external refuelling HDUs, one under each wing and one mounted on the port side of the rear fuselage. Internally the **Il-78M** has two pallet-mounted tanks in the hold; each contains 35 tonnes of fuel.

The **A-50 'Mainstay'** was developed by Beriev as an AEW and AWACS platform. It has a rotodome above the fuselage, with the nose glazing and tail turret removed and replaced by further radomes. The A-50's performance is broadly comparable to Boeing's E-3 Sentry, with an inferior absolute detection range, but a (claimed) superior ability to discriminate against ground clutter. The improved **A-50M** has the more advanced Shmel-2 radar. Related variants are the **Il-976** (**Il-76 SKIP**) range control aircraft and Iraq's indigenously developed **Adnan** and **Baghdad** AEW conversions.

Specification: Ilyushin Il-76M 'Candid-B'
Powerplant: four 117.68-kN (26,455-lb) PNPP 'Aviadvigatel' (Soloviev) D-30KP turbofans
Dimensions: wing span 50.50 m (165 ft 8 in); length 46.59 m (152 ft 10¼ in); height 14.76 m (48 ft 5 in)
Weights: max take-off 170000 kg (374,780 lb); maximum payload 40000 kg (88,183 lb)
Performance: maximum level speed 850 kmh (528 mph); cruising speed between 750 and 800 kmh (466 and 497 mph); absolute ceiling about 15500 m (50,855 ft); ferry range 6700 km (4,163 miles); range 5000 km (3,107 miles) with maximum payload
Armament: rear turret with gunner and twin radar-directed NR-23 23-mm cannon

Kaman SH-2 Seasprite

A veteran of the Vietnam war, and almost retired from US Navy service, Kaman's venerable **SH-2 Seasprite** is enjoying a new lease of life. Though the original design dates to the 1950s the Seasprite has found a new niche for itself as a compact shipboard helicopter, with advanced on-board systems.

The prototype SH-2 flew as the **HU2K-1** in July 1959, the first Kaman helicopter to have a conventional rotor configuration. The H-2 designation was applied in October 1962 and Kaman built 100 single-engined **UH-2A** and **UH-2B** aircraft for the US Navy. In 1970 the redesigned , twin-engined **SH-2D** was adopted for the ASW role, as the Navy's **LAMPS** aircraft – a small helicopter capable of operating from the decks of smaller frigates and destroyers. The definitive **LAMPS I** version was the **SH-2F Seasprite**, which entered service in 1973. This version was powered by two General Electric T58-GE-8F turboshafts, and was fitted with an LN 66HP search radar, a towed MAD, side-mounted sonobuoy rack, tactical mission system. In 1981 Kaman re-opened the Seasprite line to build 60 new SH-2Fs for the USN.

In 1985 the Navy began to upgrade its SH-2Fs to **SH-2G Super Seasprite** standard, re-engining them with T700 turboshafts and significantly increasing performance. The first SH-2F testbed flew in April 1985 and the first production-standard SH-2G conversion flew in March 1990. During the mid- to late-1990s the US Navy began to retire

Egypt has acquired 10 SH-2G(E)s to operate from its former-US Navy 'Knox'-class frigates. The Seasprites are equipped with a dipping sonar.

many of the older, smaller vessels which deployed SH-2s, and the Seasprite's place in the fleet was increasingly taken over by the Sikorsky SH-60. Currently the US Navy has just two Reserve squadrons equipped with the SH-2G.

However, the surplus of ex-US Navy aircraft allowed Kaman to embark on an aggressive export sales campaign with the Seasprite. In February 1995 Egypt ordered 10 **SH-2(GE)s** – remanufactured from SH-2F airframes – and they were delivered in 1997/98. Australia has ordered 11 SH-2G(A)s to operate from its ANZAC- class and FFG frigates. The first (remanufactured) **SH-2G(A)** flew in October 1999 and the first delivery was made to the reformed No. 805 Sqn in March 2001. The Australian aircraft are fitted with the Litton ITAS advanced cockpit and mission system. The Royal New Zealand Navy has ordered five new-build **SH-2G(NZ)**s and deliveries began in 2001. An interim batch of four unmodified SH-2Fs was acquired to provide training and familiarisation before the RNZN's Super Seasprites were delivered.

New Zealand took delivery of four T-58-powered SH-2F Seasprites as a 'bridging loan' until its full-standard SH-2G(NZ) aircraft could be delivered.

Specification: Kaman SH-2G Seasprite
Powerplant: two 1285-kW (1,723-hp) General Electric T700-GE-401 turboshafts
Dimensions: main rotor diameter 13.41 m (44 ft); length overall, rotor turning 16 m (52 ft 6 in), fuselage 12.34 m (40 ft 6 in); height overall 4.62 m (15 ft 2 in)
Weights: empty 4173 kg (9,200 lb); maximum take-off 6124 kg (13,500 lb)
Performance: maximum level speed 256 kmh (159 mph); maximum rate of climb at sea level 762 m (2,500 ft) per minute; hovering ceiling 6350 m (20,800 ft) IGE, and 5486 m (18,000 ft) OGE; maximum range 885 km (500 miles)
Armament: provision for two ASW torpedoes

Kamov Ka-50, Ka-52

Given the unflattering NATO code-name **'Hokum'**, the **Ka-50** was developed as a rival to the Mil Mi-28 in the competition to provide a new battlefield helicopter for the Soviet armed forces. Realising that it would be difficult to achieve AH-64 levels of performance with existing Soviet technology and equipment, Kamov followed an individualistic course, retaining its trademark coaxial contra-rotating rotor configuration. This was felt to give a more compact, more agile airframe, and to reduce vulnerability to hostile fire. To minimise weight, Kamov also decided to design a single-seat helicopter, using the contra-rotating coaxial's inherently good handling characteristics to make this possible, and drawing on its experience of sophisticated auto-hover systems on Kamov's naval helicopters. The single-pilot cockpit was successfully demonstrated on the testbench, and in a modified Ka-29TB. A novel feature is the pilot's Severin/Zvezda K-37 ejection seat. The ejection sequence begins with automatic rotor separation, then jettisons the doors before a rocket pack drags the seat from the helicopter.

The **V.80** prototype made its maiden flight on 27 July 1982. The competitive evaluation ended in October 1986 and the Ka-50 was reportedly selected in preference to the Mil Mi-28, although the

Kamov has marketed the Ka-50 abroad under several names, first as the 'Werewolf' but more recently as the 'Black Shark'.

The Ka-50 has yet to enter service in significant numbers, with only a handful of aircraft in use with the Russian army aviation training centre.

requirement was then revised, leading to a new competition between the night-attack optimised Mi-28N and the **Ka-50N/Ka-50Sh**, which feature advanced new avionics.

Customer resistance has led to the development of a number of two-seat derivatives of the Ka-50, including the tandem-seat **Ka-50-2** and **Ka-50-2 Erdogan** (this to meet a Turkish requirement) and the **Ka-52 Alligator**, with side-by-side seats, a mast- and roof-mounted sighting system and advanced night attack systems.

The tube-launched, laser-beam-riding Vikhr (NATO AT-9 'Whirlwind') missile forms the Ka-50's primary armament. Sixteen can be carried, augmented by the built-in 30-mm cannon. Developed for the BMP AFV, the gun has variable rates of fire and selective feed from two 250-round ammunition boxes. The gun is installed on the starboard side of the fuselage below the wing root and is electro-hydraulically driven and can be traversed through 30° in elevation, and can also move 15° in azimuth. Combat survivability is enhanced by the IR suppressors in the exhaust assemblies, the heavily armoured pressurised cockpit, the foam-filled, self-sealing fuel tanks. Wingtip pods house chaff/flare dispensers.

Specification: Kamov Ka-50
Powerplant: two 1660-kW (2,226-hp) Klimov (Isotov) TV3-117VK turboshafts
Dimensions: rotor diameter, each 14.50 m (45 ft 6.9 in); length overall, rotors turning 16.00 m (52 ft 5.9 in), and fuselage excluding probe and gun 13.50 m (44 ft 3½ in); height 5.40 m (17 ft 8.6 in)
Weights: maximum take-off 7500 kg (16,534 lb) Performance: maximum level speed 350 kmh (217 mph) maximum vertical rate of climb at 2500 m (8,200 ft) 600 m (1,969 ft) per minute; hovering ceiling 4000 m (13,125 ft) OGE; combat radius about 250 km (155 miles)
Armament: one 2A42 30-mm cannon with two 250-round drums, plus 3000-kg (6,610-lb) stores

Kawasaki T-4

The Kawasaki **T-4** is an intermediate jet trainer to replace the Lockheed T-33 and Fuji T-1A/B. Design studies were completed in 1982 and four prototypes (designated **XT-4**) were funded in 1984. The first of these made its maiden flight on 29 July 1985. The T-4 is a conventional design, featuring high subsonic manoeuvrability and docile handling characteristics. It shares a similar high-wing configuration to the Dassault-Dornier Alpha Jet, to which it bears a similar appearance – with pronounced anhedral on the wings and tailplane, and large 'dog tooth' leading edges. Visibility for both instructor and pupil is excellent, with a frameless wrap-around windscreen and a one-piece canopy. For its secondary liaison role, the T-4 has a baggage compartment fitted in the centre fuselage with external access via a door in the port side.

The T-4 is a collaborative venture, in which Fuji builds the rear fuselage, supercritical section wings and tail unit, and Mitsubishi constructs the centre fuselage and air intakes. Kawasaki builds only the forward fuselage, but is responsible for final assembly and flight test. Virtually all components are indigenously built, and most are locally designed, including the Ishikawajima-Harima F3-IHI-30 turbofan engines. A single underwing pylon on each side can accommodate a 450-litre (99-Imp gal) drop tank, and a centreline pylon can be fitted for a target towing winch, air sampling pod, ECM pod or chaff dispenser.

These T-4s wear the yellow and black checkerboard markings of 1 Koku-dan, the JASDF's 1st Air Wing and its primary jet training unit.

T-4 production deliveries began in September 1988, to meet an original Japan Air Self Defence Force requirement for some 200 aircraft, replacing the T-33 and Fuji T-1 in the basic training role. By mid-January 2001 212 T-4s had been funded. The T-4 is today in service with Nos 31 and 32 Squadrons of No. 1 Air Wing at Hamamatsu, and with some operational squadrons and wings as a liaison aircraft, sometimes wearing the same camouflage scheme and unit markings as the operational aircraft. Nine aircraft serve with the Blue Impulse aerobatic team (No.11 Squadron, No.4 Wing), having replaced T-2s in 1994. These aircraft are modified to carry smoke generators and also have a re-inforced canopy, a revised rudder limiter system, ground-proximity warning system and additional cockpit lighting and instruments to aid aerobatic flight.

An advanced version of the T-4, with more powerful engines and improved avionics, has been offered to the JASDF to replace the ageing and uneconomical T-2 in the advanced training role.

The first and third T-4 prototypes are seen here in the markings of the TRDI development and test wing, where they are retained for trials flying.

Specification: Kawasaki T-4
Powerplant: two 16.32-kN (3,671-lb) Ishikawajima-Harima F3-IHI-30 turbofans
Dimensions: wing span 9.94 m (32 ft 7½ in); length 13.00 m (42 ft 8 in); height 4.60 m (15 ft 1¼ in)
Weights: empty 3700 kg (8,157 lb); maximum take-off 7500 kg (16,534 lb)
Performance: maximum level speed 1038 kmh (645 mph); maximum rate of climb at sea level 3048 m (10,000 ft) per minute; service ceiling 15240 m (50,000 ft); ferry range 1668 km (1,036 miles) with drop tanks
Armament: structural provision for up to 2000 kg (4,409 lb) of ordnance on two underwing hardpoints

Lockheed C-5 Galaxy

The Lockheed **C-5 Galaxy** heavy logistics transport originated from a 1963 USAF **CX-HLS** (Cargo Experimental-Heavy Logistics System) requirement for a capability to carry a 113400-kg (250,000-lb) payload over 4828 km (3,000 miles) without air refuelling. The resulting design incorporates a high-wing, T-tailed configuration, powered by four underwing podded TF39 turbofans. Key to the C-5's mission is its cavernous interior and 'roll on/roll off' cargo loading capability, with access to the vast cargo bay at both front and rear via an upward-lifting visor nose and standard rear clamshell doors. The C-5A first flew on 30 June 1968 and operational C-5s were delivered between 17 December 1969 and May 1973. The C-5A suffered initially from wing crack problems and infamous cost overruns, but has served well since then and is an irreplaceable asset for the US Air Force's Air Mobility Command. To extend their service lives, 77 C-5As underwent a re-winging programme from 1981 to 1987.

In the mid-1980s, the production line was reopened to meet an urgent USAF demand for additional heavy airlift capacity. Fifty **C-5B** aircraft were built, essentially similar to the C-5A, but incorporating numerous modifications and improve-

The Galaxy is the only US aircraft able to carry the M1 main battle tank, and is also highly prized for its ability to carry large numbers of smaller vehicles.

The C-5 is still the cornerstone of the United States' heavy strategic airlift capability, and the centre of great debate about how it can ever be replaced.

ments resulting from operations with the C-5A. The C-5B model dispensed with the C-5A's complex crosswind main landing gear and introduced an improved AFCS (automated flight control system). The first production C-5B was delivered on 8 January 1986 and deliveries were completed by 1989. A further variant is the secretive **C-5C**, (two converted) which is optimised for carrying satellites and space equipment. The C-5C has a bulged rear cargo door and a sealed nose door.

Typical C-5 loads include two M1A1 Abrams MBTs, 16¾-ton trucks, 10 LAV-25s, or a CH-47. Although not usually assigned airdrop duties, the Galaxy can also drop paratroopers. C-5A/Bs serve with the USAF's AMC, AFRC, and the ANG. Galaxies have served in airlifts supporting US operations in Vietnam, Israel (October 1973 War) and Desert Shield/ Storm (1990-91), during which they flew 42 per cent of cargo and 18.6 per cent of passenger missions.

Under the recently announced C-5 Reliability Enhancement and Re-engining Program (RERP), the Galaxy will be refitted with General Electric CF6-80C2 engines and a modernised cockpit. All 126 aircraft will be upgraded between 2005 and 2014, possibly receiving the **C-5D** designation.

Specification: Lockheed C-5B Galaxy
Powerplant: four 191.27-kN (43,000-lb) General Electric TF39-GE-1C turbofans
Dimensions: wing span 67.88 m (222 ft 8½ in); length 75.54 m (247 ft 10 in); height 19.85 m (65 ft 1½ in)
Weights: operating empty 169643 kg (374,000 lb); maximum payload 118387 kg (261,000 lb); maximum take-off 379657 kg (837,000 lb)
Performance: max level speed at 7620 m (25,000 ft) 919 kmh; maximum cruising speed between 888 and 908 kmh (552 and 564 mph); (571 mph); maximum rate of climb at sea level 525 m (1,725 ft) per minute; service ceiling 10895 m (35,750 ft); range 10411 km (6,469 miles) with maximum fuel

Lockheed C-141 StarLifter

First flown on 17 December 1963, the Lockheed **C-141A StarLifter** has provided the USAF with a fast and versatile long-range jet transport since it entered service in 1964. The design features a fuselage of similar cross-section to the C-130, two large clamshell doors and a rear ramp which can be opened in flight for air-dropping. Swept wings were adopted for high-speed cruise, with powerful high-lift devices provided for good low-speed field performance. Power came from four podded TF33 fuel-efficient turbofans, and all fuel was housed in integral wing tanks. The aircraft commenced squadron operations with MAC in April 1965, supplying the war effort in Vietnam.

It soon became apparent that the C-141A's maximum payload of 32136 kg (70,847 lb) (or 41731 kg/92,000 lb on C-141As configured to carry LGM-30 Minuteman ICBMs) was rarely achieved, with the aircraft 'bulking out' before its weight limit was approached. During the 1970s, the entire fleet (minus four **NC-141A** test aircraft) was cycled through a programme to bring all 270 aircraft to **C-141B** standard. This added a 7.11-m (23-ft 4-in) fuselage stretch and an in-flight refuelling receptacle above the cockpit for true global airlift capacity. Overall cargo capacity has been increased by over 30 per cent, adding the equivalent of 90 new C-141s to the airlift fleet (in terms of capacity) at a much lower relative cost. The prototype **YC-141B** StarLifter made its first flight on 24 March 1977 and

Though the C-141B is slowly being retired, in favour of the C-17, the USAF cannot afford to replace its hard-working C-141s on a one-for-one basis.

Lockheed completed the final C-141B conversion in June 1982. USAF Special Operations Command operates 13 modified **C-141B SOLL II** (Special Operations Low-Level) aircraft with a FLIR turret and extra defensive aids.

Palletised seats can be fitted for 166 passengers, while by using canvas seats some 205 passengers or 168 paratroops can be carried. For medevac missions, the C-141B can carry 103 litter patients and 113 walking wounded. It can also carry light armoured vehicles, an AH-1 or UH-1 helicopter or five HMMWVs. Thirteen standard cargo pallets can be carried, and other loads can include aircraft engines, food supplies, fuel drums or nuclear weapons.

As the Boeing C-17 has entered service many of the older StarLifters have been retired with the AMC airlift fleet suffering a shortfall in capacity. Sixty four C-141Bs are being converted to **C-141C** standard with a 'glass' EFIS cockpit, GPS navigation, collision-avoidance systems (TCAS) and an all-weather flight control system.

While most C-141Bs are in the hands of Air Mobility Command, some are operated by the Air National Guard and the Air Force Reserve (as seen here).

Specification: Lockheed C-141B StarLifter
Powerplant: four 93.41-kN (21,000-lb) Pratt & Whitney TF33-P-7 turbofans
Dimensions: wing span 48.74 m (159 ft 11 in); length 51.29 m (168 ft 3½ in); height 11.96 m (39 ft 3 in)
Weights: operating empty 67186 kg (148,120 lb); maximum payload 41222 kg (90,880 lb); maximum take-off 155580 kg (343,000 lb)
Performance: maximum cruising speed at high altitude 910 kmh (566 mph); maximum rate of climb at sea level 890 m (2,920 ft) per minute; service ceiling 12680 m (41,600 ft); ferry range 10280 km (6,390 miles); range with maximum payload 4725 km (2,936 miles)

Lockheed S-3 Viking

United States
Carrier-based ASW and ASuV aircraft

Developed to counter the new generation of Soviet navy quiet, deep-diving nuclear-powered submarines, the Lockheed **S-3 Viking** is the US Navy's standard carrier-based, fixed-wing ASW aircraft. It is a conventional high-wing, twin-turbofan aircraft with four crew (pilot, co-pilot, tactical co-ordinator and acoustic sensor operator). The first of eight service-test **YS-3A**s made its maiden flight on 21 January 1972, and was followed by 179 production **S-3A Viking**s equipped with an AN/APS-116 search radar and OR-89 FLIR. The heart of the ASW suite is an AN/ASQ-81 MAD sensor housed in a retractable tailboom. The S-3A carried 60 sonobuoys in its aft fuselage and has a ventral bomb bay and wing hardpoints for bombs, mines torpedoes or depth charges. The S-3A entered fleet service in July 1974. Lockheed produced four **US-3A** COD aircraft which have now been retired, and a single **KS-3A** tanker demonstrator.

The current in-service **S-3B Viking** variant is the result of a 1981 upgrade programme, which added the APS-137 Inverse Synthetic Aperture Radar, the ALR-76 ESM system and the ALE-39 chaff/flare dispenser. The Viking's anti-surface warfare capability was greatly improved through the integration of the Harpoon and Maverick missiles. About 160 S-3As

For the future the US Navy is looking to its Common Support Aircraft requirement to replace the S-3 Viking, E-2 Hawkeye and C-2 Greyhound.

Each US Carrier Air Wing embarks a single S-3B squadron for battle group ASW protection, but the Vikings have many other useful functions.

were upgraded to S-3B standard. In recent years the Viking fleet has placed less emphasis on the ASW role as the Russian naval threat receded. Vikings instead took on an increased attack and special missions role, while also acting as the *de facto* tanking aircraft for carrier air wings. Specialist S-3 programmes include the **Outlaw Viking** (over-the-horizon targeting), **Beartrap Viking** (ASW development), **Orca Viking** (ASW development) and the **Grey Wolf** (overland reconnaissance, command and control with a podded SAR radar)

The **ES-3A Shadow** was a carrier-based Elint aircraft modified from the S-3A with extensive surveillance equipment. The co-pilot's position was replaced by a third sensor station and the bomb bays were modified to accommodate avionics. The ES-3A had a new radome, direction-finding antenna, and other equipment in a dorsal 'shoulder' on the fuselage, an array of seven receiving antennas on its underfuselage, an omnidirectional Elint antenna on each side of the rear fuselage, and wingtip AN/ALR-76 ESM antennas. Two squadrons operated the ES-3A from 1995 to 2000 when it was retired in favour of land-based Elint aircraft. Studies for an S-3 replacement are now being conducted under the US Navy's Common Support Aircraft programme.

Specification: Lockheed S-3B Viking
Powerplant: two 41.26-kN (9,275-lb) General Electric TF34-GE-2 turbofans
Dimensions: wing span 20.93 m (68 ft 8 in); length overall 16.26 m (53 ft 4 in) height overall 6.93 m (22 ft 9 in)
Weights: empty 12088 kg (26,650 lb); (42,500 lb); maximum take-off 23832 kg (52,540 lb)
Performance: max speed at sea level 814 kmh; (506 mph); maximum rate of climb at sea level 1280 m (4,200 ft) per minute; service ceiling 10670 m (36,000 ft); combat radius over 1751 km (1,088 miles)
Armament: maximum ordnance 3175 kg (7,000 lb) with 1814 kg (4,000 lb) carried internally

Lockheed U-2R

Early variants of the Lockheed U-2 had successful (if clandestine) careers as high-altitude reconnaissance platforms. However, these models were limited by the size and weight of sensors which they could carry, and so Lockheed developed the improved **U-2R**, which first flew in August 1967. It was larger overall, offering greatly improved range/payload, endurance and handling characteristics. Twelve early-production U-2Rs served with the USAF (in Vietnam) and with the CIA.

In 1979 the production line re-opened to provide the USAF with 37 new airframes for the **TR-1A** tactical reconnaissance programme, using the U-2R as a platform for the ASARS-2 synthetic aperture battlefield surveillance radar, the PLSS radar location system, and all-new Sigint-gathering equipment. The batch also included two two-seat **TR-1B** (later **TU-2R** and **TU-2S**) trainers and one **U-2RT**. All three two-seat trainers are identical. Finally, two 'civilianised' U-2Rs were built for NASA as **ER-2** earth resources monitoring aircraft. In 1991 the USAF abandoned the TR-1 designation and renamed all its aircraft as U-2Rs.

All U-2R and U-2RT aircraft were re-engined with the General Electric F101 (later redesignated F118-101) replacing the original J75 engine, to become the **U-2S** and the **U-2ST**, respectively. The new engine had a dramatic effect on performance and operating costs. Flight tests began in 1991 and the aircraft were redelivered between 1994 and 1998.

The chief identifying feature of the U-2R/U-2S are the 'super pods' fitted to the inboard wing. These large pods carry a range of Sigint systems

The U-2S most resembles a large powered glider. The retractable main bicycle undercarriage is aided by plug-in detachable 'pogo' outriggers. The wingtips incorporate skids, above which are RWRs. Sensors are carried in the nose, a large 'Q-bay' for cameras (behind the cockpit), smaller bays along the lower fuselage and in two removeable wing 'super pods'. Sensors include Comint and Elint recorders, imaging radars, radar locators and high resolution cameras. A common mission fit combines a nose-mounted ASARS-2 radar and the Senior Glass Elint system with its substantial 'farm' of Sigint antennas on the rear fuselage and in the 'super pods'. Recorded intelligence can be transmitted via datalink to ground stations, and some aircraft can carry the Senior Span/Spur satcom antenna in a large rear-mounted teardrop radome. The U-2S has also been re-equipped with the SYERS (Senior Year Electro-optical Relay System) camera, which uses imaging technology developed for US reconnaissance satellites. The electro-optical camera at the heart of SYERS is carried in the aircraft's nose.

The Senior Spur satellite communications antenna allows the U-2S to relay ASARS-2 imagery back to base from the other side of the world.

Specification: Lockheed U-2S
Powerplant: one 81.4-kN (18,300-lb) General Electric F118-101 non-afterburning turbofan
Dimensions: wing span 31.39 m (103 ft in); length 19.13 m (62 ft 9 in); height 4.88 m (16 ft)
Weights: operating empty about 6441 kg (14,199 lb); maximum take-off 18733 kg (41,300 lb)
Performance: maximum cruising speed at 21335 m (70,000 ft) over 692 kmh (430 mph); operational ceiling approximately 25450 m (83,500 ft); maximum range over 12500 km (7767 miles); mission endurance over 12 hours

Lockheed Martin C-130 Hercules

The **C-130 Hercules** is the world's most widely used and most versatile military transport, serving with 64 countries. The **YC-130** first flew in August 1954, and was followed by the production **C-130A** in April 1955. An entire alphabet of specialised versions followed, but the basic transport aircraft had a straightforward evolution. In 1958 the **C-130B** introduced more powerful T56-A-7A engines with four-bladed props and increased fuel tankage in the wings. In 1961 the **C-130E** arrived, with yet more fuel and higher operating weights. The **C-130H** followed, initially as an export aircraft, but it became the definitive first-generation Hercules variant. Powered by uprated T56-A-15 engines, the C-130H first flew in November 1964. The airframe featured a strengthened wing box, improved brakes and new avionics. The first production aircraft went to the RNZAF in 1965, and the USAF received its first C-130H in April 1975.

The RAF's **C-130K** (**Hercules C.Mk 1**) – based on the C-130H – has British avionics and equipment. Thirty were 'stretched' by 4.5 m (15 ft) to become **C.Mk 3**s, increasing capacity from 92 to 128 troops. With the addition of refuelling probes these aircraft became **C.Mk 1P/C.Mk 3P**s. Several nations are upgrading their older C-130s. Belgium

The most obvious difference between the C-130J and earlier models is the new aircraft's AE2100 engines and their six-bladed all-composite propellers.

This Royal Air Force of Oman C-130H is typical of the many Hercules aircraft in every-day service all around the world today.

has fitted a 'glass' cockpit and new weather radar to its C-130Hs and Marshall's of Cambridge have been doing similar work to South Africa's C-130Bs. Many other operators have fitted missile warning equipment, chaff/flare dispensers and cockpit armour to their aircraft. Production of 2,156 first-generation C-130s ended in 1998 with the delivery of a C-130H to Japan. By this time Lockheed (now Lockheed Martin) had developed its successor, the C-130J.

The **C-130J** began as a Lockheed private venture in 1991, as the '**Hercules II**'. It modernised the C-130H with new-technology engines and six-bladed props, an advanced digital cockpit for two crew with HUDs as primary flight controls, a digital engine management and diagnostic system. In 1994 the RAF became the launch customer, ordering 10 stretched **C-130J-30**s (**Hercules C.Mk 4**) and 15 C-130Js (**Hercules C.Mk 5**). Other customers include Australia, Italy, Denmark and the USA (including **EC-130J**, **KC-130J** and **WC-130J** variants). The first C-130J flew on 5 April 1996 but several unexpected problems slowed the flight test programme considerably. The first aircraft was not delivered to the UK until August 1998 and further delays prevented the C-130J from entering service with the RAF until November 2000.

Specification: Lockheed C-130J Hercules
Powerplant: four 3424-kW (4,591-hp) Rolls Royce (Allison) AE 2100D3 turboprops
Dimensions: wing span 40.41 m (132 ft 7 in); length 29.79 m (97 ft 9 in); height 11.66 m (38 ft 3 in)
Weights: operating empty equipped 34274 kg (75,562 lb); maximum payload 18955 kg (41,790 lb); maximum take-off 70,305 kg (155,000 lb)
Performance: maximum cruising speed at 9145 m (30,000 ft) 595 kmh (370 mph); maximum rate of climb at sea level 640 m (2,100 ft) per minute; service ceiling 9315 m (30,650 ft); maximum range with a 18144-kg (40,000-lb) payload 5250 km km (3,262 miles)

Lockheed Martin C-130 Specials

United States
Special missions aircraft

The versatility of the basic C-130 transport has led to conversions for specialised missions. The initial **AC-130A Spectre** gunship version introduced specialised sensors, including a searchlight, ignition sensors, a FLIR and an LLLTV camera. Successive **AC-130E** and **AC-130H** variants introduced improved armour, avionics, engines and armament (a 105-mm howitzer and 40-mm Bofors cannon). The current **AC-130U Spectre** version, developed by Rockwell, has a single GAU-12 25-mm cannon replacing the two 20-mm M61s of previous aircraft. Sensors include APQ-180 radar, AAQ-117 FLIR, all-light-level TV and ALQ-172 jammer package. The USAF Special Operations Command has acquired 13 AC-130Us, to replace the AC-130A and allow the AC-130H to be transferred to the Reserve

Several in-service variants carry the designation **EC-130**. These include the: **EC-130E (ABCCC)** Airborne Battlefield Command and Control Center; the **EC-130E(CL) 'Senior Scout'** Elint platform; the **EC-130E(RR) 'Rivet Rider'** TV and radio rebroadcast 'psy-war' aircraft; and the **EC-130H 'Compass Call'** stand-off communications jamming duties.

Long-range SAR variants include the **HC-130H**, with a large radar above the forward fuselage, the similar **HC-130H-7** for the USCG, and the **HC-130N** and **HC-130P** (HDU-equipped and used to refuel rescue helicopters). The **HC-130H(N)** has modernised avionics and lacks Fulton gear, but is equipped with underwing HDUs. Dedicated tankers

The AC-130H Spectre gunship has undergone the SOFI upgrade, adding a new mission computer, FLIR, HUD, EW fit, GPS and other systems.

include the **KC-130B**, **KC-130F** and **KC-130T** and the stretched **KC-130T-30H** (all acquired by the US Navy and Marine Corps). Not in US service, the **KC-130H** (similar to the KC-130R) has been widely exported.

The first **MC-130E** special forces insertion aircraft served in Vietnam, equipped with Fulton STAR recovery gear for retrieval of downed aircrew/recce troops. Currently there are 13 **MC-130E Combat Talon I** variants in service with AFSOC including: the **MC-130E-C** (with Fulton fitted), **MC-130E-S** and **MC-130E-Y** (no Fulton). The C-130H was used to produce 24 **MC-130H Combat Talon II**s, all with a distinctive long nose housing the APQ-170 terrain-following radar, and an AAQ-15 FLIR turret underneath. The first MC-130Hs arrived in 1991.

AFSOC has taken on the HC-130N and HC-130P aircraft and transferred them to the special forces role, as the **Combat Shadow**. They have been upgraded to **SOFI** standard by the removal of the large dorsal housing that once contained the Cook aerial tracker system, and adding an undernose FLIR and other specialist mission systems.

The EC-130(RR) carries large podded antennas on its tail and underwing for its role as a flying TV and radio station, conducting 'psychological operations'.

Specification: Lockheed AC-130U Spectre

Powerplant: four 3362-kW (4,508-hp) Allison T56-A-15 turboprops
Dimensions: wing span 40.41 m (132 ft 7 in); length 29.79 m (97 ft 9 in); height 11.66 m (38 ft 3 in)
Weights: operating empty 34356 kg (75,743 lb); normal take-off 70310 kg (155,000 lb); maximum take-off 79380 kg (175,000 lb)
Performance: maximum cruising speed 602 kmh (374 mph); service ceiling 10060 m (33,000 ft); range 7876 km (4,894 miles) with maximum fuel
Armament: one 105-mm main gun, one Bofors 40-mm cannon, one GAU-12U 25-mm five-barrelled cannon

Lockheed Martin F-16A/B

The **F-16 Fighting Falcon** is the benchmark modern combat aircraft. It was conceived as a lightweight 'no frills' fighter for air-to-air combat. The first **YF-16** service-test prototype was rolled out in December 1973 and first flew on 2 February 1974. In 1975 it won a competitive USAF evaluation against the Northrop YF-17 (later developed into the F/A-18 Hornet). The production-standard **F-16A** (which was preceded by six full scale development aircraft) was very similar to the YF-16, though it had an enlarged wing, greater fuel capacity and a deeper nose to house the APG-66 radar. The F-16 was the first 'fly-by-wire' fighter, introducing a revolutionary computer-driven flight control system, commanded by a sidestick in the cockpit.

The first F-16A deliveries to the USAF, along with the two-seat **F-16B** trainer, began in 1979. These 94 aircraft were built to **F-16 Block 1** standard, powered by the F100-PW-200 engine. They were followed by 197 **F-16 Block 5**s, fitted with the full-standard grey di-electric radome. The **F-16 Block 10** introduced minor aircraft changes and 312 were delivered to the USAF. Most Block 1 and Block 5 aircraft were brought up to this standard. Block 5 and 10 F-16A/Bs were exported to Belgium, Denmark, Israel, the Netherlands and Norway.

Portugal operates the F-16A/B Block 15 OCU, built to the same standard as the F-16 Block 15 ADF and powered by the F100-PW-220E engine.

Belgium is one of the four European Partner Air Forces currently upgrading all its early-model F16s under the European MLU programme.

The **F-16A/B Block 15** introduced the larger 'big tail' fin and wider tailplanes. The APG-66 radar was improved and new EW and IFF systems were fitted. Earlier F-16s could be updated to Block 15 standard under the **MSIP I** (Multi Staged Improvement Programme). Export sales were made to Belgium, Denmark, Egypt, Israel, the Netherlands, Norway Pakistan and Venezuela.

A specialist USAF interceptor version, armed with the AIM-7 missile, was developed as the **F-16 Block 15 ADF** (air defense fighter). These aircraft had four distinctive antennas for the APX-109 IFF system in front of the cockpit. The **F-16 Block 15 OCU** added some features of the F-16C/D, including the F100-PW-220E engine and ALQ-131 ECM pod. OCUs have been delivered to Belgium, Denmark, Indonesia, Netherlands, Norway, Pakistan, Portugal and Thailand.

The European F-16s are now undergoing the **F-16 MLU** (Mid-Life Update) bringing them up to Block 50 standard, through the addition of AIM-120 AMRAAM, AN/APG-66(V)2 radar, colour cockpit MFDs, and precision weapons capability.

The final F-16A/B variant was the **F-16 Block 20**, delivered to Taiwan, which is also virtually identical to the F-16C Block 50.

Specification: Lockheed F-16A
Powerplant: one 106-kN (23,830-lb) Pratt & Whitney F100-P-100 afterburning turbofan
Dimensions: wing span 10 m (32 ft 9¾ in) with tip-mounted AAMs; length 15.03 m (49 ft 4 in); height 5.01 m (16 ft 5.2 in)
Weights: operational empty 6607 kg (14,567 lb); maximum take-off 14968 kg (33,000 lb)
Performance: maximum level speed more than 2124 kmh (1,320 mph); maximum rate of climb at sea level more than 15240 m (50,000 ft) per minute; service ceiling more than 15240 m (50,000 ft); combat radius 547 km (340 miles)
Armament: one M61A1 Vulcan 20-mm cannon with 515 rounds; maximum ordnance 15,200 lb (6894 kg), including two AIM-9s

Lockheed Martin F-16C/D

Lockheed Martin's **F-16C/D Fighting Falcon** (Lockheed acquired General Dynamics in 1992 and became Lockheed Martin in 1995) is a development of the F-16A/B with structural, avionics and systems modifications. F-16C/Ds are distinguished by an enlarged vertical fin base. Cockpit changes include a wide-angle HUD and an improved data display for HOTAS flying. The new APG-68 multi-mode radar brought increased range, sharper resolution and expanded operating modes, and a weapons interface for AGM-65D and AIM-120 AMRAAM missiles.

The first F-16C flew on 19 June 1984 and the initial production-standard **F-16 Block 25** aircraft was acquired solely by the USAF. The Block 25 was first fitted with the Pratt & Whitney F100-PW-100 – later replaced by the more powerful -220/E engine.

The **F-16C/D Block 30**, which first flew in June 1986, introduced the General Electric F110-GE-100 engine as an alternative powerplant, and nearly all aircraft were fitted with the enlarged 'big mouth' engine inlet. Weapons capability was expanded with the integration of the AGM-45 Shrike and AIM-120 AMRAAM, while new systems included the ALE-40 RWR and ALE-47 chaff/flare dispenser. Block 30 exports went to Greece, Israel and Turkey. The **F-16C/D Block 32**, also introduced in 1986, was powered by an uprated F100-PW-220 engine. The USAF's Thunderbirds display team flies Block 32s and aircraft were delivered to Egypt, Korea.

These 35th Fighter Wing F-16CJs are carrying the AGM-88 HARM missiles and ASQ-213 HARM Targeting System specific to the Block 50/52 F-16.

The **F-16C/D Block 40 Night Falcon** introduced an all-weather precision attack capability using the LANTIRN system. The F110-GE-100-powered Block 40 has a wide-angle holographic HUD, improved APG-68(V) radar and avionics and GPS. The otherwise identical **F-16C/D Block 42** is powered by the F100-PW-220. The first USAF Block 40/42 aircraft were delivered in 1989. The Block 40 has been exported, to Bahrain, Egypt, Israel and Turkey.

The **Block 50/52 F-16C/D** incorporates all the improvements of the Block 40, more powerful engines, and integrates the AGM-88 HARM missile and HARM Targeting System. Export customers include Korea, Singapore and Turkey.

Israel has developed a 'big spine' version of the Block 30/40 F-16D, which is believed to have a dedicated SEAD combat role. Similar aircraft have been delivered to Singapore. The designation **F-16CG** has been applied to USAF Block 40/42 aircraft, and **F-16CJ** to Block 50/52s. The **Block 60** is an enhanced systems next-generation F-16 variant now under development for the UAE.

Israel and Singapore operate these specially modified F-16Ds which are believed to have a sophisticated EW system in their enlarged spines.

Specification: Lockheed Martin F-16C Block 52

Powerplant: one 129.4-kN (29,100-lb) General Electric F110-GE-129 IPE afterburning turbofan
Dimensions: wingspan, over launchers 9.45 m (31 ft); length 15.03 m (49 ft 4 in); height 5.09 m (16 ft 8½ in)
Weights: empty 8581 kg (18,917 lb); maximum take-off 12292 kg (27.099 lb)
Performance: maximum level speed Mach 2 plus; service ceiling 15240 m (50,000 ft); ferry range 4215 km (2,619 miles); combat radius 1485 km (923 miles)
Armament: one internal M61 Vulcan 20-mm cannon with 511 rounds of ammunition; maximum ordnance 7072 kg (15,591 lb)

Lockheed Martin F-22 Raptor

Designed as an 'Air Dominance Fighter', the **F-22** began from studies during the 1970s into low observable (LO) technologies, or 'stealth',and progressed to the **ATF** (**Advanced Tactical Fighter**) programme launched by the USAF in April 1980. This was spurred by Soviet fighter developments that threatened to out-perform the F-15 Eagle and the outline requirement was for 750 new aircraft. After an evaluation of seven manufacturer's proposals, Lockheed's **YF-22** and Northrop's YF-23 designs were selected for competitive evaluation (demonstration/validation, or dem/val) in October 1986. Lockheed teamed with Boeing and General Dynamics to refine (in fact completely redesign) the aircraft and to share development cost and expertise. The revised YF-22 first flew on 29 September 1990. A second prototype aircraft flew on 30 October, but was damaged beyond repair after a flight control system failure in April 1992.

The Lockheed/Boeing team won the dem/val competition in April 1991. The F-22 team was awarded an engineering and manufacturing (EMD) contract to build nine pre-production aircraft. The first of these EMD **F-22A Raptors** (Raptor 4001) flew on 7 September 1997 and the second (Raptor 4002) followed on 26 June 1998.

Once it is fully operational the F-22 will be the most capable combat aircraft in the world by far, but budget restrictions may hamper the programme.

One key element of the F-22's 'stealthy' design is the need to carry all weapons internally to eliminate the huge effect they have on overall radar cross-section.

Many fundamental aspects of the F-22's design, such as its same-plane wing and tailplane, and internal weapons bays are intended to minimise its radar cross-section, and make it 'stealthy'. Radar absorbent materials are used throughout. The lower weapons bay can carry up to six AIM-120C AMRAAMs, with two AIM-9X Sidewinders in the side bay. A pair of GBU-32 JDAM bombs can be fitted in place of four of the AMRAAMs. A 20-mm Vulcan cannon fires from a 'shoulder' compartment on the right-hand upper fuselage. The F-22 is the first aircraft to be designed from the outset for vectored-thrust control and for 'supercruise' (sustained supersonic flight without afterburner).

The APG-77 active array radar combines with sensors mounted around the airframe to create 'sensor fusion', presenting the pilot with an all-around 'big picture' of the air battle. A powerful datalink allows information to be passed between members of a flight and AWACS platforms.

Plans to acquire 648 F-22s have been cut back to 339. A lack of funds halted plans for a two-seat **F-22B** trainer in 1996. The F-22 is scheduled to enter service in 2005, but this date is sure to be delayed as the programme struggles with continuing funding cut-backs and technical hitches.

Specification: Lockheed Martin/Boeing F-22A Raptor
Powerplant: two 156-kN (35,000-lb) Pratt & Whitney F119-PW-100 turbofans
Dimensions: wing span 13.56 m (44ft 6 in); length 18.90 m (62.1 ft); height 5.02 m (16 ft 5 in)
Weights: operating empty 14365 kg (31,670 lb); maximum take-off 27216 kg (60,000 lb)
Performance: design target maximum level speed 1482 kmh (921 mph); demonstrated maximum speed (YF-22) Mach 1.7 at 9150 m (50,000 ft), and Mach 1.58 in supercruise; demonstrated ceiling (YF-22) 9150 m (50,000 ft)
Armament: one M61A1 Vulcan 20-mm cannon with 480 rounds; three internal weapons bays

Lockheed Martin F-117 Nighthawk

With the lessons of the Vietnam and Yom Kippur Wars in mind, in 1974 the United States' Defense Advanced Research Projects Agency (DARPA) began to look for ways to build a 'stealthy' aircraft. Using a mix of radar absorbent materials and a radar-reflective internal/external structure it was possible to dramatically decrease an aircraft's radar cross-section (RCS). Lockheed demonstrated its expertise in this field (which began with the SR-71) when the 'Skunk Works' classified projects development centre built two sub-scale **'Have Blue'** technology demonstrators, which flew in 1977. They utilised a unique faceted structure to reduce RCS and, although both aircraft crashed during tests, the experience gained was sufficient to win Lockheed a contract to develop a full-scale operational tactical fighter. This was signed on 16 November 1978 and, under the 'Senior Trend' codename, Lockheed built five **F-117 FSD** prototypes, with a revised outboard-canted tail configuration. The first example flew on 18 June 1981 and the entire development programme and entry into service was conducted in total secrecy.

As production of 59 **F-117A**s continued at a low rate, the USAF began establishing a base at Tonopah Test Range in Nevada. In October 1983, the first unit was declared operational, undertaking only night flights until November 1988, when the F-117 was publicly unveiled. The F-117 is commonly referred to as the **'Stealth Fighter'**, even though it

The F-117 is a key USAF asset, offering a combat-proven survivable precision-attack capability that is unique – apart from the B-2 Stealth Bomber.

is purely an attack aircraft. The official name **Nighthawk** has been adopted, but it is also widely referred to simply as **'The Black Jet'**.

The F-117's 1989 unspectacular combat debut in Operation Just Cause in Panama was overshadowed by its crucial contribution to Operation Desert Storm, when an eventual total of 42 aircraft flew from Saudi Arabia on nightly precision-attack missions destroying the most important targets in Iraq and occupied Kuwait. The F-117 repeated this role during Operation Allied Force in 1999, when the F-117 suffered its only combat loss.

The F-117 is used for attacks against 'highly leveraged' targets such as communications and command centres, air defence centres, bridges and airfields. It uses a system of two FLIR sensors to select targets before dropping laser-guided bombs from its internal weapons bay. A post-Gulf War Offensive Capability Improvement Program (OCIP) has added two colour MFDs, a moving map display and auto-throttles. Further improvements will add a new IR acquisition and designation sensor.

From this angle it is easy to see why one of the less flattering nick-names that has been applied to the F-117 is the 'cockroach'.

Specification: Lockheed Martin F-117A
Powerplant: two 48.04-kN (10,800-lb) General Electric F404-GE-F1D2 non-afterburning turbofans
Dimensions: wing span 13.20 m (43 ft 4 in); length 20.08 m (65 ft 11 in); height 3.78 m (12 ft 5 in)
Weights: empty about 13608 kg (30,000 lb); maximum take-off 23814 kg (52,500 lb)
Performance: maximum level speed 1040 kmh (646 mph); normal maximum operating speed at optimum altitude Mach 0.9; combat radius about 1112 km (691 miles) with maximum ordnance
Armament: maximum ordnance 2268 kg (5,000 lb), carried internally

Lockheed Martin P-3 Orion

Based on the Lockheed L-188 Electra medium-range passenger airliner, the P-3 Orion was developed to meet a 1957 US Navy requirement for a new anti-submarine aircraft to replace the Lockheed P-2 Neptune. An initial batch of seven **P-3A**s was ordered and the Orion entered service in mid-1962. The following **P-3B** variant introduced uprated Allison T56-A-14 engines, higher weights and provision for AGM-12 Bullpup ASMs. The **P-3C** variant entered service in 1969 and remains the US Navy's primary land-based ASW aircraft. US Navy Orions have undergone several systems updates over the years. The **P-3C Update I** (1975) added more modern mission systems. **P-3C Update II** (1977) added an undernose FLIR to 44 aircraft. **P-3C Update III** (1984) added a new acoustic processor and other modernised systems.

The US Navy employs a fleet of 12 specially-modified Orions to perform the Elint-gathering role as the **EP-3E 'Aries II'**. The **EP-3J** is a US Navy EW jamming trainer fitted with internally- and pod-mounted jamming equipment. Five Orions are used for range support work, comprising two **EP-3A** SMILS (Sonobuoy Missile Impact Locating System) aircraft and three **RP-3A (EATS)** (Extended Area Test System) aircraft used for accurate tracking and

The P-3 Orion is essentially the world's standard maritime patrol and anti-submarine warfare aircraft. It also has a very effective surface attack capability.

14 Wing of the Canadian Armed Forces has two component squadrons which pool operations of the CAF's 13 CP-140s and three CP-140As.

instrumentation of missile tests. Further variants include the oceanographic reconnaissance **RP-3A**, weather reconnaissance **WP-3A/D**, **VP-3A** executive transport, **TP-3A** aircrew trainer, **UP-3A** utility transport and **NP-3A/B** trials aircraft. The **P-3 AEW&C** is fitted with an APS-145 airborne early warning radar (adopted from the E-2 Hawkeye) in a dorsal rotodome, and is used by the US Customs Service on anti-drug patrols.

The **CP-140 Aurora** is a version of the P-3C purchased in 1976 by the Canadian Armed Forces. It is configured internally to Canadian requirements, and is equipped with an avionics system based on that of the S-3A Viking. Three CP-140s have been converted to **CP-140A Arcturus** standard, with their ASW equipment removed. They serve as environmental, Arctic and fishery patrol aircraft.

Export customers for the Orion include Australia, New Zealand, Iran, Pakistan, Portugal, Greece, Japan, Argentina, Chile, South Korea, the Netherlands, Spain and Thailand (**P-3T/UP-3T**). Japan's P-3s were built by Kawasaki and include a number of EP-3 electronic reconnaissance versions. Australia's **P-3**s are currently being upgraded to **AP-3C** standard with new radars and improved onboard mission systems.

Specification: Lockheed P-3C Orion
Powerplant: four 3661-kW (4,910-hp) Allison T56-A-14 turboprops
Dimensions: wing span 30.37 m (99 ft 8 in); length 35.61 m (116 ft 10 in); height 10.27 m (33 ft 8½ in)
Weights: empty 27890 kg (61,491 lb); maximum take-off 64410 kg (142,000 lb)
Performance: maximum level speed 761 kmh (473 mph); patrol speed 381 kmh (237 mph); service ceiling 8625 m (28,300 ft); maximum mission radius 3835 km (2,383 miles); mission endurance 17 hours 12 minutes (two engines)
Armament: maximum expendable load 9072 kg (20,000 lb) on 10 stores stations and in internal weapons bay

Lockheed Martin X-35 JSF

The US **Joint Strike Fighter** (**JSF**) programme is an ambitious effort to develop a replacement for an entire generation of USAF, US Navy and US Marine Corps aircraft using one common 'stealthy' airframe. The JSF is earmarked to replace the F-16, F/A-18, AV-8B and other types in the US inventory, and will also be exportable to customers worldwide. The JSF has its roots in a number of studies for advanced, affordable combat aircraft that were launched in the early 1990s. These were merged into the **JAST** (**Joint Advanced Strike Technology**) programme in 1995, which later became JSF.

Three contractors – Boeing, Lockheed Martin and McDonnell Douglas – were selected by the US DoD to submit JSF designs. In November 1996 Boeing and Lockheed Martin were chosen to build two demonstrator aircraft, essentially JSF prototypes, to conduct a Concept Demonstration Program. At the end of this period one contractor would be chosen to build its JSF design. Lockheed Martin's CDP aircraft was given the designation **X-35**.

While the JSF concept demands a common airframe, there will be different versions for the three main US users. The USAF and the US Navy are looking for a conventional take-off and landing (CTOL) capability, though Navy CV aircraft will have to be modified for carrier operations. The Marines need aircraft with short take-off and vertical landing (STOVL) capability to replace the Harrier, so the USMC's JSF variant will have to have a modified

The CV-configured X-35C is similar to the CTOL X-35A, but has larger wings and empennage, a refuelling probe, re-inforced landing gear and a hook.

propulsion system for vertical lift. Britain's Fleet Air Arm (Royal Navy) has also signed up to acquire the STOVL JSF to replace its Sea Harriers.

Lockheed has built three CDP aircraft. The CTOL **X-35A**, the STOVL **X-35B** and the CV **X-35C**. The X-35A made its maiden flight on 24 October 2000, the X-35C flew next on 16 December 2000. In March 2001 the X-38B completed its 'hover pit' testing, in preparation for its first flight. The X-35 design is more conventional than Boeing's rival X-32, but Lockheed as adopted a completely new propulsion solution. The X-35B's -611 STOVL engine uses a vectoring lift fan for vertical flight which can be coupled/decoupled to/from the main engine using a gear/clutch mechanism. The engine also has a swivelling exhaust nozzle, and bifurcated intakes (between which the lift fan is positioned).

A decision date on the winning design has been delayed several times, but is now planned before the end of 2001. The first operational JSFs are expected to be the Marines' STOVL variants in 2008, followed by the CTOL aircraft in 2010.

Lockheed Martin's X-35 design looks very different to the the rival Boeing X-32 – but both aircraft must meet the same mission requirements.

Specification: Lockheed X-35B JSF

Powerplant: one 173.55-kN (39,000-lb) Pratt & Whitney JSF119-611 turbofan engine, with two-stage shaft-driven counter rotating lift fan (STOVL version)
Dimensions: wing span 10.7 m (35 ft 10 in); length 15.47 m (50 ft 9 in); wing area 42.7m^2 (459.6 sq ft)
Weights: maximum take-off 16692 kg (36,800 lb)
Performance: maximum level speed over Mach 1.0;
Armament: one internal Bk 27 27-mm cannon
(Full specification not available)

McDonnell Douglas A-4 Skyhawk

The **Douglas A-4 Skyhawk** first flew in prototype form on 22 June 1954, and entered service in October 1956. It provided the US Navy and the US Marine Corps with their principal light attack platform for over 20 years. Total production of all variants reached 2,960. Early models comprised the J65-powered **A-4A**, **A-4B** and **A-4C** (differing in avionics and engine power), and the the J52-engined **A-4E**, and **A-4F** with a dorsal avionics hump. Export models included the **A-4G** (Australia), **A-4H** (Israel), **A-4K** (New Zealand), **A-4PTM** (Malaysia), **A-4S** (Singapore) and **A-4KU** (Kuwait). The **A-4L** was a rebuilt A-4C for the USN Reserve. The last major production model was the **A-4M**, based on the A-4F but with a J52-P-408A engine and new canopy. **A-4N**s for Israel were similar, but featured uprated avionics, including a HUD.

Skyhawks bore the brunt of the naval air war in Vietnam, flying the most missions and suffering the heaviest losses. A-4s have also seen combat with Israel, Argentina and Indonesia.

The **TA-4F** two-seat variant came along late, but was used first as a FAC by the USMC and later as the main jet trainer for the USN. It features two cockpits in tandem with a single canopy. The USMC's **OA-4M** was a specialised two-seater used

The RNZAF modernised all its Skyhawks to Kahu standard, with APG-66 radar and cockpit MFDs. This TA-4K is carrying a buddy refuelling pod.

Argentina acquired 32 rebuilt and upgraded A-4ARs between 1997 and 2000. They are fitted with a version of the APG-66 multi-mode radar, the ARG-1.

for FAC duties. The definitive **TA-4J** trainer was a simplified TA-4F which usually lacked cannon armament and combat capability. The last USN Training Command A-4s were retired in 1999, but one squadron retains TA-4Js for adversary and fleet support duties.

Although Australia, Malaysia and Kuwait have retired their A-4s, the other export users continue to operate them. New Zealand bought the remaining A-4Gs and upgraded them with the APG-66 radar, new avionics, AIM-9L Sidewinder and Maverick-missile capability, under project **Kahu**. The Argentine air force bought surplus A-4/OA-4Ms and also upgraded them as the **A-4AR Fightinghawk**. Brazil bought the former-Kuwaiti T/A-4KUs for service on its recently acquired former-French aircraft carrier *Foch* (now renamed *Sao Paulo*) as the **AF-1A** and **AF-1B**.

Singapore has the most highly modified Skyhawks, having upgraded surplus A-4B/Cs as **A-4S**s and **TA-4S**s trainers with seperate rear canopies. These aircraft were first upgraded to **T/A-4S-1 Super Skyhawk** standard, re-engined with the GE F404 turbofan. A follow-on upgrade brought them up to **T/A-4SU Super Skyhawk** standard, with a new digital avionics suite.

Specification: McDonnell Douglas A-4M Skyhawk II
Powerplant: one 50-kN (11,280-lb) Pratt & Whitney J52-P-408 non-afterburning turbojet
Dimensions: wing span 8.38 m (27 ft 6 in); length 12.72 m (41 ft 8½ in) height 4.57 m (14 ft 11¾ in)
Weights: operating empty 4747 kg (10,250 lb); maximum take-off 10206 kg (24,000 lb)
Performance: maximum level speed 1102 kmh 685 mph); service ceiling 12190 m (40,000 ft); combat radius 547 km (345 miles) with a 1814-kg (4,000-lb) warload
Armament: two Mk 12 20-mm cannon, maximum ordnance 4153 kg (9,155 lb)

McDonnell Douglas F-4 Phantom

The McDonnell F-4 Phantom was originally designed as a shipboard interceptor for the USN and USMC. The prototype (**XF4H-1**) first flew on 27 May 1958. The first production version was the **F-4B**. None of the naval versions remain in use as fighters and even the handful operated by test agencies have now been retired, leaving only **QF-4N/S** drones in service. The USAF's initial **F-4C** variant was followed by the **F-4D** optimised for air-to-ground operations. All US F-4C/Ds have been retired, but the model remains active in Iran and South Korea.

The definitive **F-4E** for the USAF first flew in June 1967, and introduced a 20-mm cannon fitted under the nose. F-4Es remains in service with Egypt, Greece, Iran, Israel, South Korea and Turkey. The type has been withdrawn from US service and many have been converted to **QF-4E** target drones.

The **F-4G 'Wild Weasel'** anti-radar variant resulted from the conversion of 116 F-4E airframes, deleting the integral cannon and adding an APR-38 RHAWS. They were the last US Phantoms to see active service, in the 1991 Gulf War. The survivors have been converted to **QF-4G** drones.

Five major Phantom operators have upgraded their surviving aircraft, extending airframe lives and adding modern radar, improved avionics and self-defence systems. In the mid-1980s Israeli launched the **Kurnass 2000** upgrade, which adds a completely new mission avionics package to its

The first upgraded Peace Icarus F-4E for Greece made its maiden flight on 28 April 1999 . The bulk of the actual upgrade is being handled by HAI.

remaining F-4Es and **RF-4E/RF-4E(S) Oref** (raven) reconnaissance aircraft. Israel is now upgrading Turkish F-4Es to **Phantom 2000** standard with EL/M-2032 multi-mode radars, a digital cockpit and enhanced weapons capability.

The Luftwaffe's **F-4F ICE** (Improved Combat Efficiency) upgrade added the APG-65 radar and AMRAAM capability to about 150 aircraft. DASA is also upgrading 39 Greek F-4Es to a similar level, under the **Peace Icarus** programme. Japan operates about 90 upgraded **F-4EJ Kai**s, with APG-66 radars, expanded weapons capability and updated avionics.

The reconnaissance-configured **RF-4C** and **RF-4E** have a modified nose housing optical cameras, electronic equipment, IR sensors and a mapping/terrain avoidance radar. RF-4Es remain active with Greece, Iran, Turkey and Israel, while Spain operates modernised RF-4Cs. Israel's armed RF-4Es are equipped with indigenous reconnaissance and avionics equipment and have fixed refuelling probes. Japan operates 14 upgraded **RF-4EJ Kai**s with new radars and modernised recce systems.

Israel's Elbit is upgrading Turkey's F-4Es, substantially improving their attack capability by integrating the Popeye stand-off missile.

Specification: McDonnell Douglas F-4E Phantom II

Powerplant: two 79.62-kN (17,900-lb) General Electric J79-GE-17A afterburning turbojets
Dimensions: wing span 11.71 m (38 ft 5 in); length 19.20 m (63 ft); height 5.02 m(16 ft 5½ in)
Weights: basic empty 13757 kg (30,328 lb); combat take-off 18818 kg (41,487 lb); maximum take-off 28030 kg (61,795 lb)
Performance: maximum level speed 2390 kmh (1,485 mph); maximum rate of climb at sea level 18715 m (61,400 ft) per minute; service ceiling 18975 m (62,250 ft); area interception combat radius 1266 km (786 miles)
Armament: one M61 20-mm cannon with 640 rounds, maximum ordnance 7258 kg (16,000 lb)

McDonnell Douglas KC-10 Extender

The McDonnell Douglas **KC-10A Extender** strategic tanker/transport is based on the DC-10 Series 30CF commercial freighter/airliner and was developed to satisfy the USAF's **ATCA** (Advanced Tanker Cargo Aircraft) requirement. An initial batch of 16 aircraft was first ordered in 1977 and procurement was later increased to 60 aircraft. The first Extender made its maiden flight on 12 July 1980 and deliveries to SAC took place between March 1981 and November 1988.

Changes from the commercial DC-10 standard include provision of an IFR receptacle above the cockpit, an improved cargo handling system and some military avionics. A McDonnell Douglas Advanced Aerial Refuelling Boom (AARB) is fitted beneath the aft fuselage. The digital FBW control boom can transfer fuel at a rate of 5678 litres (1,249 Imp gal) per minute. The KC-10 is also fitted with a hose and reel unit in the starboard aft fuselage and can thus refuel Navy and USMC aircraft during the same mission. This is a unique capability and one that makes it much more versatile than the KC-135. More recently, wing-mounted HDU pods have been fitted to all KC-10s so that three receiver aircraft may be refuelled simultaneously with this very capable system.

The KC-10's substantial fuel-offload and cargo-carrying ability makes it well suited to supporting fighter deployments over long distances.

The KC-10A Extender is a more capable tanker/transport than the Boeing KC-135, but it is available in far fewer numbers.

The wing and fuselage fuel cells contain approximately 68610 litres (15,092 Imp gal) and are interconnected with the aircraft's own basic fuel system. The KC-10 is able to transfer 90718 kg (200,000 lb) of fuel to a receiver 3540 km (2,200 miles) from its home base and return to base. For conventional strategic transport missions the KC-10 has a port-side cargo door and carries standard USAF pallets, bulk cargo or wheeled vehicles. Dual tanker/transport missions include accompanying deploying fighters.

Two ex-Martinair DC-10-30CFs were procured by the Netherlands for conversion by McDonnell Douglas to tanker configuration, and entered service with the KLU in 1995 as the **KDC-10**. Unlike the KC-10 refuelling operator who guides the refuelling through an optical window, the KDC-10 'Boomer' uses a three camera TV system to give a 'three dimensional' view. The Dutch tankers have been used to support F-16 deployments to 'Red Flag' and other exercises in the US.

The USAF now has a fleet of 59 KC-10s after one was destroyed in an accident on the ground. All active aircraft are operated by Air Mobility Command, based principally at McGuire AFB (305th AMW) and Travis AFB (60th AMW).

Specification: McDonnell Douglas KC-10A Extender
Powerplant: three 233.53-kN (52,500-lb) General Electric CF6-50C2 turbofans
Dimensions: wing span 47.34 m (155 ft 4 in); length 55.35 m (181 ft 7 in); height 17.70 m (58 ft 1 in)
Weights: operating empty 108891 kg (240,065 lb); maximum take-off 267620 kg (590,000 lb) maximum payload 76843 kg (169,409 lb) of cargo
Performance: maximum level speed 982 kmh (610 mph); maximum cruising speed 908 kmh (564 mph); maximum rate of climb at sea level 884 m (2,900 ft) per minute; maximum range with maximum cargo 7032 km (4,370 miles)

MD Helicopters MD 500, MD900

Hughes' **YHO-6** design was developed to meet a 1960 US Army requirement for a light observation helicopter. The production **OH-6A Cayuse** entered service in 1965 and was widely used in Vietnam. The civilian **Hughes 500** introduced an uprated engine, increased fuel and a revised interior. The first military variant was the **Model 500M Defender**. The **500M/ASW** has a MAD 'bird' and can carry torpedoes. The civilian 500D variant introduced a slow-turning five-bladed rotor and a T-tail. It was built under licence in Japan as the **OH-6D**.

The military **Model 500MD Defender** had armour protection and IR exhaust suppressors. Variants have been developed for ASW, anti-tank and scout duties. The **Model 500E** introduced a revised, pointed nose, more spacious interior and an Allison 250-C20B engine. Dedicated military models are designated **500MG Defender**. The up-engined **530MG Defender** had options for a mast-mounted TOW sight, FLIR, RHAW gear, IFF and a laser rangefinder, and can be armed with TOW 2 missiles, 2.75 in rockets and Stinger AAMs.

The US Army has developed a family of special-missions variants called the 'Little Birds', which are operated by the 160th Special Operations Aviation Regiment. Current service variants include the FLIR-equipped **MH-6H** special forces insertion aircraft, and the armed **AH-6G**. Equivalent aircraft fitted with the NOTAR (NO TAil Rotor) system are designated **MH-6J** and **AH-6J**.

The MD530MG Defender is based on the civil MD530F model and is the latest in a long-line of military MD 500 variants.

In the mid-1990s South Korea developed the licence-built armed **MD520MK Black Tiger**. The assembly work was undertaken by the engineering department at Korean Air Lines.

Hughes helicopters was acquired by McDonnell Douglas in 1984. When Boeing merged with McDonnell Douglas in 1997, McDonnell Douglas Helicopters was sold off, and acquired by a Dutch company to become MD Helicopters. MD Helicopters continues to offer military variants of the MD 530MG model, but is also working on armed versions of the **MD 900 Explorer**.

The Explorer, which first flew in December 1992, is much larger and more advanced than the Model 500/520 and uses the NOTAR anti-torque system instead of a conventional tail rotor. A proposed combat-capable version was announced in 1995, designated the **Combat Explorer**, but in 2000 MD Helicopters developed a simplified gun/rocket package to equip the Explorers already in service with the Mexican navy. The Explorer was also evaluated by the US Coast Guard.

Mexico became the fist customer for a militarised MD 900 Explorer and can arm its aircraft with 70-mm rockets and 0.50-in machine guns.

Specification: MD Helicopters Model 500
Powerplant: one 236-kW (317-hp) Allison 250-C18A turboshaft
Dimensions: main rotor diameter 8.03 m (26 ft 4 in); length overall, rotors turning 9.24 m (30 ft 3¾ in); height 2.48 m (8 ft 1½ in)
Weights: empty 493 kg (1,088 lb); maximum take-off 1361 kg (3,000 lb)
Performance: maximum level speed 244 kmh (152 mph); maximum rate of climb at sea level 518 m (700 ft) per minute; service ceiling 4390 m (14,400 ft); hovering ceiling 2500 m (8,200 ft) IGE, 1615 m (5,300 ft) OGE; range 606 km (307 miles)
Armament: two external hardpoints for gun pods, rockets or TOW missiles

Mikoyan MiG-21 'Fishbed'

The original **MiG-21** was developed as a light, high performance, short-range interceptor. Early **MiG-21F-13 'Fishbed-Cs'** were armed with one NR-30 cannon, and two AA-2 'Atoll' AAMs, while the **MiG-21P 'Fishbed-D'** dispensed with the cannon armament altogether, but introduced R1L radar. The R-11F2-300-engined **MiG-21PF** was similar, although late **MiG-21PF 'Fishbed-Es'** introduced a broader-chord fin and provision for an external GP9 cannon pod. The R-11F-300-engined **MiG-21FL** was for export. The **MiG-21PFS** and **MiG-21PFM** had two-piece canopies, blown SPS flaps and the R-11F2S-300 engine.

All later variants had blown flaps, two-piece canopies, broad-chord tailfins and four pylons. The MiG-21PFM-based reconnaissance **MiG-21R** had an enlarged dorsal fairing and provision for centre-line reconnaissance pods. The **MiG-21S** was similar, with a centreline GP9. The R-13-300-engined **MiG-21SM** put the GSh-23L cannon in a fixed installation, instead of in the removeable GP9 gondola. The R-11F2S-300 engined export **MiG-21M** was built under licence in India, while the **MiG-21MF** introduced AAM capability on all four pylons. The **MiG-21MT** used the more powerful R-13F-300 engine, while the **MiG-21SMT 'Fishbed-K'** was fitted

Aerostar has upgraded 10 of the Romanian air force's two-seat MiG-21 trainers to Lancer II standard (service designation Lancer B).

This Russian MiG-21 is carrying the R-27 (AA-10 'Alamo') and R-72 (AA-11 'Archer') air-to-air missiles offered for the upgraded MiG-21-93.

with a further enlarged spine. Significant numbers of MiG-21Rs, MiG-21Ms and MiG-21MFs remain in service. The multi-role R-25-300-powered **MiG-21bis** introduced improved avionics, AA-8 'Aphid' AAMs, and improved Sapphire-21 radar.

The **MiG-21U 'Mongol-A'** tandem two-seat trainer could carry a centreline gun pod and had two underwing pylons. The **MiG-21US 'Mongol-B'** had increased fin chord, improved ejection seats, a bigger spine, a retractable periscope and blown SPS flaps, while the **MiG-21UM** was similar, with updated instruments and avionics.

The number of MiG-21s in service has declined dramatically since the end of the Cold War, with force reductions and a growing trend for ex-Warsaw Pact nations to turn to the West for combat aircraft. Aerostar and Elbit are jointly upgrading 110 Romanian air force MiG-21s to **Lancer** standards, with new radar, digital databus, cockpit, avionics and weapons. Romania's **Lancer I**s are upgraded MiG-21M/MFs, while the **Lancer II** is an upgraded MiG-21UM/US. The **Lancer III** is aimed at the export market, and based on the MiG-21bis.

Mikoyan and the Sokol plant are upgrading 125 MiG-21s to **MiG-21-93** standard for the Indian Air Force, adding new radar, weapons and systems.

Specification: MiG-21bis 'Fishbed-M'
Powerplant: one Tumanskii R-25-300 turbojet rated at 69.58 kN (15,650 lb)
Dimensions: wing span 7.15 m (23 ft 5½ in); length 15.76 m (51 ft 8½ in) including probe; height 4.12 m (13 ft 6.2 in)
Weights: empty 5350 kg (11,795 lb); maximum take-off 9661 kg (21,299 lb)
Performance: maximum level speed 2230 kmh (1,385 mph); maximum rate of climb at sea level 7200 m (23,622 ft) per minute; service ceiling 19000 m (62,336 ft); typical combat radius 450-500 km (280-311 miles)
Armament: one centreline twin-barrelled GSh-23 23-mm cannon, with 2000-kg (4,409-lb) of ordnance on four underwing hardpoints

Mikoyan MiG-23, MiG-27 'Flogger'

Soviet Union (Russia)
Tactical fighter bomber

The **MiG-23** was developed as a MiG-21 replacement, with greater range and firepower. It was ordered into production as the **MiG-23S**. The **MiG-23M** and export **MiG-23MF 'Flogger-B'** had 'High Lark' pulse-Doppler radar, an IRST, AA-7 'Apex' missiles, and a shortened rear fuselage. Some remain in use with Bulgaria, Cuba, India, Romania and Syria. The down-graded **MiG-23MS** **'Flogger-E'** was an export version with 'Jay Bird' radar, and no BVR missile, and remains in service with Algeria, Libya and perhaps Syria.

The lightweight **MiG-23ML 'Flogger-G'** introduced airframe, engine, radar and avionics improvements. Aircraft remain in service in Angola, Bulgaria, Cuba, Iraq, North Korea, Syria and Yemen. The **MiG-23P** was a dedicated PVO interceptor. The final **MiG-23MLD 'Flogger-K'** fighter variant is still used by Belarus, Kazakhstan and Bulgaria.

The attack-dedicated **MiG-23B/BN 'Flogger-F'** had an upgraded nav/attack system and a derated R-29B-300 engine. The **'Flogger-H'** introduced a new RWR. MiG-23BNs were exported to Algeria, Angola, Bulgaria, Cuba, Czechoslovakia, East Germany, Ethiopia, India, Iraq and Syria. The **MiG-23UB 'Flogger-C'** is a tandem two-seat trainer version delivered to all MiG-23/-27 operators.

The **MiG-27** remedied the deficiencies and reduced the cost of the ground-attack 'Flogger'. It introduced simplified, fixed intakes, and an engine with a two-position afterburner nozzle. Fuel economy

Libya was a typical customer for the down-graded export version of the MiG-23MF, the MiG-23MS. This aircraft is armed with AA-2 'Atoll' air-to-air missiles.

is improved and weight reduced, at the expense of performance. A new GSh-6-30 30-mm cannon replaced the original 23-mm cannon. The **MiG-27 'Flogger-D'** had the same avionics as the MiG-23BN, with a Fone laser rangefinder and it first flew in prototype form in 1972.

The 'straight' MiG-27 was soon replaced by the **MiG-27M 'Flogger-J'**, which was equipped with the PrNK-23M nav/attack system and a Klyon laser rangefinder, and which introduced fixed wing leading edge root extensions housing Beryoza RWR antennas. India was the only export customer for the MiG-27, and builds the type under licence.

The most advanced member of the family was the **MiG-27K 'Flogger-J2'**, deployed from 1977. This had a Kaira-24 laser designator in an under-nose fairing with a TV system in the enlarged, oval nose window, with a Delta-2NG missile guidance transmitter antenna in a 'pimple' on the tip of the nose, re-located from its usual location on the glove pylons. The twin pitot probes were mounted low on the nose.

This is a 'Flogger-J2' the most advanced version of the ground-attack MiG-27. Unlike the MiG-23BN, the MiG-27 had fixed engine intake ramps.

Specification: MiG-23ML 'Flogger-G'
Powerplant: one 127.49-kN (28,660-lb) MNPK 'Soyuz' (Khachatourov) R-35-300 afterburning turbojet
Dimensions: wing span 13.97 m (45 ft 10 in) spread and 7.78 m (25 ft 6¼ in) swept; length 16.70 m (54 ft 9½ in); height 4.82 m
Weights: empty 10200 kg (22,487 lb); maximum take-off 17800 kg (39,242 lb)
Performance: maximum level speed 2500 kmh (1,553 mph); maximum rate of climb at sea level 14400 m (47,244 ft) per minute; service ceiling 18500 m (60,695 ft); combat radius 1150 km (715 miles) with six AAMs
Armament: one GSh-23 23-mm cannon; maximum ordnance 3000 kg (6,613 lb)

Mikoyan MiG-25 'Foxbat' High speed interceptor/reconnaissance aircraft

The **MiG-25** (NATO code-name **'Foxbat'**) was developed to counter the high-flying Mach 3 XB-70 strategic bomber. It featured advanced construction techniques, using tempered steel for most of the airframe with titanium for the leading edges. The prototype **Ye-155P-1** flew on 9 September 1964, powered by a pair of 100-kN (22,500-lb) Mikulin R-15B-300 turbojets.

Production of the refined **MiG-25P 'Foxbat-A'** fighter began in 1969, and it entered service in 1973. The definitive **MiG-25PD 'Foxbat-E'** featured a new RP-25 look-down/shoot-down radar, an IRST, more powerful R-15BD-300 turbojets and provision for a large 5300-litre (1,166-Imp gal) belly tank. About 370 surviving 'Foxbat-As' were brought up to PD standard, as the **MiG-25PDS**. Some MiG-25PDs were fitted with a 250-mm (10-in) nose plug to allow installation of a retractable IFR probe, taking overall length to 24.07 m (78 ft 11.67 in). The **MiG-25PU 'Foxbat-C'** conversion trainer lacks radar and has a new instructor's cockpit stepped down in an elongated nose in front of the standard cockpit. MiG-25 fighters were exported to Algeria, Iraq, Libya and Syria, and also remain in small-scale service in Russia and a handful of former Soviet states.

The MiG-25 PU and MiG-25RU 'Foxbat-C' trainers were largely identical, but the MiG-25RU was not fitted with the underwing pylons of the MiG-25PU

This 'Foxbat-B' is a MiG-25RBT, fitted with the Tangazh Sigint system in its nose (note the grey di-electric antenna panel).

The MiG-25 was also developed for use in the high-speed, high altitude reconnaissance role. The prototype **Ye-155R-1** flew on 6 March 1964, six months before the prototype fighter and the production **MiG-25R 'Foxbat-B'** recce variant passed state acceptance tests in 1969. The **MiG-25RB** was a dual-role reconnaissance bomber able to drop stores from high altitudes at supersonic speeds. Sigint models were the **MiG-25RBK 'Foxbat-D'**, with Kub Sigint equipment (subsequently upgraded as **MiG-25RBF**s with Shar-25), the **MiG-25RBV** with Virazh, and the **MiG-25RBT** with Tangazh. Radar recce versions included the **MiG-25RBS** with Sablya SLAR, most of which were upgraded to **MiG-25RBSh** with the improved Shompol radar. MiG-25RBs were exported to Algeria, Bulgaria, India, Iraq, Libya, Peru and Syria. The dedicated **MiG-25RU** recce trainer has no cameras, but like other reconnaissance aircraft has reduced wing span and a constant-sweep leading edge, instead of the fighter's 'cranked' leading edge.

The dedicated defence-suppression **MiG-25BM 'Foxbat-F'** was armed with four underwing AS-11 'Kilter' missiles. The prototype first flew in 1976, and limited deployment of the 100 or so built began in 1982. The type became operational in 1988.

Specification: MiG-25PDS 'Foxbat-E'
Powerplant: two 109.83-kN (24,691-lb) MNPK 'Soyuz' (Tumanskii) R-15BD-300 turbojets
Dimensions: wing span 14.02 m (45 ft 11¾ in); length 23.82 m (78 ft 1¾ in); height 6.10 m (20 ft ¼ in)
Weights: normal take-off 34920 kg (76,894 lb); maximum take-off 36720 kg (80,952 lb)
Performance: maximum level speed Mach 2.8 (3000 kmh,1,864 mph); climb to 20000 m (65,615 ft) in 8 minutes 54 seconds; service ceiling 20700 m (67,915 ft); range with internal fuel 1730 km (1,075 miles) subsonic
Armament: Four underwing hardpoints for four or six AAMs, with centreline hardpoint for drop-tank

Mikoyan MiG-29 'Fulcrum'

The **MiG-29** (NATO code-name **'Fulcrum'**) was developed to meet a 1971 requirement for a lightweight fighter to replace Frontal Aviation MiG-21s, MiG-23s and Su-17s in the battlefield air superiority and ground- attack roles. Design work began in 1974, and the first prototype flew on 6 October 1977. Deliveries began in 1983.

The baseline **MiG-29 'Fulcrum-A'** carries two BVR AA-10 'Alamo-As' inboard and four short-range AA-8 'Aphid' or AA-11 'Archer' IR-homing missiles outboard, backed by an internal 30-mm cannon. Early Russian MiG-29 regiments included a 'strike' squadron, its aircraft using the 30-kT RN-40 nuclear weapon on the port inboard pylon. The MiG-29 has an N-019 pulse-Doppler radar and a passive IRST system. This can detect, track and engage a target while leaving the radar in a non-emitting mode. For close-in engagements, a helmet-mounted sight can be used to cue IR-homing missiles onto an off-boresight target.

More than 450 single-seat 'Fulcrums' are estimated to be in service with the VVS, and other former Soviet states including Belarus, Kazakhstan, Moldova, Turkmenistan, Ukraine and Uzbekistan. The aircraft has also been acquired by Bangladesh, Bulgaria, Cuba, Czech Republic, East Germany, West Germany, Hungary, India, Iran, Iraq, North Korea, Malaysia, Peru, Poland, Romania, Slovakia, South Yemen, Syria and Yugoslavia. MiG-29s have been evaluated by Israel and by the USA.

The MiG-28SE demonstrator was based on the 'fat back' 'Fulcrum-C' and was intended as an improved export version of the first-generation MiG-29.

The **MiG-29UB (9-51) 'Fulcrum-B'** trainer has no radar, but retains the IRST and has a weapons system simulator, allowing the instructor to generate HUD, IRST and radar symbology in the front cockpit. An improved single-seater (**Model 9-13**, known to NATO as the **'Fulcrum-C'**) introduced a bulged spine, housing additional fuel and an active jammer. None have been exported outside the former USSR, except a handful of Moldovan aircraft supplied to the USA.

MiG-29S, **SD**, **SE** and **SM** designations were applied to planned late production variants and upgrade configurations, while the **MiG-29M (9-15)** was an advanced derivative with revised structure, increased fuel and genuine multi-role capability. This reached the prototype stage, as did the carrier-borne **MiG-29K (9-31)**. A handful of MiG-29S aircraft entered service with Russian regiments, and the SD formed the basis of the **MiG-29N** for Malaysia. A number of upgrade programmes are underway in Germany (DASA), Romania (**Aerostar Sniper**) and Russia itself.

The Luftwaffe's 'Fulcrum-As', inherited from the former East German air force, have been overhauled by DASA to make them more reliable and economic.

Specification: Mikoyan MiG-29 'Fulcrum-A'
Powerplant: two 81.39-kN (18,298-lb) Klimov/Leningrad RD-33 afterburning turbofans
Dimensions: wing span 11.36 m (37 ft 31/4 in); length 17.32 m (56 ft 10 in); height 4.73 m (15 ft 6.2 in)
Weights: empty 10900 kg (24,030 lb); maximum take-off 18,500 kg (40,785 lb)
Performance: maximum level speed 2445 kmh (1,519 mph); maximum rate of climb at sea level 19800 m (64,961 ft) per minute; service ceiling 17000 m (55,775 ft); ferry range 2100 km (1,305 miles), 1500 km (932 miles) with internal fuel
Armament: one GSh-301 30-mm cannon, maximum stores of 3000 kg (6,614 lb)

Mikoyan MiG-29SMT

The first attempt to produce a 'second-generation' multi-role MiG-29 resulted in the **MiG-29M** (**9.15**), six prototypes of which were constructed and flown from April 1986. This featured a redesigned airframe, with deleted overwing intake ducts and with extensive use of composites and advanced welded aluminium-lithium alloy components, giving increased internal volume with the minimum weight penalty. The aircraft also featured aerodynamic refinements, including 'sharp' LERXes and increased span ailerons. The aircraft also had a revised weapons system, with RLPK-29M (N010) Zhuk radar, and new TV and laser guidance systems for PGMs. The aircraft impressed during acceptance trials, but did not enter production, due to the high cost of re-tooling. Two prototypes of a carrierborne derivative, the **MiG-29K** (**9.31**) were also built, with an increased span, reduced-sweep folding wing and extended chord flaps, drooping ailerons and enlarged tailplanes. Development ceased in 1992, after the less versatile Su-27K was selected for Russia's carrier.

Instead of procuring a new-build second-generation MiG-29, it was eventually decided to produce such an aircraft by upgrading existing MiG-29s. The **MiG-29SMT** (**9.17**) can be manufactured using

The two-seat MiG-29 UBT development prototype, which first flew in 1998, was converted from MiG's existing MiG-29UB testbed

The MiG-29SMT upgrade is the latest in a series of attempts to improve the range and performance of the MiG-29 'Fulcrum'.

existing jigs, or produced by upgrade. It has a new glass cockpit, and new multi-role avionics, and has a massive swollen spine to provide the necessary extra internal fuel capacity. This covers the old 'split-beaver tail' airbrakes, and requires the addition of a large dorsal airbrake, like that used on the MiG-29M. The aircraft also features a bolt-on retractable refuelling probe and has an extra pair of underwing hardpoints. The airframe is strengthened to allow operation at much higher weights, and has an extended airframe life. An avionics prototype first flew on 29 November 1997, and an aircraft with a mock-up of the new spine followed on 22 April 1998. A fully converted prototype flew on 14 July 1998. Current plans call for about 180 Russian air force MiG-29s to be upgraded to SMT standard. This includes the two-seat **MiG-29UBT** version, which can also be configured for a combat role.

The MiG-29SMT forms the basis of a new carrierborne version (using the MiG-29K's wing, landing gear and other navalised features) known as the **MiG-29SMTK**. A further sub-variant, the **MiG-29MTK** or **MiG-29K-2002** offers folding tailplanes and a narrow-span inboard wing fold, and has been offered to India to equip the newly-acquired and converted carrier *Gorshkov*.

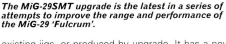

Specification: Mikoyan MiG-29SMT
Powerplant: planned to receive two 98.1-kN (22,050-lb) Klimov/Leningrad RD-333 (RD-43) turbofans
Dimensions: wing span 11.36 m (37 ft 3¼ in); length 17.32 m (56 ft 10 in); height 4.73 m (15 ft 6.2 in)
Weights: maximum take-off 21,000 kg (46,297 lb) in ground attack configuration
Performance: maximum level speed 2445 kmh (1,519 mph); maximum rate of climb at sea level 19800 m (64,961 ft) per minute; service ceiling 17000 m (55,775 ft); ferry range 3500 km (2,714 miles); combat radius 1550 km (963 miles)
Armament: one GSh-301 30-mm cannon, plus 5000-kg (11,023-lb) of ordnance

Mikoyan MiG-31 'Foxhound'

The **MiG-31 'Foxhound'** was developed to counter the threat posed by new low-level strike aircraft and cruise missiles, complementing the Su-27 in service, and using its ultra-long-range capability to fill gaps in Russia's ground-based radar chain. A two-seat derivative of the MiG-25 'Foxbat' airframe, the 'Foxhound' introduced an all-new structure, a new wing planform with small LERXes, Soloviev D-30F-6 turbofans and a new undercarriage. The **Ye-155MP** prototype flew on 16 September 1975 and series production of 280 MiG-31s began in 1979.

The MiG-31 featured a flat belly with four missile recesses for its primary armament, which consisted of R-33 (AA-9 'Amos') AAMs. The 'Foxhound' also carries a scabbed-on GSh-6-23 six-barrelled 23-mm cannon pod and has underwing pylons for two AA-6 'Acrid' or four AA-8 'Aphid' missiles. The new 'Zaslon' radar had a phased-array antenna, increasing range and allowing faster, more accurate beam pointing. Ten targets can be tracked simultaneously, and four engaged. Groups of four MiG-31s can operate independently of ground control, covering a 900-km (560-mile) swathe of territory, with the leader automatically controlling his wingmen.

The **MiG-31 01-DZ** introduced a retractable inflight refuelling probe, while the **MiG-31B** also had an improved radar with better ECCM, and a new digital processor. Existing aircraft brought up to the same standard were designated **MiG-31BS**.

This is one of the improved MiG-31 development aircraft, identifiable by its wingtip fairings. It is carrying a load of R-77 (AA-12 'Adder') missiles.

Two **MiG-31D** prototypes were produced as testbeds for a new anti-satellite missile. The **MiG-31E**, **MiG-31F** and **MiG-31FE** designations were applied to unbuilt export and upgrade configurations, while the **MiG-31BM** is a proposed defence suppression variant.

The improved **MiG-31M** interceptor variant was built in prototype form only. The MiG-31M carried six R-37 long-range AAMs in three side-by-side recesses under the belly, each accommodating tandem pairs of missiles. Its new radar had a 1.4-m diameter antenna and could simultaneously engage six targets. A fully-retractable IRST was fitted, and MiG-31Ms also have a redesigned rear cockpit, with three CRT MFDs. Other changes include a one-piece canopy and windscreen, a retractable IFR probe, large wingtip ESM pods, and aerodynamic refinements. Redesigned LERXes improved high AoA handling, and a bulged spine gave increased fuel capacity, but development was abandoned due to lack of funding. The first of six prototypes made its maiden flight on 21 December 1985.

This 'Foxhound' is the one-off MiG-31LL flying testbed, operated by the LII flight test and development institute, at Zhukhovskii.

Specification: Mikoyan MiG-31 'Foxhound-A'

Powerplant: two 151.9-kN (34,170-lb) Aviavidgatel D-30F6 turbofans
Dimensions: wing span 13.464 m (44 ft 2 in); length 22.69 m (74 ft 5¼ in) including probe; height 6.15 m (20 ft 2¼ in)
Weights: empty 21825 kg (48,115 lb); maximum take-off 46200 kg (101,850 lb)
Performance: maximum level speed 3000 kmh (1,865 mph); service ceiling 20600 m (67,600 ft); combat radius with maximum internal fuel and four R-33 AAMs 1200 km (745 miles)
Armament: one GSh-6-23 23-mm cannon with 260 rounds, hardpoints for four missiles under the fuselage, and two underwing pylons.

Mikoyan MiG-AT

During the late 1980s MiG began design work on a new type of advanced trainer. The Russian air force had an emerging requirement to replace its Czech-built L-29 and L-39 jet trainers and opened up the search for the new aircraft to Russian industry. Submissions from Sukhoi and Myasischev were rejected, but the **MiG-AT** proposal was selected to go forward with the Yakovlev Yak-130 for evaluation.

The MiG-AT was a more conventional design than the Yak-130, using a low-wing configuration, mid-set tailplane and over-wing inlets for its Turbomeca-SNECMA Larzac turbofans. The original design featured a 'T-tail' and the PS/ZMK DV-2 (R-35) engine, but these plans were abandoned - as was an intended industrial co-operation with Korea's Daewoo.

In addition to its French-supplied engines the MiG-AT also features French-supplied cockpit avionics, from Sextant and Thomson-CSF (now Thales). Each cockpit is fitted with a pair of colour multi-function displays and provision for helmet-mounted sights, while the front cockpit had a wide-angle HUD for the student. MiG designed the MiG-AT to have a re-configurable three-axis digital flight control system, allowing the aircraft to

Development and acquisition funding for the MiG-AT have been hard to come by in recent years, as post Cold War military budget cuts have bitten deeply.

The MiG-AT's distinctive 'overwing' intakes have recently been replaced by Hawk-style oval intakes, extending just ahead of the leading edge.

replicate the handling characteristics of a number of different front-line combat types.

MiG has proposed two versions of the basic trainer, the **MiG-ATR** for Russian air force service (with Russian engines and avionics) and the export **MiG-ATF** with Sextant Topflight avionics. The MiG-ATR would be powered by the Soyuz/CIAM RD-1700 engine which is currently under development. The **MiG-ATS** (or **MiG-AT-UTS**) is a combat-capable/weapons training version, fitted with under-wing hardpoints and a centreline stores station. The second MiG-AT prototype was built to this standard. MiG is also proposing a dedicated light-attack variant, the single-seat **MiG-AS**, with a built-in gun, radar and air-to-air missiles.

The first MiG-AT made its official maiden flight on 21 March 1996. The MiG-AT is being adopted by the Russian air force, though Yakovlev claims to have received air force orders for the Yak-130 also. Russia has a requirement for between 200 and 250 MiG-ATs, and MiG is building an initial batch of 18 aircraft. The MiG-AT is also being promoted on the export market - most recently in South Africa and India. In both cases it was beaten by the BAE SYSTEMS Hawk, but MiG is optimistic that the MiG-AT will find new customers.

Specification: MiG-AT
Powerplant: Two 14.12-kN (3,175-lb) Turbomeca-SNECMA Larzac 04-R20 turbofans;
Dimensions: wing span 10.16 m (33 ft 4 in); length 12.01 m (39 ft 5 in) excluding probe; height 4.42 m (14 ft 6 in)
Weights: normal take-off 4610 kg (10,163 lb); maximum take-off 7800 kg (17,196 lb)
Performance: maximum level speed 1000 kmh (621 mph); maximum rate of climb at sea level 4140 m (13,580 ft) per minute; service ceiling 15500 m (50,860 ft); ferry range 2600 km (1,615 miles)
Armament: maximum ordnance 2,000 kg (4,410 lb) on seven underfuselage and wing hardpoints.

Mil Mi-8, Mi-17 'Hip'

Mil's **Mi-8** (NATO code-name **'Hip'**) helicopter was designed as a turbine-engined Mil Mi-4 derivative, using the same tailboom and rotors. The new Isotov turboshaft was relocated above the fuselage, allowing a simpler transmission and bigger cabin for up to 28 troops. The single-engined prototype **V-8 'Hip-A'** flew during 1961, followed by the **V-8 'Hip-B'**, powered by twin TV2 engines. The **Mi-8P 'Hip-C'** was a transport, while the **Mi-8S Salon** was a passenger/VIP transport with toilet and galley, and square cabin windows

The **Mi-8T/AT 'Hip-C'** is a utility transport with circular cabin windows, and optional outriggers carrying four weapons pylons. The **Mi-8TB 'Hip-E'** is a dedicated assault derivative, with a nose-mounted machine-gun. It has new outriggers with three underslung pylons per side. Above the outer four pylons are launch rails for the AT-2 'Swatter' ATGM. The export **Mi-8TBK 'Hip-F'** had six 'over-wing' launch rails for the AT-3 'Sagger' ATGM. To improve performance, the Mi-8 was re-engined with uprated TV3-117MTs to produce the **Mi-17 'Hip-H'**. The new aircraft has PZU intake filters, and the tail rotor is relocated from starboard to port. CIS/Russian air forces use the **Mil Mi-8MT** or **Mi-8TV** designations depending on equipment fit.

The **'Hip-D'** was a command post/radio relay platform, with a pair of tubular antennas above the rear fuselage, and a V-shaped antenna mast under the tailboom. The **Mi-9 'Hip-G'** is another command

Kazan Helicopters has refined the 'Hip' design to produce the round-nosed Mi-17MD/Mi-8MTV-5. Note the cockpit armour and IR jammer.

post/radio relay variant, with 'hockey stick' antennas under the tailboom. The **Mi-8SMV 'Hip-J'** operates in the ECM jamming role. The **Mil Mi-8PPA 'Hip-K'** is a communications jammer, with box fairings on the fuselage sides, a complex mesh-on-tubular-framework antenna array on the rear fuselage and six side-by-side heat exchangers below the forward fuselage. The **Mi-17P** or **Mi-17PP 'Hip-H (EW)'** has the same heat exchangers and box-like fairings on the fuselage sides but has a solid array in place of the mesh antenna.

Since the break-up of the Soviet Union, the plants building Mil helicopters have begun marketing their own versions. These include Kazan, Ulan Ude and the Mil Moscow Helicopter Plant. Ulan Ude has offered an export Mi-17 with Western avionics called the **Mi-171** and also the **Mi-8AMT(Sh) 'Terminator'** which has a four hardpoint stub wing. Kazan's main version is the **Mi-8TV-3** (similar to the 'Terminator', with the **Mi-172** as the export version. Kazan also makes the **Mi-17MD** with a rear loading ramp and capacity increased to 40 passengers.

The Mi-8AMT(Sh) 'Terminator' is the latest model of the Mi-8 armed transport on offer from the Mil Bureau and its associated Ulan-Ude plant.

Specification: Mil Mi-8 'Hip-C'
Powerplant: two 1257-kW (1,700-hp) Klimov (Isotov) TV2-117A turboshafts
Dimensions: rotor diameter 21.29 m (69 ft 10¼ in); length overall, rotors turning 25.24 m (82 ft 9¾ in) and fuselage 18.17 m (59 ft 7.35 in); height overall 5.65 m (18 ft 6½ in)
Weights: typical empty 7260 kg (16,007 lb); maximum payload 4000 kg (8,818 lb); maximum take-off 12000 kg (26,455 lb);
Performance: maximum level speed 260 kmh (161 mph); maximum cruising speed 225 kmh (140 mph); service ceiling 4500 m (14,760 ft); hovering ceiling 1900 m (6,235 ft) IGE and 800 m (2,625 ft) OGE; ferry range 1200 km (746 miles); range 465 km (289 miles), standard fuel

Mil Mi-24 'Hind'

The Mil **Mi-24 'Hind'** was developed from the Mi-8, using the same engines and rotor. It was designed as a flying APC, to carry soldiers and provide its own suppressive fire, while relying on speed for protection. A **V-24** prototype flew in 1970 and the production **'Hind-A'** entered service during 1973, armed with AT-2 'Swatter' missiles. During production the TV3-117 engine (used by the Mi-17) was introduced, leading to repositioning of the tail rotor to the port side of the tailboom.

The Mi-24's anti-tank capability became more important, but the original heavily-glazed cockpit provided inadequate visibility and little protection. The solution was an entirely new nose, with separate, stepped, heavily armoured tandem cockpits for the pilot (rear) and gunner (front). Under the nose was a stabilised turret housing a four-barrelled 12.7-mm gun. The new aircraft was the **Mi-24D 'Hind-D'** (**Mi-25** for export). This was soon replaced by the **Mi-24V 'Hind-E'** (**Mi-35** for export) armed with tube-launched AT-6 'Spiral' missile.

Combat experience in Afghanistan proved that the Mi-24 was a sound design. However, the original 12.7-mm machine-gun proved ineffective against some targets, and the 'Hind' needed a bigger gun. Accordingly, Mil designed the **Mi-24P 'Hind-F'**

Poland operates a mix of 'Hind-Ds' and 'Hind-Es' and has announced plans to upgrade and modernise its Mi-24s, adapting some for the C-SAR role.

The Mi-24D 'Hind-D' introduced the redesigned armoured cockpits that now characterise the 'Hind'. This is a Hungarian air force aircraft.

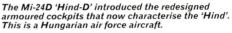

which mounts a GSh-30K twin-barrelled 30-mm cannon on the starboard forward fuselage. This was followed by the **Mi-24VP**, armed with the smaller twin-barrelled GSh-23L 23-mm cannon in its nose turret. Export versions of the 'Hind-F' were designated **Mi-25P** and **Mi-35P**. Over 35 countries, most recently Macedonia, have taken delivery of 'Hind' variants and they have seen combat in numerous conflicts, including Ethiopia-Eritrea, Nicaragua, Sri Lanka, and various parts of the former Soviet Union, notably Chechnya.

The **Mi-24M** is an upgraded night-capable version for the Russian forces with the rotor and transmission system of the Mi-28 and a turret for a twin 23-mm cannon. This is offered for export as the Mi-35M, while the Russian army has gone for a less sophisticated **Mi-24VM** with new avionics. A second phase will see the Mi-28 rotor/transmission introduced, as well as a lightweight fixed undercarriage. Israel's Tamam (a division of IAI) and South Africa's ATE have offered upgrades with western avionics and weapons capabilities. ATE's **'Super Hind'** has a 20-mm chain gun cannon and new night vision systems. The first 'Super Hind' customer is Algeria, while the Tamam upgrade is thought to encompass 25 Mi-25s for India.

Specification: Mil Mi-24D 'Hind-D'
Powerplant: two 1640-kW (2,200-hp) Klimov (Isotov) TV3-117 Series III turboshafts
Dimensions: main rotor diameter 17.30 m (56 ft 9 in); length overall, rotors turning 19.79 m (64 ft 11 in) and fuselage 17.51 m (57 ft 5½ in) excluding rotors and gun; height overall 6.50 m (21 ft 4 in) with rotors turning
Weights: empty 8400 kg (18,519 lb); maximum take-off 12500 kg (27,557 lb)
Performance: maximum level speed 310 kmh (192 mph); service ceiling 4500 m (14,765 ft); combat radius 160 km (99 miles) with maximum military load
Armament: one four-barrelled JakB 12.7-mm gun, maximum ordnance 2400 kg (5,291 lb)

Mil Mi-28 'Havoc'

M il's **Mi-28** (NATO code-name **'Havoc'**) is a successor to the Mi-24 and a direct rival to the Kamov Ka-50. Born in the Soviet era, the post Cold War years have seen funding for new programmes collapse and the Mi-28's progress has been slow. The first of three Mi-28 attack helicopter prototypes flew on 10 November 1982. The basic production-standard **Mi-28A** flew in 1987 and was first seen in the West at the 1989 Paris Air Show. Since then it has not entered production.

The Mi-28's conventional layout has stepped armoured cockpits accommodating a pilot (rear) and gunner (forward), with an undernose cannon. A conventional three-bladed tail rotor was abandoned and replaced on the second and third prototypes by a 'scissor'-type tail rotor, with two independent two-bladed rotors on the same shaft, set at approximately 35° to each other and forming a narrow X.

The Mi-28 is armed with a single-barrelled 2A42 30-mm cannon, with twin 150-round ammunition boxes co-mounted to traverse, elevate and depress with the gun itself, reducing the likelihood of jamming. The stub wings have four pylons, each able to carry 480 kg (1,058 lb), typically consisting of four tube-launched AT-6 'Spiral' missiles or a variety of rocket pods. The wingtip houses a chaff/flare dispenser.

The cockpit is covered by flat, non-glint panels of armoured glass, and is protected by titanium and ceramic armour. Vital components are protected and duplicated, and shielded by less important

This is the first production Mi-28A 'Havoc' which introduced the definitive downward-pointing exhaust suppressors for its TV3-117VMA engines.

items. In the event of a catastrophic hit the crew are protected by energy absorbing seats. An emergency escape system is installed which blows off the doors and inflates air bladders on the fuselage sides. The crew roll over these before pulling their parachute ripcords.

Mil's development effort has now moved on to the radar-equipped **Mi-28N** all-weather day/night attack helicopter. This aircraft is fitted with a mast-mounted Kinzhal V or Arbalet millimetre-wave radar, like that of the Longbow Apache, with FLIR and LLLTV sensors in the nose. The Mi-28N has an NVG-compatible cockpit with multi-function displays. Only four Mi-28s have been completed to date and they have undergone numerous detail changes. The first Mi-28N demonstrator was modified from the Mi-28A prototype. It had its formal roll out in August 1996 and first flew on 30 April 1997. The names **Night Hunter** and **Night Pirate** have been applied to the Mi-28N, by Mil. Officially, the Russian army has adopted the Ka-50, but Mi-28N development continues.

The black radome on the nose of the Mi-28N houses the radio guidance system for its 9M114 Shturm (AT-6 'Spiral') anti-tank missiles.

Specification: Mil Mi-28A 'Havoc'
Powerplant: two 1640-kW (2,200-hp) Klimov (Isotov) TV3-117VMA turboshafts
Dimensions: main rotor diameter 17.20 m (56 ft 5 in); wing span 4.87 m (16 ft); length overall, rotors turning 19.15 m (62 ft 10 in) and fuselage 16.85 m (55 ft 3½ in)
Weights: empty 8095 kg (17,846 lb); maximum take-off 11500 kg (25,353 lb)
Performance: maximum level speed 300 kmh (186 mph); service ceiling 5800 m (19,025 ft); hovering ceiling 3600 m (11,810 ft) OGE; range 470 km (292 miles); endurance 2 hours
Armament: one single-barrelled 2A42 30-mm cannon with two 150-round drums, maximum ordnance approximately 1920 kg (4,233 lb)

Mitsubishi F-2

Japan has established a tradition of military self-sufficiency, preferring to licence-build or indigenously develop its military hardware, despite the higher financial costs that such small-scale production inevitably incurs. When the JASDF launched its **FS-X** competition to find a replacement for its attack-dedicated Mitsubishi F1s – and ultimately its upgraded F-4EJs – the solution came in an interesting hybrid. Japan decided to adopt a modified F-16C, redesigned in conjunction with Lockheed Martin and built by Mitsubishi (with Kawasaki, Fuji and Lockheed Martin as important sub-contractors). The new aircraft was given the designation **F-2**.

Mitsubishi modified the F-16 by adding an entirely new, and larger, composite materials wing, a longer mid-fuselage, wider tailplanes, a slightly elongated nose and a brake-chute housing. The F-2 is powered by a General Electric F110 IPE turbofan. It is fitted with a Mitsubishi Electric active phased array radar, and a cockpit with LCD MFDs and a wide-angle holographic HUD – all of Japanese origin. A new integrated EW system has also been developed by Mitsubishi.

The Mitsubishi proposal was selected as the winning FS-X design in October 1987 and Mitsubishi was appointed as the prime contractor

The fourth and final XF-2 prototype – the second two-seat XF-2B operational trainer – was painted in a representative blue/grey camouflage.

The larger wing and revised tailplane configuration of the Mitsubishi F-2, when compared to the F-16C, are clear in this view of the first prototype XF-2A

in November 1988. After some early difficulties with the allocation of workshare and technology transfer between the US and Japan were ironed out, the initial airframe development contract was awarded in March 1989.

Mitsubishi has built four flying prototypes – two single-seat **XF-2A**s and two two-seat **XF-2B**s. The first prototype XF-2A made its maiden flight on 7 October 1995 and the first XF-2B flew on 17 April 1996. In May 1996 the Japanese government approved the production of 130 aircraft, comprising 83 F-2As and 47 **F-2B** trainers (and, at the same time, officially allocated the F-2 designation).

On 22 March 1996 the first XF-2A was handed over to the Japan Defence Agency. The XF-2 test fleet was transferred to the Air Development and Test Wing at Gifu AB. During 1998/99 serious problems were uncovered when the composite wing began to show signs of cracking when carrying heavy loads. This caused a nine-month delay in the programme while the wingtips and pylon attachments were redesigned. Mitsubishi delivered the first production F-2A aircraft to the Japan Defence Agency in a ceremony at its Komaki-South facility in September 2000. By the end of March 2001, 18 F-2s had been delivered to the JDA.

Specification: Mitsubishi F-2A
Powerplant: one 131.7-kN (29,600-lb) General Electric F110-GE-129 IPE afterburning turbofan (licence-built by IHI)
Dimensions: wing span 11.13 m (36 ft 6¼ in), over missile rails; length 15.52 m (50 ft 11 in); height 4.96 m (16 ft 3¼ in)
Weights: empty, equipped 12000 kg (26,455 lb); maximum take-off 22100 kg (48,722 lb)
Performance: maximum level speed approximately Mach 2.0
(Detailed performance figures not available)
Armament: one internal M61A1 Vulcan 20-mm cannon, plus 13 external stores stations

Nanchang (HAIG) Q-5, A-5 'Fantan'

Development of the Nanchang **Q-5 'Fantan'** began in 1958 to meet a PLA requirement for a dedicated attack aircraft. Although based on the MiG-19, Nanchang's design retained only the rear fuselage and main undercarriage, introducing a new, stretched, area-ruled fuselage with an internal weapons bay, new conical-section nose, wings of greater area and less sweep, larger tailplanes and lateral air intakes. A prototype made its delayed maiden flight on 4 June 1965, but extensive modifications proved necessary to solve problems with the hydraulics, brakes, fuel and weapons systems. Two new prototypes flew in October 1969 and the type was ordered into production.

Little is known about the dedicated **Q-5A** tactical nuclear strike version, which carries a single 5- to 20-kT free-fall bomb. The **Q-5I** is an extended-range variant with a new ejection seat, two additional hardpoints and a new Wopen WP6 engine. Some Q-5Is were modified to serve as missile-carriers with the PLA navy, and some of these may have Doppler nose radar. C-801 anti-ship missiles and torpedoes could also be carried. The **Q-5IA**, certified for production in 1985, was fitted with an additional underwing hardpoint and introduced a new gun/bomb sighting system and new defensive avionics. The **Q-5II** received an RWR but was otherwise similar. The **A-5C** (**Q-5III**) was an export Q-5IA for Pakistan with substantially improved avionics and compatibility with AIM-9 AAMs. The A-5Cs

The A-5C is still on offer to export customers, but its bargain-basement price brings with it outdated technology and debatable effectiveness.

serve with two squadrons at Peshawar, one having been disbanded due to the high accident rate. A programme to rebuild A-5Cs in Pakistan has been turning out refurbished aircraft at about 10 per year for very low cost compared to new-build examples.

Production of the Q-5/A-5 continues by Hongdu Aviation Industry Group (HAIG) – which Nanchang became in 1998 – though only at a low rate as attrition replacements. Over 1,000 are believed to have been delivered. Approximately 500 Q-5s serve with 12 regiments of the PLAAF.

The A-5 has been exported to Bangladesh, North Korea, Pakistan and Myanmar (Burma). Several programmes were launched to upgrade Q-5s with Western avionics and/or equipment. The **A-5K Kong Yun** (Cloud) was equipped with a French-built laser rangefinder. The **A-5M** programme began in conjunction with Italy and added a ranging radar, an INS, a HUD and new IFF and RWR equipment. An extra wing hardpoint was added, along with compatibility with the PL-5 AAM. All western-aided upgrade work on the A-5 has now ceased.

The PLAAF relies heavily on the Q-5 as its primary tactical strike/attack aircraft. It has no obvious successor in the Chinese inventory.

Specification: Nanchang Q-5 IA 'Fantan'
Powerplant: two 39.7-kN (8,930-lb) Liming (LM) Wopen-6A afterburning turbojets
Dimensions: wing span 9.68 m (31 ft 9 in); length 15.65 m (51 ft 4¼ in) including probe; height 4.333 m (14 ft 2¼ in)
Weights: empty 6375 kg (14,054 lb); maximum take-off 11830 kg (26,080 lb)
Performance: maximum level speed 1190 kmh (740 mph); maximum rate of climb at 5000 m (16,400 ft) 4980-6180 m (16,340-20,275 ft) per minute; service ceiling 15850 m (52,000 ft); combat radius with maximum external stores, 400 km (248 miles)
Armament: two Type 23-2K 23-mm cannon with 100 rpg, plus 2000-kg (4,409-lb) ordnance

N H Industries NH90

France/Germany/Italy
Advanced multi-role helicopter

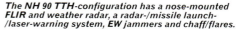

A longside the EH101 the N H Industries **NH 90** is the most important European collaborative helicopter programme. In terms of planned production numbers it is certainly the largest. The NH 90 is being developed by a consortium of manufacturers from France, Germany, Italy and the Netherlands with Eurocopter and Agusta (now AgustaWestland) as the senior partners. Two versions, the multi-role naval **NFH** and the battlefield tactical transport **TTH** are being developed from a common airframe.

The NH 90 programme can trace its beginnings back to the mid-1980s (its very name betrays the fact that was intended as a helicopter for the 1990s). The first NATO Industrial Advisory Group studies were launched in 1983/84 and a five-nation MoU (including Britain) was signed in 1985. The initial design phase was launched in 1986, but in 1987 the UK withdrew and the German and Italian work-shares had to be renegotiated in 1990/91. Further design and development MoUs were finally signed in 1992, agreeing to the production of five flying prototypes – nearly 10 years after the NH90 programme began.

The NFH (**NATO Frigate Helicopter**) is designed for ASW and ASuW tasks, with a secondary SAR and transport role. The TTH (**Tactical Transport**

In its NFH configuration, the NH 90 is fitted with a 360° search radar in a ventral radome. It will also have a dipping sonar, FLIR, MAD, ESM and datalink.

The NH 90 TTH-configuration has a nose-mounted FLIR and weather radar, a radar-/missile launch-/laser-warning system, EW jammers and chaff/flares.

Helicopter) is an army/air force version for airmobile operations. The twin-engined NH 90 will be the world's first fly-by-wire helicopter, using a quadruplex digital flight control system. The fuselage is built entirely from composite materials, as are the main rotor blades (which use an advanced aerofoil section with curved tips). The NFH cockpit has a five-screen EFIS layout, while the TTH has four.

The first of the five NH 90 prototypes was built to a common basic configuration and made its first flight on 18 December 1995, powered by RTM 322 engines. It flew with the NH 90's alternate T700 powerplants in March 1998. The first full TTH mission system was flown in 1999 on the fourth prototype, while the first full NFH system flew later that year on the fifth prototype.

In June 2000 the partner nations gave the go-ahead for full NH 90 production. A month later, in July, they signed a firm order for the first batch of 298 NH 90s, comprising 70 TTHs and 46 TTHs for Italy (plus one option), 27 NFHs for France, 80 TTHs for Germany (plus 54 options) and 20 NFHs for the Netherlands. The initial NH 90 production commitment is for 366 helicopters and the total European requirement for the NH 90 stands at 595 aircraft. The first (TTH) deliveries will begin in 2003.

Specification: NH 90 TTH
Powerplant: two 1253-kW (1,680-hp) class Rolls-Royce/Turbomeca RTM322-01/9 or Alfa Romeo/GE T700-T6E turboshafts
Dimensions: rotor diameter 16.30 m (53 ft 5½ in); length overall, rotors turning 19.56 m (64 ft 2 in) and fuselage 15.89 m (52 ft 1½ in); height overall 5.44 m (17 ft 10 in)
Weights: typical empty 5400 kg (11,905 lb); mission payload 2500 kg (5,512 lb); maximum take-off 10000 kg (22,046 lb);
Performance: maximum cruising speed 291 kmh (181 mph); service ceiling 4250 m (13,940 ft); hovering ceiling 3500 m (11,480 ft) IGE and 2900 m (9,520 ft) OGE; ferry range 1204 km (748 miles); mission radius 250 km (155 miles)

Northrop Grumman EA-6B Prowler

Designed and built for the US Navy, Grumman's **EA-6B Prowler** is now the United States' only dedicated lethal SEAD (Suppression of Enemy Air Defences) and high-performance jamming platform. Experience with the two-crew **EA-6A** EW aircraft led to the development of an advanced, lengthened four-seat A-6 variant, seating a pilot and three electronic warfare officers (EWOs) to manage the sophisticated array of ECM and ESM systems. Entering service during 1971, it introduced a tactical jamming system (TJS) which employs 'noise' jamming originating from a maximum of five transmitter pods. The first 23 production aircraft were to 'Basic' standard with ALQ-99 TJS and ALQ-92 communications jamming system.

These were followed in 1973 by 25 **EXCAP** (Expanded Capability) airframes with the ALQ-99A TJS. In 1976, the **ICAP** (Improved Capability) standard was applied to 45 new-build and 17 earlier aircraft and introduced new displays, AN/ ALQ-126 multiple-band defensive breakers and updated radar deception gear. All 55 surviving ICAPs were upgraded with software and display improvements to **ICAP-I** standard. This also introduces upgraded jamming pods and is able to handle groups of weapons systems with improved identification of hostile emitters and improved reliability and maintainability. The **ICAP-I/Block 86** introduced 'hard kill' capability with AGM-88A HARMs.More recently, EA-6Bs have been upgraded to two **ADVCAP** configurations. The

The EA-6B is now a key element of US (and Allied) air operations, because of its powerful jamming capability and HARM anti-radar missiles.

basic ADVCAP has new jammer transmission and passive detection capabilities and an expanded AN/ALE-39 chaff dispenser fit. An Avionics Improvement Program was to lead to a remanufactured **ADVCAP/Block 91** EA-6B with new displays, radar improvements, an improved tactical support jamming suite, AN/ALQ-149 communications jamming system and a digital autopilot. In fact, only three prototypes were tested, and a new upgrade, **Block 86**, proceeded instead. This included new radios, a digital fuel indicator and other cockpit improvements. All surviving aircraft then became **Block 89**, with new 'safety of flight' features such as halon fire extinguishers and hardened control rods, and were followed by **Block 89A** rebuilds with improved instrumentation and imbedded GPS.

With the retirement of the USAF's F-4G 'Wild Weasel's and EF-111 jamming aircraft, a joint-service agreement allocated four Prowler squadrons to Air Force use when needed. These units have a mix of USAF and USN crews and first saw action during Operation Allied Force in 1999.

In addition to the US Navy's 16 Prowler squadrons, the US Marine Corps operates another four. This aircraft is from VMAQ-1 'Banshees'.

Specification: EA-6B Prowler
Powerplant: two 49.8-kN (11,200-lb) Pratt & Whitney J52-P-408 turbojets
Dimensions: wing span 16.15 m (53 ft); width folded 7.87 m (25 ft 10 in); length 18.24 m (59 ft 10 in); height 4.95 m (16 ft 3 in)
Weights: empty 14321 kg (31,572 lb); normal carrier take-off 24703 kg (54,461 lb), or from land 27493 kg (60,610 lb)
Performance: maximum level speed with five jammer pods 982 kmh (610 mph); service ceiling with five jammer pods 11580 m (38,000 ft); range 1769 km (1,099 miles) with maximum external load
Armament: up to four AGM-88A HARM anti-radar missiles

Northrop Grumman B-2

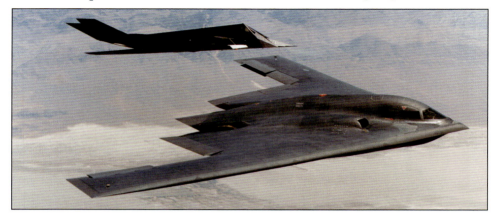

The Northrop **B-2 Spirit** flying wing was developed in great secrecy as a 'stealthy', radar-evading, bomber for the Cold War mission of attacking Soviet targets with stand-off nuclear weapons. B-2 development was a 'black' programme, known in its infancy as Project Senior C.J. and later as the **ATB (Advanced Technology Bomber)**.

The B-2's four F118 turbofans are non-afterburning variants of the F110 turbofan and have intakes and exhausts located above the aircraft to shield them from detection. The crew/payload section of the aircraft starts aft of the apex of the wing, ends at the wing trailing edge and is smoothly blended on the upper surfaces of the wing. The crew compartment provides side-by-side seating for two pilots, seated in zero-zero ACES II ejection seats.

The first flight of a B-2 took place on 17 July 1989. Test flying to evaluate low observables technology began on 30 October 1990. The USAF received is first operational B-2 in December 1993 and the last was delivered to the 509th Bomb Wing at Whiteman AFB, MO in December 1997. As later aircraft were delivered, early examples were upgraded to **Block 20** and **Block 30** standard. Block 30 bombers have full PGM and terrain-following capability and improved stealth measures.

The B-2 has a nuclear strike role, armed with cruise missiles or bombs. This aircraft was involved in inert drop tests of the B61-11 penetrating nuclear bomb.

The B-2 used stealth technology developed a generation after the F-117 Stealth Fighter, and the differences between the two are striking.

Total procurement, reduced initially from 132 to 75, has been curtailed to just 20 front-line aircraft due to the enormous $2.25 billion cost of each B-2. The need for secrecy and problems with the Defensive Management System (DMS) contributed to the ballooning of costs. Maintenance costs are also very high due to the need to preserve the smooth, RAM-coated surface finish.

Although many observers thought that the USAF would never risk the costly B-2 in anything other than all-out nuclear war, the Spirit saw action against Yugoslav forces in Kosovo in 1999. Non-stop 15-hour missions were flown all the way from Whiteman to the Balkans and back, in which up to 16 GPS-guided 2,000-lb JDAMs were dropped on targets such as airfields and air defence sites with 16 direct hits, and complete surprise from the defenders. The USAF plans to build special dedicated B-2 hangars at forward locations such as RAF Fairford, in the UK, to support future deployed operations and reduce the strain on aircrews from such extremely long missions. With possible changes to US defence strategy forthcoming, Northrop Grumman has offered to reopen the production line for an improved version at a cost of $700 million each for a batch buy.

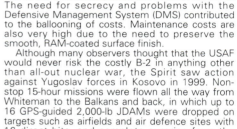

Specification: Northrop B-2A
Powerplant: four 84.52-kN (19,000-lb) General Electric F118-GE-110 non-afterburning turbofans
Dimensions: span 52.43 m (172 ft); length 21.03 m (69 ft); height 5.18 m (17 ft)
Weights: empty between 45360 and 49900 kg (100,000 and 110,000 lb); maximum take-off 181437 kg (400,000 lb)
Performance: maximum level speed 764 kmh (475 mph); service ceiling 15240 m (50,000 ft); range with a 10886-kg (24,000-lb) warload 12231 km (7,600 miles) on a hi-hi-hi mission or 8339 km (5,182 miles)on a hi-lo-hi mission
Armament: maximum ordnance 50,000 lb (22680 kg)

Northrop Grumman E-2 Hawkeye

The **E-2 Hawkeye** has been the US Navy's airborne early warning platform since entering service in 1964. It has a rotodome (mounted above the rear upper fuselage) housing antennas for the main radar and IFF systems. Including prototypes and development aircraft, a total of 59 E-2As was built, equipped with the APS-96 surveillance radar. Most were later converted to **E-2B** standard with a general-purpose computer and retired from service in the mid-1980s.

Current generation Hawkeyes are built to **E-2C** standard, the first example of which flew on 20 January 1971. Identified by a cooling intake behind the cockpit, the E-2C introduced a new APS-125 radar and improved signal processing capability. The basic E-2C has been the subject of continual updating over the years. Radar units have changed to the APS-138 (**E-2C Group 0**), the APS-139 (**E-2C Group I**, from 1989) and the APS-145 (**E-2C Group II**) now fitted to all aircraft. APS-145 offers improved resistance to jamming and better overland surveillance capability.

Production of the Hawkeye by Grumman on Long Island finished in 1994 with the 139th example, but was reinstated at St. Augustine, Florida to turn out four Group II aircraft per year plus export aircraft. In the AEW role, the E-2C extends the detection range of the battle group by about 480 km (300 miles) for aircraft and 258 km (160 miles) for cruise missiles. Small surface vessels can be located

Until the delivery of the far-larger E767, the E-2C Hawkeye was the sole AEW and ABCCC asset of the Japan Air Self Defence Force.

at 231 km (143 miles). Communication is maintained with the carrier's Combat Information Centre and patrolling fighters by means of a datalink. The Hawkeye can also act as an airborne control and command post, feeding directions to attack aircraft and escorting fighters to deconflict them, in addition to providing warnings of hostile aircraft.

In US Navy service, the E-2C flies with 11 active-duty units, two training units and two Reserve squadrons. E-2Cs have been exported to the air forces of Egypt (six), Japan (13), Singapore (four plus two on option) and Taiwan (four **E-2T**s). Israel had four aircraft fitted with refuelling probes but has now retired them. The French navy is acquiring four E-2Cs to operate from its new carrier, *Charles De Gaulle*.

The next-generation **Hawkeye 2000** will integrate into the USN's Co-operative Engagement Capability network. Northrop Grumman also has plans for an **Advanced Hawkeye** with a new multi-bladed propeller and a tactical cockpit giving the pilots access to the overall sensor 'picture'.

The US Navy is investing in future developments of the E-2 Hawkeye, while beginning to explore options for its replacement by 2020.

Specification: Grumman E-2C Hawkeye
Powerplant: two 3661-kW (4,910-hp) Allison T56-A-425 turboprops
Dimensions: wing span 24.56 m (80 ft 7 in); folded width 8.94 m (29 ft 4 in); length 17.54 m (57 ft 6¾ in); height 5.58 m (18 ft 3¾ in)
Weights: empty 17265 kg (38,063 lb); maximum take-off 23556 kg (51,933 lb)
Performance: maximum level speed 598 kmh (372 mph); maximum rate of climb at sea level 767 m (2,515 ft) per minute; service ceiling 9390 m (30,800 ft); minimum take-off run 610 m (2,000 ft); minimum landing run 439 m (1,440 ft); 1,605 miles); operational radius 320 km (200 miles) for a patrol of 3 to 4 hours

Northrop Grumman E-8 JSTARS

Making a 'star' appearance in Operation Desert Storm years before it was truly operational, the Boeing/Grumman **E-8** represents a major advance in battlefield command and control, introducing the capability for monitoring and controlling the land battle that the E-3 provides in the air battle.

Two **E-8A** prototypes were converted from former Boeing 707 airliners, with the first flying in operational configuration in 22 December 1988. The E-8A had a cabin configured with 10 operator consoles. It introduced the Norden AN/APY-3 multimode side-looking phased array radar (housed in a forward ventral canoe fairing). Its synthetic aperture radar gives a high resolution radar picture out to 257 km (160 miles) from the orbiting aircraft, while two pulse-Doppler modes provide moving target indication (MTI).

A wide area search MTI mode monitors a large sector of land, while an MTI sector search mode is used to target smaller areas of interest to follow individual vehicles. The antenna can be electronically slewed 120° to either side of the aircraft to cover nearly 50,000 km² (19,305 sq miles) and the radar has some capability to detect helicopters, rotating antennas and low slow-moving fixed wing aircraft. A datalink is used to transmit intelligence gathered

The AN/APY-3 radar is housed in a canoe fairing under the forward fuselage. It uses an electronically-scanned, mechanically-steered (in elevation) array.

A former Southern Air Transport Boeing 707 was used to provide the first full-scale development E-8C aircraft, which will serve as a permanent testbed.

in near real-time to mobile ground consoles, similar to those on the E-8. Using the various modes, the **JSTARS (Joint Surveillance Target Attack Radar System)** can be used for general surveillance and battlefield monitoring to provide the 'big picture' to commanders, stand-off radar reconnaissance or individual targeting functions for attacking vehicles and convoys.

In January 1991 both E-8As deployed to Riyadh to fly combat missions in Desert Storm. Forty-nine war missions were flown, for a total of 535 hours, a sizeable portion of which was spent on the search for Iraqi 'Scud' missiles.

In service, the JSTARS system was to have been carried on the new-build **E-8B** aircraft with F108 (CFM56) turbofans but, despite one **YE-8B** being procured (later sold), the production-standard platform is the **E-8C** based on converted 707 airliner airframes. The first production E-8C and a pre-production aircraft made their operational debut over Bosnia in 1996, but IOC with the 93rd Air Control Wing was not declared until December 1997. The E-8C crew consists of four flight crew and 18 operators. Current plans are for 14 E-8Cs to be in service by 2003. The USAF is already working on the RTIP radar upgrade for the JSTARS.

Specification: Northrop Grumman E-8C
Powerplant: four 84.52-kN (19,000-lb) Pratt & Whitney JT3D-7 turbofans
Dimensions: wing span 44.42 m (145 ft 9 in); length 46.61 m (152 ft 11 in); height 12.93 m (42 ft 5 in)
Weights: empty 77564 kg (171,000 lb); maximum take-off 152407 kg (336,000 lb)
Performance: max cruising speed at 7620 m (25,000 ft) 973 kmh (605 mph); economical cruising speed at 10670 m (35,000 ft) 860 kmh (534 mph); maximum rate of climb at sea level 1219 m (4,000 ft) per minute; service ceiling 12800 m (42,000 ft); range with maximum fuel 9266 km (5,758 miles); endurance 11 hours unrefuelled, 20 hours refuelled

Northrop Grumman F-5 Tiger

In 1954 the US government initiated a study for a simple lightweight fighter to be supplied via the Military Assistance Program. Northrop's private-venture **N-156C** design made its first flight on 30 July 1959, and was selected in 1962 by the USAF as the required '**FX**' fighter. It was designated **F-5**, and an **F-5A** prototype flew in May 1963. A corresponding two-seat **F-5B** trainer entered service in April 1964, four months ahead of the F-5A. Northrop also developed the reconnaissance **RF-5A**, equipped with four nose-mounted cameras.

First generation F-5s were exported to Brazil, Greece, Jordan, Morocco, Philippines, Saudi Arabia, South Korea, Spain, Thailand, Turkey, Venezuela and Yemen. Improved versions were built by Canadair as the **CF-5A** and **CF-5D** and were later upgraded by Bristol Aerospace. Some were later sold to Botswana. The Royal Netherlands air force ordered 105 **NF-5A**s with leading-edge manoeuvre flaps and Doppler radar.

The **F-5E/F Tiger II** incorporated uprated J85 engines, an integrated fire control system, additional fuel and a larger, modified wing with LERXes and manoeuvring flaps. The F-5E is the single-seat variant and was first flown on 11 August 1972. The combat-capable F-5F trainer had a lengthened fuselage first delivered to the USAF in 1973, to prepare the aircraft for foreign users. F-5E/Fs later served for aggressor training with the USAF until the late 1980s and still fly with the USN.

Chile's F-5E Tigre III upgrade was carried out in conjunction with Elbit and added a new EL/M-2032 radar, helmet-mounted sight and Python III missiles.

Some 1,300 F-5E/Fs were supplied to 20 air forces. Current operators are Bahrain, Botswana, Brazil, Chile, Honduras, Indonesia, Iran, Jordan, Kenya, Malaysia, Mexico, Morocco, Saudi Arabia, Singapore, South Korea, Sudan, Switzerland, Taiwan, Thailand, Tunisia, USN/USMC, Venezuela and Yemen. It was also built under licence in South Korea, Switzerland and Taiwan.

Many F-5 upgrade programmes are now available. Chile, Brazil, Indonesia, Singapore and Taiwan have all modernised their aircraft with new radars, cockpit systems and weapons.

A specialised **RF-5E Tigereye** reconnaissance version, retaining full combat capability, first flew in 1978. A modified lengthened nose houses a single camera. This can be augmented by two inter-changeable pallets, containing combinations of panoramic cameras and an IR linescanner. The RF-5E has been exported to Malaysia and Saudi Arabia. Singapore Aerospace has converted some of its F-5Es to **RF-5S** configuration and others to **RF-5E TigerGazers** for Taiwan.

The last F-5s in US service are the aggressor F-5Es operated by the US Navy's VFC-13 'Saints' (seen here) and the USMC's VMFT-401 'Snipers'.

Specification: Northrop F-5E Tiger II
Powerplant: two 22.24-kN (5,000-lb) General Electric J85-GE-21B afterburning turbojets
Dimensions: wing span 8.53 m (28 ft) with tip-mounted AAMs; length 14.45 m (47 ft 4¾ in) including probe; height 4.08 m (13 ft 4½ in)
Weights: empty 4349 kg (9,558 lb); maximum take-off 11187 kg (24,664 lb)
Performance: maximum level speed 1700 kmh (1,056 mph); maximum rate of climb at sea level 10455 m (34,300 ft) per minute; service ceiling 15590 m (51,800 ft); combat radius 1405 km (875 miles) with two AIM-9 AAMs
Armament: two M39A2 20-mm revolver cannon with 280 rounds per gun; maximum ordnance 3175 kg (7,000 lb)

Northrop Grumman F-14 Tomcat

Designed as a successor to the F-4 in the fleet air defence role, the Grumman **F-14A Tomcat** was conceived to engage and destroy targets at extreme range using the AWG-9 fire control system and AIM-54 Phoenix missiles. It remains the US Navy's standard carrier-based interceptor. The first development aircraft flew on 21 December 1970. Deliveries to the Navy began in October 1972, with the first operational cruise in 1974.

Problems with the F-14A's TF-30 turbofan were a key factor in the development of re-engined and upgraded Tomcat variants. One airframe was fitted with F401-PW-400s and tested as the **F-14B** as early as 1973-74. This aircraft later re-emerged as the **F-14B Super Tomcat** with F101DFE engines. This engine was developed into the GE F100-GE-400 turbofan, which was selected to power improved Tomcat variants. Two re-engined variants were proposed: the **F-14A+** was to be an interim type, while the **F-14D** would introduce improved digital avionics. Subsequently, the **F-14A(Plus)** was redesignated as the **F-14B**, 38 new-build examples being joined by 32 F-14A rebuilds by 1988. These incorporated some avionics changes, including a modernised fire control system, new radios, upgraded RWRs, and various cockpit changes.

VF-102 'Diamondbacks' operates the F-14B, one of five F-14B Tomcat squadrons currently active in the overall US Navy Tomcat force.

The US Navy's F-14 fleet is gradually being scaled back and many famed fighter squadrons have been disbanded as a result.

The first new-build F-14D made its first flight on 9 February 1990. The F-14D added digital radar processing and displays to the AWG-9, resulting in a designation change to APG-71, and a dual under-nose TCS/IRST sensor pod. Other improvements include NACES ejection seats, and AN/ALR-67 RWR equipment. Defence cuts resulted in the service receiving only 37 new-build aircraft, with deliveries beginning in 1990. Deliveries of rebuilt F-14D rebuilds finished at 110, in 1995. A proposed **Tomcat 21** strike fighter lost out against the F/A-18E/F Super Hornet.

In late 1990 the air-ground potential of the F-14 began to be exploited as the '**Bombcat**' entered the fleet, albeit with 'dumb' bombs only. LGBs were cleared for use in 1994 and in September 1995 VF-41 dropped them in action against Bosnian Serb forces. LANTIRN has been integrated with the F-14 allowing self-designation for LGBs, and has seen action over Yugoslavia and Iraq. Other new Bombcat weapons include JDAM and JSOW.

From 2002, the F-14 will be progressively replaced by the F/A-18F Super Hornet, and will be completely phased out by 2010. Until then, the F-14 continues to be upgraded, most recently with a Digital Flight Control System (DFCS).

Specification: Northrop Grumman F-14D
Powerplant: two 102.75-kN (23,100-lb) General Electric F110-GE-400 turbofans
Dimensions: wing span 19.54 m (64 ft 1½ in) spread, 11.65 m (38 ft 2½ in) swept and 10.15 m (33 ft 3½ in) overswept; length 19.10 m (62 ft 8 in); height 4.88 m (16 ft)
Weights: empty 18951 kg (41,780 lb); maximum take-off 33724 kg (74,349 lb)
Performance: maximum level speed 1997 kmh (1,241 mph); max rate of climb at sea level more than 9145 m (30,000 ft) per minute; service ceiling more than 16150 m (53,000 ft); combat radius on a CAP 1994 km (1,239 miles)
Armament: one M61 Vulcan 20-mm cannon; maximum ordnance 6577 kg (14,500 lb)

Panavia Tornado IDS, ECR

The Panavia **Tornado**, initially known as the **Multi-Role Combat Aircraft** (**MRCA**), was designed to fulfil a tri-national requirement for a strike, interdiction, counter-air, close air support, reconnaissance, and maritime attack aircraft. The prototype flew on 14 August 1974. The **Tornado IDS** (interdictor/strike) variant was a compact variable geometry (swing-wing) aircraft, optimised for low level penetration by day or night, in all weathers. The aircraft was designed around sophisticated attack and terrain following radars.

Nine prototypes were followed by six pre-production aircraft, before production began. RAF orders totalled 228 production **GR.Mk 1**s including 14 new **GR.Mk 1A** reconnaissance aircraft (and 14 GR.Mk 1A conversions). Some 26 were converted to **GR.Mk 1B** standards for the maritime attack role with BAe Sea Eagle anti-ship missiles, and eighteen more were converted to carry the BAe ALARM anti-radar missile, with no change of designation.

A mid-life update planned for the early 1990s was cut-back to cover the provision of a new HUD, a FLIR, a digital moving map, a colour displays, and an updated weapon control system. A total of 142 aircraft are being converted to **GR.Mk 4** and **GR.Mk 4A** standard, although major problems were encountered with integrating new equipment and software. Upwards of 80 had been re-delivered the squadrons before the aircraft was capable of even the most limited operational flying.

The fleet-wide GR.Mk 4 upgrade gives the Tornado force an enhanced ground attack capability. Note the new undernose FLIR housing.

In Germany, the Luftwaffe received 212 aircraft and the Marineflieger received 112 while Italy received 100. The German and Italian reconnaissance requirements were initially met using a simple multi-sensor pod on standard IDS aircraft. The Luftwaffe and AMI did opt for a more sophisticated variant for defence suppression. The **Tornado ECR** (Electronic Combat and Reconnaissance) variant incorporates an advanced emitter location system, and has provision for two AGM-88 HARM missiles under the fuselage. The last 35 German IDS aircraft were completed as ECRs, with an IR linescan mounted in a blister under the forward fuselage and with a FLIR immediately ahead. The linescan was subsequently removed and added to a new Tornado recce pod. Italy produced 16 ECRs (without FLIR or linescan) by converting existing aircraft.

A total of 96 IDS aircraft were delivered to the Royal Saudi Arabian Air Force under the Al Yamamah and Al-Yamamah II contracts, some with Sea Eagle and ALARM missiles, and some in GR.Mk 1A – **IDS(R)** – recce configuration.

Saudi Arabia was the only customer for the Tornado, outside the original partner nations of Britain, Germany and Italy.

Specification: Panavia Tornado GR.Mk 1
Powerplant: two 71.50-kN (16,075-lb) Turbo-Union RB.199 Mk 103 turbofans
Dimensions: wing span 13.91 m (45 ft 7½ in) minimum sweep and 8.60 m (28 ft 2⅖ in) maximum sweep; length 16.72 m (54 ft 10¼ in); height 5.95 m (19 ft 6¼ in)
Weights: operating empty 14091 kg (31,065 lb); maximum take-off 27951 kg (61,620 lb)
Performance: limiting IAS 1482 kmh (921 mph); service ceiling more than 15240 m (50,000 ft); combat radius 1390 km (863 miles) on a typical hi-lo-hi attack mission
Armament: two 27-mm IWKA-Mauser cannon with 180 rpg; maximum ordnance over 9000 kg (19,841 lb)

Panavia Tornado ADV

Long-range interceptor and air defence aircraft

Developed from the Tornado interdictor to meet a unique British requirement, the **Tornado ADV** (**Air Defence Variant**) was optimised for long-range, all-weather interception. Its primary mission is the defence of the UK Air Defence Region and UK maritime forces, with an important out-of-area commitment. The ADV was designed around the Marconi AI.Mk 24 Foxhunter radar and an armament of four Sky Flash AAMs. One 27-mm cannon was retained, but the other was removed to make room for a fully-retractable inflight refuelling probe. The radar suffered development problems and delays, before being brought to an acceptable standard by 1990. Carrying the primary missile armament semi-recessed under the fuselage necessitated a lengthened airframe and increased internal fuel capacity.

The first of three prototypes flew on 27 October 1979 and these were followed by 18 interim **Tornado F.Mk 2**s with RB.199 Mk 103 engines. These early aircraft initially flew with lead ballast in place of radar and performed only conversion training duties until January 1988. Plans for their conversion to operational standards as **F.Mk 2A**s were never implemented, and they were scrapped.

The definitive **Tornado F.Mk 3** first flew in November 1985. BAe produced 144 aircraft (38

This Tornado F.Mk 3 was a development aircraft for the CSP upgrade and is carrying four AMRAAM missiles, replacing the less capable Sky Flash.

The Royal Saudi Air Force's Tornado ADVs serve alongside the RSAF's F-15s to provide air defence for the Kingdom.

with dual-controls), including a cancelled Omani order for eight aircraft which were transferred to the RAF before completion. Some 24 more were built for Saudi Arabia from 1989, but a second Saudi batch was cancelled. 24 ex-RAF Tornado F.Mk 3s were leased to Italy from 1995 as a stop-gap measure, pending the availability of the Eurofighter Typhoon. Their replacement by F-16s was announced in 2001.

The Tornado F.Mk 3 introduced Mk 104 engines, a second INS, and provision for four AIM-9L Sidewinders (instead of two). Upgrades in service 'fixed' the radar problems, added HOTAS controls, added Hermes RHAWS and other defensive systems improvements. A **Tornado Capability Sustainment Programme** launched in 1996 will provide a MIL STD 1553B databus and an enhanced main computer. It will also integrate the AIM-120 AMRAAM and the short range ASRAAM on the Tornado F.Mk 3, and will parcel together a number of other improvements, some of which were already underway, including provision for JTIDS and a towed radar decoy.

Five front-line RAF units operate the Tornado F.Mk 3, and the type has seen extensive operational service in the Middle East and the Balkans.

Specification: Panavia Tornado F.Mk 3
Powerplant: two 73.48-kN (16,520-lb) Turbo-Union RB.199-34R Mk 104 turbofans
Dimensions: wing span 13.91 m (45 ft 7½ in) spread and 8.60 m (28 ft 2½ in) swept; length 18.68 m (61 ft 3½ in); height 5.95 m (19 ft 6¼ in)
Weights: operating empty 14502 kg (31,970 lb); maximum take-off 27986 kg (61,700 lb)
Performance: maximum level speed 'clean' at 10975 m (36,000 ft) 2338 kmh mph (1,453); operational ceiling about 12192 m (40,000 ft); combat radius more than 1852 km (1,151 miles)
Armament: one internal 27-mm Mauser cannon, plus four semi-recessed Sky Flash/AMRAAM and four AIM-9L/M AAMs

Pilatus PC-7, PC-9

Switzerland's Pilatus **PC-7** is derived from the piston-engined P-3, but with a PT6A-25 turboprop, a new wing, bubble canopy and six hardpoints for up to 1040 kg (2,293 lb) of stores.

The first production **PC-7 Turbo Trainer** made its maiden flight on 18 August 1978. First deliveries were to Burma in 1979. With the Beech T-34C Turbo Mentor then its sole production competitor, the PC-7 achieved growing export success, supplemented (after a two-year evaluation) in June 1981 by a Swiss order for 40.

Over 500 PC-7s have been sold to military customers in 20 countries including are Abu Dhabi, Angola, Austria, Bolivia, Bophuthatswana, Botswana, Burma, Brunei, Chile, France, Guatemala, Iran, Iraq, Malaysia, Mexico, the Netherlands, Nigeria, South Africa, Surinam, Switzerland and Uruguay. PC-7s are believed to have been used operationally by both sides in the Iran/Iraq war. In 1985, Pilatus offered an optional installation of twin Martin-Baker CH Mk 15A lightweight ejection seats.

The prototype Pilatus **PC-9** made its first flight on 7 May 1984, was powered by an 857-kW (1,150-hp) P&WC PT6A-62 turboprop. Although derived from the PC-7, there is only 10 per cent structural commonality between the two. The PC-9 is dimensionally similar, but is distinguished by its larger canopy, 'stepped' tandem cockpits with ejection seats, ventral airbrake and four-bladed propeller.

The Royal Thai Air Force took delivery of 36 PC-9 trainers, beginning in 1991. They are operated by the Flying Training School at Kamphaeng Saen.

Approximately 250 PC-9s have been acquired Angola, Australia Croatia, Cyprus, Iraq, Myanmar, Saudi Arabia, Slovenia, Switzerland. Thailand and the US Army. Most of Australia's 67 PC-9As were licence-built with a Bendix EFIS cockpit.

Pilatus teamed with Beech (now Raytheon) to win the USAF/USN JPATS (Joint Primary Aircraft Training System) contest in June 1995 with the re-engineered **PC-9 Mk 2** (**Beech Mk II**). Featuring almost a 70 per cent redesign of the basic PC-9, the new aircraft introduced a strengthened fuselage, a PT6A-68 engine and a pressurised cockpit with new digital avionics. The JPATS PC-9 has been given the service designation **T-6A Texan II**. The prototype flew in 1992, the first production aircraft in 1998, and the first T-6A was delivered to Randolph AFB, Texas in March 2000 for operational test and evaluation. The T-6A became operational with the USAF in 2001 the US Navy will follow in 2003. Total US orders for the T-6 exceed 700. Canada is to acquire 24 **T-6A-1**s as the **CT-156 Harvard II** while Greece has ordered 45 Texan IIs.

The subtle differences in line between the PC-7 and the PC-9 are evident in this formation of a green Burmese air force PC-9 with a PC-7 demonstrator.

Specification: Pilatus PC-7 Turbo-Trainer
Powerplant: one 485-kW (650-hp) Pratt & Whitney Canada PT6A-25A turboprop
Dimensions: wing span 10.40 m (34 ft 1 in); length 9.78 m (32 ft 1 in); height 3.21 m (10 ft 6 in)
Weights: basic empty 1330 kg (2,932 lb); normal take-off 1900 kg (4,188 lb) for aerobatics; maximum take-off 2700 kg (5,952 lb)
Performance: never exceed speed 500 kmh (311 mph); maximum cruising speed at 6095 m (20,000 ft) 412 kmh (256 mph); max rate of climb at sea level 655 m (2,150 ft) per minute; climb to 5000 m (16,400 ft) in 9 mins; service ceiling 10060 m (33,000 ft); range 1200 km (746 miles); endurance 4 hours 22 minutes

Rockwell B-1 Lancer

Suffering one of the more protracted development periods of any recent military aircraft, today's Rockwell **B-1B Lancer** long-range multi-role strategic bomber is derived from the preceding **B-1A** design. The B-1A programme was cancelled in 1977, and then resurrected in September 1981 with an order for 100 B-1Bs. The design features a blended low-wing/body configuration with VG outer wing panels and advanced high-lift devices, four GE F101 turbofans (mounted in pairs below the wing) with fixed intake geometry, a strengthened landing gear, three internal weapons bays, optional weapons bay fuel tanks for increased range, and external under fuselage stores stations for additional fuel or weapons. A moveable bulkhead in the forward weapons bay allows for the carriage of a diverse range of different sized weapons including ALCMs . The low-altitude, high-speed penetration role against sophisticated air defence systems was to be carried out using electronic jamming equipment, IR countermeasures, radar warning systems and the application of 'low observable' technology.

The offensive avionics system is centred around the AN/APQ-164 multi-mode radar, which includes a low-observable phased-array antenna for low-altitude terrain following and accurate navigation. The

For much of its career the B-1B was sidelined as its specialist nuclear strike role became less and less relevant. Now it is an important combat asset.

The B-1B's designation (B-one) has led to its 'Bone' nick-name . As is often the case, its official title of Lancer is almost never used by B-1B crews.

AN/ALQ-161A system is the core of the B-1B's continuously upgraded defensive capability.

The first production B-1B flew on 18 October 1984. Deliveries began on 27 July 1985 with SAC achieving IOC exactly a year later. Today the Lancer equips three Air Combat Command and two ANG wings. Until 1991, the B-1B was tasked with the strategic role and is compatible with a variety of nuclear devices, which it can deliver over an unrefuelled range of approximately 12000 km (7,455 miles). A conventional munitions upgrade programme (CMUP) was begun in 1993, with block numbers denoting successive improvements. **Block D** is the current standard, allowing use of many precision weapons such as JSOW and WCMD (Wind-Corrected Munitions Dispenser), and **Block F** (to be completed in 2009) will see the defensive systems upgraded to meet the highest threat levels. The capacity for regular Mk 82 bombs is 84 in the three bomb bays and another 44 on the external pylons, which are rarely, if ever, used.

The B-1 saw its combat debut in Operation Desert Fox during December 1998, and later in 1999 against Yugoslavia in Operation Allied Force where over 100 sorties were flown and more than 5,000 Mk 82 bombs dropped.

Specification: Rockwell B-1B Lancer
Powerplant: four 36.92-kN (30,780-lb) General Electric F101-GE-102 turbofans
Dimensions: wing span 41.67 m (136 ft 8½ in) (at 15°) and 23.84 m (78 ft 2½ in) (at 67° 30'); length 44.81 m (147 ft); height 10.36 m (34 ft 10 in)
Weights: empty equipped 87091 kg (192,000 lb); maximum take-off 216365 kg (477,000 lb)
Performance: maximum level speed at high altitude about Mach 1.25 or (1324 kmh, 823 mph); penetration speed at 61 m (200 ft) more than 965 kmh (600 mph); range 12000 km (7,455 miles) with standard fuel
Armament: maximum internal payload of 34020 kg (75,000 lb)

Saab 37 Viggen

Saab's **System 37**, the **Viggen** (thunderbolt) was developed as a relatively low-cost Mach 2 fighter capable of deployed short-field operations. The design pioneered the use of flap-equipped canards with a stable delta-wing configuration. The selected RM8A turbofan was based on the commercial P&W JT8D-22 and equipped with a thrust reverser and Swedish afterburner.

The initial **AJ 37 Viggen** all-weather attack variant featured sophisticated nav/attack and landing systems and the PS-37 multi-role radar. The first of seven Viggen prototypes initially flew on 8 February 1967 and deliveries of the first of 109 AJ 37s began in 1971. The primary armament comprised Saab Rb 04E anti-ship missiles (replaced by the far more capable long-range Rbs 15) and licence-built AGM-65 Maverick ASMs.

Several AJ 37-based variants were developed. The **SF 37** was tasked with all-weather day and night overland reconnaissance. It is equipped with various optical and IR cameras, and carries podded sensors. The **SH 37** was modified for all-weather sea surveillance and patrol with a secondary maritime strike role. It has a modified radar, ventral night reconnaissance and long-range camera pods. A tandem two-seat **SK 37** trainer was also developed with a stepped rear cockpit fitted with a bulged canopy and twin periscopes.

The next-generation **JA 37 Jakt Viggen** (fighter Viggen) was developed as a dedicated interceptor.

The Viggen's operational career is being cut short by budget cuts and the arrival of the next generation Gripen. The last JA 37s will be withdrawn in 2003.

It introduced a new pulse-Doppler look-down/shoot-down PS-47 radar, new avionics, an uprated and modified RM8B engine and a ventral 30-mm cannon. A modified AJ 37 was flown as the JA 37 prototype on 27 September 1974. Overall production of this variant was increased to 149, taking total Viggen procurement to 330. JA 37s entered service in 1978. A number of aircraft have now undergone the **JA 37 Mod D** upgrade, giving them AIM-120 AMRAAM capability.

Force cuts during the 1990s brought about the retirement of many AJ 37s as squadrons were disestablished and aircraft were scrapped. The advent of the JAS 39 Gripen brought about a rationalisation of the Viggen fleet. The attack/recce Viggens were upgraded to a new 'multi-role' standard, allowing them to familiarise pilots with Gripen weapons and procedures. Under this upgrade AJ 37s became **AJS 37**s, SF 37s became **AJSF 37**s and SH37s became **AJSH 37**s. A number of two-seat SK 37s have also been radically modified to serve as **SK 37E** EW/SEAD aircraft.

Sweden's fighter Viggens wear a mix of overall grey and green/brown splinter camouflage. The splinter scheme was applied to all attack/recce Viggens.

Specification: Saab JA 37 Viggen
Powerplant: one 125.04-kN (28,110-lb) Volvo Flygmotor RM8B turbofan with Swedish afterburner and thrust reverser
Dimensions: wing span 10.60 m (34 ft 9¼ in); length 16.40 m (53 ft 9¾ in) including probe; height 5.90 m (19 ft 4¼ in)
Weights: normal take-off 15000 kg (33,069 lb); maximum take-off 17000 kg (37,478 lb)
Performance: maximum level speed 2126 kmh (1,321 mph); combat radius more than 1000 km (622 miles) on hi-lo-hi profile
Armament: one ventral 30-mm Oerlikon KCA cannon with 150 rounds; maximum ordnance 13,000 lb (5897 kg)

Saab JAS 39 Gripen

Following the cancellation of the Saab B3LA light-attack/advanced trainer project in 1979, Saab began development of the **JAS 39 Gripen** (gryphon) as an advanced lightweight multi-role successor to the Viggen. The JAS designation (Jakt Attack Spaning – fighter, attack, reconnaissance) underlined the fact that one aircraft (and one pilot) would be able to undertake all the combat tasks of the mission-specific Viggen family. The Gripen was designed to carry the advanced Ericsson PS-05/A multi-mode radar, integrated with the D80 mission computer. The cockpit featured the Ericsson EP-17 display system with three monochrome screens and a wide-angled HUD. The Gripen uses a highly-developed version of Sweden's tactical airborne datalink system that allows rapid real-time exchange of complex mission data between aircraft and ground stations. Power was supplied by the Volvo RM12 turbofan, an improved licence-built version of the General Electric F404. Above all the Gripen was designed to be rapidly deployable and easily maintainable. It was intended to use Sweden's Bas 90 system of dispersed 800-m (2,624-ft) long roadstrips, and to be re-armed, refuelled and maintained in the field by a team of just five ground personnel.

The two-seat JAS 39B was drawn up as a trainer, but it will be fielded as a fully-operational mission-specific aircraft, perhaps with a dedicated SEAD

The heavyweight Rbs 15F anti-ship missile gives the Gripen an unparalleled maritime attack capability. This JAS 39A is carrying two Rbs 15s and AGM-65s.

Five **JAS 39A** prototypes were built, with the first flying on 9 December 1988. The first production JAS 39A Gripen flew on 16 December 1992. The development programme was slowed by the loss of two aircraft in 1989 and 1993. These incidents led to a redesign of the Gripen's pioneering digital fly-by-wire system.

The Gripen was declared fully operational with the lead Swedish unit, F7 Wing, on 1 November 1997. A second squadron at F7 followed on 30 December 1998. Deliveries to the second Gripen wing, F10, are now underway. The Swedish air force will acquire a total of 204 Gripens, including 28 two-seat combat-capable **JAS 39B**s. Sweden's Gripens are being delivered in three batches, each with improving levels of capability.

The ultimate Batch Three evolution (designated **JAS 39C** and **JAS 39D**) will be delivered from 2003 to 2007. These 64 aircraft will have the EP22 full colour cockpit with enlarged displays, air-to-air refuelling capability, upgraded D96 computer systems. Future Gripen upgrade options include a re-engining plan and conformal fuel tanks to extend range. In 1998 South Africa ordered 25 Gripens which will be equivalent to Sweden's Batch Three aircraft, for delivery beginning in 2007.

Specification: SAAB JAS 39A Gripen
Powerplant: one 80,5-kN (18,100-lb) Volvo Aero RM12 turbofan
Dimensions: wing span 8.40 m (27 ft 6¾ in), over missile rails; length 14.10 m (46 ft 3 in) including probe; height 4.50 m (14 ft 9 in)
Weights: operating empty 6622 kg (14,600 lb); maximum take-off 13000 kg (28,600 lb)
Performance: supersonic all altitudes; landing and take-off distance less than 800 m (2,625 ft); combat radius approximately 800 km (497 miles)
Armament: one 27-mm Mauser BK 27 cannon, plus six external hardpoints, and wingtip missile launchers; maximum ordnance approximately 4500 kg (9,920 lb)

SEPECAT Jaguar

Designed to meet a 1965 joint Anglo-French specification for an advanced trainer, the SEPECAT **Jaguar** was transformed into a potent low-level all-weather fighter-bomber The first prototype flew on 8 September 1968. The RAF received 200 Jaguars, comprising 165 single-seat **GR.Mk 1**s (**Jaguar S**) with Ferranti LRMTS in a re-profiled nose and a tail-mounted RWR and 35 **T.Mk 2** trainers (**Jaguar B**), all fitted with a sophisticated NAVWASS nav/attack system. They equipped a three-squadron Wing at Coltishall, operating in the conventional attack and reconnaissance roles, and with an out-of-area, rapid reinforcement commitment. The Jaguar also equipped a four-squadron Wing at RAF Bruggen in Germany (with a further recce unit at RAF Laarbruch) until 1988, with an additional nuclear strike commitment.

The RAF's Jaguars received more powerful Adour Mk 104 engines from 1978-84, while the **GR.Mk 1A/T.Mk 2A** upgrade added a FIN1064 INAS to 75 single-seaters, and 14 trainers. The aircraft also received AIM-9G Sidewinders, AN/ALE-40 flare dispensers, Phimat chaff/flare dispensers and AN/ALQ-101 jamming pods. For Operation Granby in 1991, the RAF's Jaguars received defensive systems improvements, overwing AIM-9Ls, CRV-7 rockets and CBU-87 cluster bombs. Since 1994, the surviving Jaguars been upgraded (to **GR.Mk 3A** standards) adding GPS, TERPROM, the TIALD laser designator, an advanced NVG-compatible cockpit,

Unlike their French counterparts British single-seat Jaguars have a chisel nose housing a laser range-finder and marked target seeker.

helmet mounted sight and a sophisticated new mission planner. They are due to serve until 2008-2009, and perhaps even longer.

The French Armée de l'Air received 160 single-seat **Jaguar A**s and 40 **Jaguar E** trainers with more austere avionics. Some had an undernose TAV-38 laser rangefinder, and all had an OMERA 40 vertical camera. The French Jaguars equipped EC.7 (operating in the attack and, until 1991, strike roles), EC.11 (with out-of-area and defence suppression commitments) and one escadron of EC.3. The surviving French Jaguars, still powered by the original Adour 102, will be withdrawn by 2004. The aircraft now use ATLIS laser designator pods, AS30 missiles and various LGBs. French Jaguars have seen action in Mauritania, Chad, the Gulf and the Balkans.

The **Jaguar International** (based on the RAF variants) was sold to Ecuador, India, Nigeria and Oman. India also builds the type under licence, (93 so far, with production continuing). India's Jaguars include some **Jaguar IM** maritime attack aircraft, with Agave radar and BAe Sea Eagle missiles.

The British Jaguar T.Mk 2A and (as seen here) the French Jaguar E trainers have a stepped tandem cockpit configuration in an elongated nose.

Specification: SEPECAT Jaguar A
Powerplant: two 32.49-kN (7,305-lb) Rolls-Royce/Turboméca Adour Mk 102 turbofan
Dimensions: wing span 8.69 m (28 ft 6 in); length 17.53 m (57 ft 6¼ in) including probe; height 4.89 m (16 ft ½ in)
Weights: empty equipped 7000 kg (15,432 lb); maximum take-off 15700 kg (34,612 lb)
Performance: maximum level speed at 10975 m (36,000 ft) 1699 kmh (1,056 mph); combat radius 852 km (530 miles) on a hi-lo-hi attack mission with internal fuel
Armament: two DEFA 553 30-mm cannon with 150 rpg; maximum load of 4536 kg (10,000 lb) on four underwing and one centreline hardpoints

Shenyang J-8, F-8 'Finback'

C hina's **J-8** (NATO code-name **'Finback'**) originated from a 1964 PLA requirement for an indigenous fighter with performance superior to that of the MiG-21. Shenyang's twin-engined design incorporated a scaled-up configuration of the MiG-21's 'tailed delta', with a ranging radar in the intake centre-body, similar to MiG's own Ye-150. The first of two prototypes flew on 5 July 1969. These undertook a protracted flight test programme (lasting 10 years), which was interrupted and delayed by political upheaval. The resulting J-8 was armed with a single 30-mm cannon and up to four PL-2 AAMs.

The improved **J-8 I 'Finback-A'** was designed as an all-weather fighter, and featured a new Sichuan SR-4 radar in an enlarged intake centrebody, some aerodynamic refinements and a two-piece canopy with a fixed windscreen. It introduced a twin-barrelled 23-mm 23-III cannon, and provision for four rocket pods as an alternative to the AAMs. A prototype flew on 24 April 1981. J-8 and J-8 I production totalled about 100 aircraft, and some J-8 Is have been converted to serve in the reconnaissance role, with an undernose sensor package..

Development of the further improved **J-8 II 'Finback-B'** began in May 1981, leading to first flight of a prototype on 12 June 1984. The J-8 II

The original J-8's MiG-21 heritage is clear to see in this line-up of 'Finback-As'. Despite its limited capability the J-8A is still in PLAAF service.

The J-8 II was a radical re-design of the original J-8. The F-8 IIM is a further improved export version equipped with Russian-supplied radar and missiles.

introduced a nose-mounted radar, and relocated new lateral air intakes for its 69-kN (15,430-lb) WP-13B turbojets and a ventral folding fin. An export **F-8 IIM** version has been offered, with a pulse-Doppler look-down radar and digital avionics, including a HUD and two HDDs, but this has not yet won any orders.

On 5 August 1987 Grumman received a contract to design, develop and test the **Peace Pearl** avionics upgrade for the J-8 II. This introduced a modified AN/APG-66 radar, giving compatibility with BVR SARH missiles like the AIM-7. The aircraft would also have received a modern HUD, a US ejection seat and an INS, and a bubble canopy and frame-less wrap-around windscreen. However, the Tienanmen Square massacre led to an immediate halt on work on the project.

J-8IIs of the PLA Air Force and PLA Navy Air Force are being upgraded with new RWRs (intro-duced in the second production block), and some are fitted with fixed inflight refuelling probes as **J-8 IV**s (also referred to as the **J-8D**). They are also being equipped with the PL-8 AAM (a copy of the Israeli Python III). The J-8 hit the headlines in April 2001 when one was lost after a collision with a US Navy EP-3E over the South China Sea.

Specification: Shenyang J-8 II 'Finback-B'
Powerplant: two 65.90-kN (14,815-lb) Liyang (LMC) Wopen-13A II afterburning turbojets
Dimensions: wing span 9.34 m (30 ft 8 in); length 21.59 m (70 ft 10 in) including probe; height 5.41 m (17 ft 9 in)
Weights: empty 9820 kg (21,649 lb); maximum take-off 17800 kg (39,242 lb)
Performance: maximum level speed 2338 kmh (1,453 mph); maximum rate of climb at sea level 12000 m (39,370 ft) per minute; service ceiling 20200 m (66,275 ft); ferry range 2200 km (1,367 miles); combat radius 800 km (497 miles)
Armament: one ventral Type 23-3 twin-barrelled 23-mm cannon with 200 rounds; ordnance PL-2B, PL-8 and PL-10 missiles

Sikorsky H-3, S-61 Sea King

Sikorsky developed the **S-61 Sea King** to replace its previous S-58 design, combining dual ASW hunter/killer roles in a single airframe. The prototype **YHSS-2** first flew on 11 March 1959 and was followed by 245 production **SH-3A**s for the USN. The primary sensors were an AQS-10 dipping sonar and an APN-130 search radar; in the 'killer' role the SH-3A carried two torpedoes or depth charges.

The 74 **SH-3D**s that followed introduced uprated T58-GE-10 engines, AQS-13A sonar and APN-182 radar. The **SH-3G** conversion modified 105 SH-3A/Ds to act as general-purpose rescue platforms and transports. Some 116 SH-3A, SH-3D, SH-3Gs were later converted to perform the inner-zone anti-submarine mission as **SH-3H**s with AQS-13B dipping sonar, LN66HP search radar, chaff dispensers and an ASQ-81 towed MAD bird. ESM equipment and the radar were later replaced by a modern tactical navigation suite and improved sonobuoy and sonar processing capability.

By 2001 only a handful of SH-3Hs remained in US Navy service, stripped of their ASW equipment and used for utility and SAR duties by second-line units, along with small numbers of **UH-3A** and **VH-3A** utility transports. The VIP-dedicated **VH-3D** is also still in service, used as a Presidential transport by Marine Corps squadron HMX-1.

Of the military **S-61R**s, which featured rear-loading ramps and a more conventional, non-boat-hulled fuselage, the USAF's **CH-3C**, **CH-3E**, and probe-

Italy's Agusta-built AS-61Rs differ from the basic S-61/SH-3 design with their high-raised tailbooms, rear ramps and water-right hulls.

equipped **HH-3E 'Jolly Green Giants'** have all been retired, as have the US Coast Guard's similar **HH-3F** Pelicans. Two are still flown in Argentina, however, and about 33 Agusta-built **AS-61R Pelican**s remain operational in the SAR role in Italy. Some of these aircraft have been armed and upgraded with FLIRS for the combat SAR role.

The basic Sikorsky-built S-61/SH-3 Sea King was exported to a number of countries, and remains operational in Argentina, Brazil, Denmark, Namibia and Spain. Licence manufacture was under-taken by Canada, Italy and Japan. Canada's surviving **CH-124A**s have been updated for continued ASW service, but are now overdue for replacement. About 48 of the Japan Maritime Self Defence Force's 100 Mitsubishi-built **HSS-2**, **HSS-2A** and **HSS-2B** helicopters are still operated on ASW, utility and SAR tasks. Agusta-built **ASH-3D** and **ASH-3H** ASW, logistic, and VIP transport derivatives for a number of customers, and they remain operational in Argentina, Brazil, Egypt, Iran, Iraq, Italy, Libya, Malaysia, Peru, and Venezuela.

Only small numbers of H-3 Sea Kings remain in US Navy service today, serving largely as base SAR and utility transport aircraft.

Specification: Sikorsky S-61 (SH-3H)
Powerplant: two 1044-kW (1,400-hp) General Electric T58-GE-10 turboshafts
Dimensions: main rotor diameter 18.90 m (62 ft in); length overall, rotors turning 22.15 m (72 ft 8 in), fuselage 16.69 m (54 ft 9 in); height overall 5.13 m (16 ft 10 in)
Weights: empty 5601 kg (12,350 lb); maximum take-off 9526 kg (21,000 lb)
Performance: maximum level speed 267 kmh (166 mph); economical cruising speed 219 kmh (136 mph); maximum rate of climb at sea level 670 m (2,200 ft) per minute; service ceiling 4480 m (14,700 ft); hovering ceiling 3200 m (10,500 ft) IGE and 2500 m (8,200 ft) OGE; range 1005 km (625 miles)

Sikorsky CH-53 (S-80)

Heavy-lift assault and special missions helicopter

The Sikorsky **CH-53** (**Model S-65**) heavy-lift helicopter first flew in prototype form on 14 October 1964 and, as the **CH-53A Sea Stallion**, it became the USMC's principal heavy-lift helicopter in Vietnam, entering service in 1965. The **CH-53D** introduced uprated engines and a revised interior for increased troop accommodation. In the air assault role, it carried 55 troops or 3630 kg (8,000 lb) of cargo internally. Four USMC units (all in Hawaii) operate the surviving 45-50 CH-53Ds today. S-65s were exported to Austria (two **S-65C-2** or **S-65O** aircraft, later sold to Israel), West Germany (112 **CH-53G**s) and Israel (about 40 **S-65C-3**s and ex-USMC **CH-53A**s). 30 of 38 surviving Israeli CH-53s are undergoing the **Yasur-2000** upgrade, which adds new EW and cockpit systems.

The **RH-53D** was a US Navy mine sweeping variant, able to tow a mine countermeasures 'sled', and introduced uprated engines and an optional IFR probe and sponson tanks. Now withdrawn by the US Navy, two remain operational in Iran.

The first-generation H-53 remains active with the USAF. The service has retired its early **HH-53B/53C** SAR platforms and **CH-53C** transports have gone, but the type remains active in the CSAR role. The **HH-53H Pave Low III** introduced APQ-158 terrain-

The Pave Low IV is a special-forces dedicated infiltration/exfiltration helicopter, which has take over the combat search and rescue role for the USAF.

The three-engined CH-53E Super Stallion is the US Marines' primary heavylift helicopter. It can carry 55 equipped troops or 14545 kg (32,000 lb) of cargo

following radar, LLLTV, a FLIR turret, and other improvements, and led to the current **MH-53J Pave Low III Enhanced**. This has uprated engines, TFR, FLIR, NVG, RWRs, IR jammers, chaff/flare dispensers, GPS, IFR probe, external tanks, titanium armour and provision for three door/rear ramp-mounted 7.62-mm Miniguns. The fleet are now being upgraded further to **Pave Low IV** standards, with EFIS cockpits and improved defensive aids. A handful of earlier variants are used for training.

The improved, three-engined **CH-53E Super Stallion** (**S-80**) variant flew in prototype form on 1 March 1974, and introduced a seven-bladed main rotor, a lengthened airframe and fuselage sponsons as well as the third engine,. IOC was achieved in 1981 and the type now forms a vital part of USMC amphibious operations. The VIP-configured **VH-53E** serves with HMX-1. In 2000 Turkey ordered eight **S-80E** (**CH-53E**) transports.

The current CH-53E-based **MH-53E Sea Dragon** features enlarged fuselage sponsons with increased fuel capacity and modernised mine countermeasures systems. A total of 46 were delivered to the US Navy to replace the RH-53D, equipping two squadrons. The JMSDF operates 11 similar **S-80M-1**s.

Specification: Sikorsky CH-53E
Powerplant: three 2756-kW (3,696-hp) General Electric T64-GE-416 turboshafts
Dimensions: main rotor diameter 24.08 m (79 ft); length overall, rotors turning 30.19 m (99 ft ½ in), fuselage 22.35 m (73 ft 4 in); height overall, rotors turning 8.97 m (29 ft 5 in)
Weights: empty 15072 kg (33,338 lb); maximum take-off 33340 kg (73,500 lb); maximum payload 16330 kg (36,000 lb)
Performance: maximum level speed 315 kmh (196 mph); maximum rate of climb at sea level with 11340-kg (25,000-lb) payload 762 m (2,500 ft) per minute; service ceiling 5640 m (18,500 ft); operational radius 925 km (575 miles) with 9072-kg (20,000-lb) external payload

Sikorsky UH-60 (S-70A)

Sikorsky's **S-70** design was developed to meet the US Army's 1972 requirement for a utility/tactical transport helicopter to replace the UH-1, offering far better performance, crashworthiness and all-round survivability. The **YUH-60A** prototype first flew on 17 October 1974 and featured a broad, squat cabin for one crew chief/door gunner and 11 troops. A production **UH-60A Black Hawk** first flew in 1978, and the type entered service in June 1979. The cheaper **UH-60L** (delivered from 1989) has uprated engines and other improvements.

Other US Army models include the **EH-60C** Quick Fix battlefield jamming system variant, which has two tailboom dipole antennas. A **UH-60C** command post is under development. The Army has a number of dedicated medevac **UH-60Q Dustoff Hawks**, and converted **MH-60A** and **MH-60L 'Velcro Hawks'** with FLIR, extra nav/comms, auxiliary fuel tanks and Miniguns for special operations support, and rocket-armed **AH-60L 'Direct Action Penetrators'**. The definitive, new-production Special Operations **MH-60K** has TFR, FLIR, pintle-mounted 0.50-in machine-guns, ESSS wings for fuel tanks, IFR probe, HIRSS, comprehensive comms/nav equip-ment, and defensive warning receivers and countermeasures. The US Army hopes to procure at least 1,400 UH-60A/L models, and is upgrading many to **Enhanced Black Hawk** standards. The USMC use nine **VH-60N White Hawk**s in the VIP transport role.

The External Stores Support System (ESSS) was built into late-model UH-60A/Ls. It can carry fuel and weapons loads of up to 2268 kg (5,000 lb).

Export models (sometimes designated as **S-70A**s) are in widespread service worldwide, including Argentina, Australia, Bahrain, Brazil, Brunei, Chile, China, Colombia, Egypt, Hong Kong, Israel, Jordan, Malaysia, Mexico, Morocco, the Philippines, Saudi Arabia, Taiwan and Turkey. Licence-production is undertaken in South Korea (**UH-60P**) and Japan (**UH-60J**).

The USAF also uses the type for SAR and CSAR. The planned **HH-60D/E Night Hawk** was cancelled, and instead the USAF pursued a three-phase procurement process; the Phase One **UH-60A Credible Hawk** has an IFR probe, provision for additional fuel and door guns. The Phase Two **MH-60G Pave Hawk** added new avionics (radar, GPS, INS, secure comms equipment and full countermeasures) and Phase Three added a HUD and FLIR. Sixteen special operations **MH-60G** support helicopters (with 0.50-in machine-guns) retained the MH- designation prefix, but aircraft with Phase Two avionics and lower calibre door weapons were re-designated as **HH-60G**s.

Turkey is an important Black Hawk customer with over 100 S-70A (UH-60A) aircraft in service with the army and para-military police units.

Specification: Sikorsky UH-60A
Powerplant: two 1151-kW (1,560-hp) General Electric T700-GE-700 turboshafts
Dimensions: main rotor diameter 16.36 m (53 ft 8 in); length overall, rotors turning 19.76 m (64 ft 10 in), fuselage 15.26 m (50 ft ¾ in); height overall 5.13 m (16 ft 10 in)
Weights: empty 5118 kg (11,284 lb); maximum take-off 9185 kg (20,250 lb); maximum internal payload 1197 kg (2,640 lb) and 3629 kg (8,000 lb) carried externally
Performance: maximum level speed 296 kmh (184 mph); maximum vertical rate of climb at 1220 m (4,000 ft) 125 m (411 ft) per minute; service ceiling 5790 m (19,000 ft); range 592 km (368 miles) with standard fuel

Sikorsky SH-60 (S-70B)

United States
Shipboard ASW/ASuV helicopter

Sikorsky's navalised **S-70B** was developed to meet the USN's **LAMPS III** requirement. This called for a helicopter capable of providing an over-the-horizon search and strike capability for ASW frigates and destroyers, using radar, MAD, sonobuoys and ESM to detect its targets. A prototype **YSH-60B** flew on 12 December 1979, followed by the first production **SH-60B Seahawk** in 1983. Retaining 83 per cent commonality with the UH-60A, it introduced airframe anti-corrosion treatment, T700-GE-401 engines, a folding tailboom, modified undercarriage and RAST (recovery assist secure and traverse) gear. Mission equipment comprises APS-124 ventral search radar, a 25-tube sonobuoy launcher, ASQ-81(V)2 towed MAD, and ALQ-142 ESM, with an armament of two Mk 46 torpedoes. It has a hoist for the secondary SAR role. S-70Bs have been exported to Australia (with MEL Super Searcher radar), Japan, Spain, Thailand and Turkey.

The **SH-60F Ocean Hawk** variant performs the CVW (carrier-based) inner zone ASW mission. Initially deployed in 1991, it lacked radar and RAST but instead had AQS-13F dipping sonar, FLIR and ESM and was armed with three Mk 50 torpedoes. Greece received a hybrid version with SH-60B type radar, but with provision for dipping sonar and with

This Royal Australian Navy S-70B-2 wore a special scheme to mark the 50th anniversary of its squadron, the NAS Nowra-based HS 816.

The evolved CH-60S has a combination of Black Hawk and Seahawk design features, and will provide the US Navy with a new multi-role transport.

SH-60F ESM. Taiwan bought 21 similar **S-70C(M)-1** and **S-70C(M)-2 Thunderhawk**s. The SH-60F-based **HH-60H Rescue Hawk** is the USN's strike rescue platform, and entered service in 1989. It has a secondary covert SEAL team infil/exfil role.

Some 273 of the Navy's SH-60Bs, SH-60Fs and HH-60Hs are being re-manufactured to a common **SH-60R** standard, optimised for littoral operations with new passive and active detection and ECM systems, including a new AN/APS-147 ISAR radar, and new sonar equipment. The MAD is deleted, and computer and navigation systems are replaced. The prototype flew on 22 December 1999.

The **CH-60S** is a new-build multi-role VERTREP, SAR and CSAR derivative of the Seahawk, intended to replace the HH-60H, CH-46 and HH-3. It combines a UH-60L fuselage with the dynamics system, folding rotors and tailboom and other features of the SH-60B. The aircraft will also have a glass cockpit (also being adopted for the SH-60R) and flew in prototype form on 6 October 1997.

The USCG's SAR **HH-60J Jayhawk** replaced the Sikorsky HH-3F in the SAR, patrol and smuggling interdiction roles, and featured a search/weather radar, a searchlight, an NVG-compatible cockpit and an optional fuel tank.

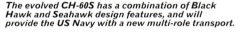

Specification: Sikorsky SH-60B Seahawk
Powerplant: two 1417-kW (1,900-hp) General Electric T700-GE-401C turboshafts
Dimensions: main rotor diameter 16.36 m (53 ft 8 in); length overall, rotors turning 19.76 m (64 ft 10 in), fuselage 15.26 m (50 ft 0¾ in); height overall, rotor turning 5.18 m (17 ft)
Weights: empty 6191 kg (13,648 lb) for the ASW mission; maximum take-off 9926 kg (21,884 lb) for the utility mission; maximum payload 3629 kg (8,000 lb)
Performance: dash speed 234 kmh (145 mph); operational radius 278 km (173 miles) for a one-hour loiter
Armament: AGM-119B Mod 7 Penguin ASM, and pintle-mounted 0.50-in machine-guns

Sukhoi Su-17, Su-22 'Fitter'

To improve the payload/range and STOL capability of the Su-7, Sukhoi built an improved derivative with a variable-geometry ('swing') wing. The result was the Sukhoi **S-22I** (**Su-7IG 'Fitter-B'**) prototype flew on 2 August 1966. The production **Su-17M 'Fitter-C'** introduced the 109.83-kN (24,690-lb) AL-21F-3 engine and a new nav/attack system. A handful of 'Fitter-Cs' were built for reconnaissance duties, with provision for multi-sensor reconnaissance pods as **Su-17R**s. All 'Fitter-Cs' have been retired from use in Russia, and Poland, and similar export aircraft (designated **Su-20**) delivered to Afghanistan, Algeria, Angola, Egypt, Iraq, North Korea, Syria and probably Vietnam are all also believed to have been retired.

The **Su-17M-2D 'Fitter-D'** introduced a lengthened, drooping nose and revised avionics. The ranging radar was replaced by a laser ranger and Doppler was added below the nose. A sanitised, less-sophisticated version, the **Su-17M-2K 'Fitter-F'**, was built for export to Angola, Libya and Peru. These aircraft were powered by Tumanskii R-29BS-300 engines. A handful remain active in Peru, upgraded with new avionics and refuelling probes.

The **Su-17UM-2D 'Fitter-E'** was a two-seat trainer based on the Su-17M-2D airframe, but with no port cannon. Export Su-17UM-2Ks used the R-29BS-300 engines and aircraft were delivered to Afghanistan, Algeria, Angola, Iraq, Libya, Peru, Vietnam and North and South Yemen.

This Russian air force 'Fitter-K' represents the most modern version of the Su-17/Su-22 family, which has gained a reputation for rugged dependability.

The **Su-17M-3 'Fitter-H'** for Frontal Aviation had a deepened forward fuselage, a tall tailfin and a removable ventral fin, like the trainer, but with two wingroot cannon and a single cockpit. A dedicated AAM launch rail was added beneath each inner wing. It was supplied to Frontal Aviation and Afghanistan only. The similar **Su-22M-3K 'Fitter-J'** (with the Tumanskii R-29BS engine) was exported to Iran, Iraq, Libya, Peru, Syria, Vietnam and both Yemens, and remains in service with most of these operators. The **Su-22UM-3K** was a trainer based on the tall-tailed Su-17M-3 airframe, produced with Lyul'ka and Tumanskii engines.

The final production variant, the **Su-22M-4 'Fitter-K'** introduced new avionics and compatibility with an even wider range of weapons, and was distinguished by a small intake at the base of the tailfin. The type is in limited service with a number of former Soviet states, and in Angola, the Czech and Slovak Republics, and Poland. The Su-22M-4 was also exported to Afghanistan, and the former East Germany.

Many surviving 'Fitter' operators like the Czech Republic, are faced with the difficult choice of upgrading their aircraft, or retiring them.

Specification: Sukhoi Su-17M-4 'Fitter-K'
Powerplant: one 110.32-kN (24,802-lb) NPO Saturn (Lyul'ka) AL-21F-3 afterburning turbojet
Dimensions: wing span 13.80 m (45 ft 3 in) spread and 10 m (32 ft 10 in); length 18.75 m (61 ft 6¼ in); height 50 m (16 ft 5 in)
Weights: normal take-off 16400 kg (36,155 lb); maximum take-off 19500 kg (42,989 lb)
Performance: maximum level speed 1400 kmh (870 mph); service ceiling 15200 m (49,870 ft); combat radius 1150 km (715 miles) on a hi-lo-hi attack mission with a 2000-kg (4,409-lb) warload
Armament: two wingroot-mounted NR-30 30-mm cannon with 80 rpg; maximum practical ordnance load 1000 kg (2,205 lb) plus drop tanks

Sukhoi Su-24 'Fencer'

The **Su-24** (NATO code-name **'Fencer'**) was intended as an all-weather low-level supersonic bomber able to attack fixed and mobile targets with pinpoint accuracy and with a secondary photographic reconnaissance role. It was developed from the unsuccessful **T-6-1** delta-winged VTOL bomber prototype, which had separate cruise and lift engines. The heavy lift jets were removed to leave space for fuel or weapons and a variable-geometry wing was added to produce the **T-6-2IG** prototype, which made its maiden flight during May 1970.

The production **Su-24 'Fencer-A'** was powered by a pair of Perm/Soloviev AL-21F-3 turbofans. The **Su-24 'Fencer-B'** had an extended-chord tailfin giving a distinctive 'kinked' tailfin, and introduced a heat exchanger above the fuselage. Late-model 'Fencer-Bs' had a refined rear fuselage (more closely following the jet pipes), and a brake chute fairing below the rudder. The **Su-24 'Fencer-C'** had triangular RWR fairings on the sides of the fin-tip and on the engine intakes.

The improved **Su-24M 'Fencer-D'** attack variant entered service in 1986 and introduced a retractable IFR probe above the nose, an upgraded avionics suite and provision for a UPAZ-A buddy refuelling pod. Its shortened, reshaped radome

The Su-24M 'Fencer-D' is the second-generation strike/attack version of the Su-24. It has a new nav/attack fit and a laser/TV targeting system.

The Su-24MR 'Fencer-E' is a tactical reconnaissance version equipped with a sideways-looking airborne radar, IR line-scan and cameras.

houses Orion-A forward-looking attack radar and Relief TFR. The Kaira 24 laser and TV sighting system gives compatibility with the newest Soviet TV- and laser-guided ASMs.

Soviet Su-24 bombers could carry free-fall TN-1000 and TN-1200 nuclear bombs, and a variety of conventional free-fall bombs and guided ASMs. 'Fencer-Bs', '-Cs' and '-Ds' remain in widespread front-line use with Russia, and with a number of former Soviet states. Belarus is reported to have sold eight aircraft to UNITA in Angola. Downgraded, non-nuclear capable export **Su-24MK**s have been delivered to Algeria, Iran, Iraq, Libya and Syria. The 24 Iraqi aircraft that fled to Iran during the 1991 Gulf War, were absorbed by the IIAF.

The **Su-24MR 'Fencer-E'** tactical reconnaissance aircraft uses internal and podded sensors of various types, and is able to transmit data from some sensors to a ground station in real time. The **Su-24MP 'Fencer-F'** is believed to have a primary Elint-gathering role and is similar in appearance to the Su-24MR. It can be distinguished from the earlier aircraft by a prominent undernose fairing below the nose and swept-back intake-mounted 'hockey stick' antennas. The Russian air force is now examining a range of Su-24 upgrade options.

Specification: Sukhoi Su-24 'Fencer-C'
Powerplant: two 110.32-kN (24,802-lb) NPO Saturn (Lyul'ka) AL-21F-3A turbofans
Dimensions: wing span 17.63 m (57 ft 10 in) spread and 10.36 m (34 ft) swept; length 24.53 m (80 ft 5¾ in) including probe; height 4.97 m (16 ft 3¾ in)
Weights: empty equipped 19000 kg (41,887 lb); normal take-off 36000 kg (79,365 lb); maximum take-off 39700 kg (87,522 lb)
Performance: maximum level speed 2320 kmh (1,441 mph); service ceiling 17500 m (57,415 ft); combat radius 1050 km (650 miles) on a hi-lo-hi attack mission
Armament: one GSh-6-23M 23-mm cannon; maximum ordnance 8000 kg (17,637 lb)

Sukhoi Su-25 'Frogfoot'

The **Su-25** was developed during the late 1960s, as a jet *shturmovik*, using the tried and trusted weapons system of the Su-17M-2. A prototype flew on 22 February 1975 with RD-9 engines and a depressing GSh-23 cannon under the nose. Further prototypes introduced the R-95Sh turbojet (a non-afterburning version of the MiG-21's R-13-300), a twin-barrelled AO-17 30-mm cannon and the upgraded weapons system of the Su-17M3.

The production **Su-25 'Frogfoot-A'** introduced enlarged engine intakes and increased armour around cockpit and critical components, and was evaluated under combat conditions in Afghanistan led to the addition of bolt-on chaff/flare dispensers, and an exhaust IR suppressor. From 1987 the R-195 engine was introduced, as fitted to all two-seaters, and to 50 **Su-25BM** dual-role attack/target-towing aircraft. Single-seat Su-25 production ended in 1989, after 330 aircraft had been delivered, including export **Su-25K**s to Angola, Bulgaria, Czechoslovakia, Iraq and North Korea, and, according to some reports, Afghanistan. Peru has recently taken delivery of a number of probably second-hand Su-25s, while Iran obtained ex-Iraqi aircraft during the Gulf War.

The **Su-25UB 'Frogfoot-B'** trainer featured a lengthened fuselage with stepped tandem cockpits, and a taller tailfin. Similar **Su-25UBK**s were provided to export customers. The **Su-25UT** (later **Su-28**) had all armament and weapons systems removed

The first export customer for the Su-25K was Czechoslovakia. Its Su-25s were later split between the independent Czech and Slovakian air forces.

and was intended for the pilot training role with the VVS and DOSAAF. The **Su-25UTG** was a carrier trainer with strengthened undercarriage and hook.

The **Su-25T** and **Su-25TM** (briefly the **Su-34**) are extensively modernised Su-25 derivatives – single-seaters based on the Su-25UB airframe, using the rear cockpit to house avionics and fuel. To give true night capability, the aircraft have new avionics, sensors and systems, including provision for podded radars or LLLTV/FLIR systems. Eight Su-25Ts were reportedly built for Frontal Aviation, plus a handful completed as Su-25TMs. The Russian air forces reportedly have an outstanding requirement for 24 Su-25TMs to meet regional reinforcement and out-of-area requirements, while Georgia has a requirement for 50 aircraft. The export **Su-25TK** or **Su-39 Strike Shield** has also been offered to Abu Dhabi and Bulgaria.

In April 2001 Israel's Elbit and Georgia's TAM unveiled the **Su-25 Scorpion** upgrade, featuring a modernised cockpit with two MFDs, HUD and a new weapons delivery and navigation system.

The Su-25 'Frogfoot-A' has remained largely unchanged throughout its front-line career, and proved its combat worth in Afghanistan.

Specification: Sukhoi Su-25K 'Frogfoot-A'
Powerplant: two 44.13-kN (9,921-lb) MNPK 'Soyuz' (Tumanskii) R-195 turbojets
Dimensions: wing span 14.36 m (47 ft 1.4 in); length 15.53 m (50 ft 11½ in); height 4.80 m (15 ft 9 in)
Weights: empty equipped 9500 kg (20,944 lb); maximum take-off 17600 kg (38,801 lb)
Performance: maximum level speed 'clean' at sea level 975 kmh (606 mph); service ceiling 7000 m (22,965 ft); combat radius 550 km (342 miles) on hi-lo-hi attack mission with a 4000-kg (8,818-lb) warload and two drop tanks
Armament: one 30-mm AO-17A cannon with 250 rounds; maximum ordnance 4400 kg (9,700 lb)

Sukhoi Su-27 'Flanker'

Sukhoi began work on a new long range heavy fighter for Frontal Aviation in 1969. This was to be a highly manoeuvrable aircraft, with long range, heavy armament and modern sensors, capable of intercepting low-flying or high-level bombers, and of out-fighting the F-15. The requirement was re-drafted to cover two separate but complementary designs, one heavy and with a long range, and the other a cheaper, lower cost tactical fighter.

Sukhoi was awarded a contract to develop the heavy aircraft, as the **T10**. The **T10-1 'Flanker-A'** prototype flew on 20 May 1977, but testing revealed serious problems and the type underwent a total redesign. Four T10s (**T10-1** to **-4**) were built in the OKB's own workshops, and five more (**T10-5, -6, -9, -10** and **-11**) at Komsomolsk. The planned seventh prototype (**T10-7**) was completed as the **T10S-1 'Flanker-B'** with a redesigned wing, under-carriage and fuselage, and a spine-mounted airbrake, and flew on 20 April 1981. An early T10S was stripped and lightened and fitted with uprated engines. As the **P-42** this aircraft set a series of time-to-height records between 1986 and 1988. The new configuration formed the basis of the production **Su-27 'Flanker-B'**, which entered service in 1985, and was officially 'accepted' in 1990.

The Su-27 'Flanker-B' can carry up to 10 modern and effective air-to-air missiles, a load that gives it immense combat persistence.

The Su-27 shocked Western air forces, because it combined long-range and a heavy warload, with dramatic manoeuvrability.

The 'Flanker-B' has an advanced pulse-Doppler radar, backed up by a sophisticated EO complex with an IRST system and a laser rangefinder. This allows the Su-27 to detect, track and engage a target without using radar. The Su-27 is also compatible with a helmet-mounted target designation system. The prototype **Su-27UB 'Flanker-C'** trainer featured a lengthened fuselage with stepped tandem cockpits under a single canopy and increased height/area tailfins and airbrake and flew on 7 March 1985.

About 600 Su-27s have been built, and 567 were estimated to be in service by the end of 1999. About 395 of these were in service with the Russian air forces, serving with Frontal Aviation and the PVO air defence force. Most of the remainder served in small numbers with former Soviet republics, including Armenia, Azerbaijan, Belarus, Georgia, Ukraine, Uzbekistan. Some of these aircraft have been sold on, to Angola, and Ethiopia. Fifty new-build export **Su-27SK**s and two-seat **Su-27UBK**s have been delivered to the People's Republic of China, where 200 more are to be built under licence by Shenyang as the **J-11**. The first Chinese-built Su-27 flew in December 1998. Some 12 aircraft have also been delivered to Vietnam.

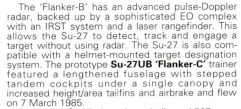

Specification: Sukhoi Su-27 'Flanker-B'
Powerplant: two 122.58-kN (27,557-lb) NPO Saturn (Lyul'ka) AL-31F turbofans
Dimensions: wing span 14.70 m (48 ft 2¾ in); length 21.935 m (71 ft 11½ in) excluding probe; height 5.932 m (19 ft 5½ in)
Weights: empty 17700 kg (39,021 lb); maximum take-off 30000 kg (66,138 lb)
Performance: maximum level speed 2500 kmh (1,553 mph); maximum rate of climb at sea level 18300 m (60,039 ft) per minute; service ceiling 18000 m (59,055 ft); combat radius 1500 km (932 miles) with four AAMs
Armament: one 30-mm GSh-30-1 cannon in starboard wingroot with 150 rounds; maximum ordnance 6000 kg (13,228 lb)

Sukhoi Su-30, Su-30M 'Flanker'

The **Su-27PU** (later **Su-30**) was designed to fulfil a long-standing requirement for a long-range fighter-interceptor to replace the Tu-128 in defending Russia's northern frontiers. The basic Su-27's long range was further improved through the use of inflight refuelling, (the aircraft being fitted with a retractable AAR probe), long range navigation equipment was provided and systems were tested and proved for long endurance use. The IA-PVO received about five Su-27PUs before production was halted by funding constraints, and the type was marketed to export customers as the **Su-30K**. Sukhoi also designed and built a single-seat **Su-27P** with the same systems as the Su-27PU, but its single cockpit made it difficult to exploit the aircraft's long endurance potential operationally, and none were delivered to frontline customers. At least one example was built to become the **Su-30KI** demonstrator, in anticipation of an Indonesian order. Two more long-endurance were delivered as aerobatic demonstration aircraft, as the **Su-27PD**.

Sukhoi added limited air-to-ground capabilities to the two-seat Su-30 to produce the **Su-30M** (M for multi-role) marketing the aircraft to export customers as the **SU-30MK**. Although a succession of aircraft appeared at international airshows in colourful ground attack camouflage colour schemes, festooned with dummy weapons, most of these were standard Su-27UB trainers, and it

The vectored-thrust Su-30MKI strike/attack aircraft, now under development for the Indian Air Force, is fitted with canards and AL-37FP engines.

took some time for the Su-30MK's multi-role avionics to catch up with the marketeers' promises. Thus, when India took delivery (late) of eight **Su-30MKI**s in 1997 the aircraft were little more than probe-equipped Su-27UBs, and it will be some time before ground-attack capable aircraft are delivered.

China has ordered 60 of the baseline aircraft as the **Su-30MKK**, and Chinese 'Flanker' production will switch to this version after the 80th Su-27SK. Vietnam has also ordered the type, under the simple designation Su-30K.

India's full-standard Su-30MKIs are planned to be much more capable aircraft, with canard fore-planes, thrust-vectoring engines and advanced air-to-ground precision weapon capability. Sukhoi is now flying aircraft to this standard, but production deliveries are not yet imminent. Some sources expect this two-seat configuration (sometimes referred to as the **Su-35UB** or **Su-37UB**) to replace the vectored-thrust Su-37 single-seater as the Russian air forces' next-generation 'Super Flanker' of choice.

Small numbers of the baseline Su-30 long-range interceptor have entered service with Russian units, such as the 54 IAP operational training regiment.

Specification: Sukhoi Su-30
Powerplant: two 122.58-kN (27,557-lb) NPO Saturn (Lyul'ka) AL-31F afterburning turbofans
Dimensions: wing span 14.70 m (48 ft 2¾ in); length 21.935 m (71 ft 11½ in) excluding probe; height 6.36 m (20 ft 10¼ in)
Weights: empty 17700 kg (39,021 lb); maximum take-off 33,500 kg (73,850 lb)
Performance: maximum level speed 2500 kmh (1,550 mph); service ceiling 17500 m (57,420 ft) combat radius 1500 km (932 miles) on a hi-hi-hi interception mission with four AAMs
Armament: one 30-mm GSh-30-1 cannon in starboard wingroot with 150 rounds; maximum ordnance 6000 kg (13,228 lb)

Sukhoi Su-32, Su-34 'Flanker'

With its long range and heavy load-carrying capability the Su-27 offered considerable potential as a tactical strike/attack aircraft, and as a replacement for the Su-24. The **Su-27IB** fighter bomber began life as a carrier-based trainer aircraft for Su-27K pilots, initially designated **Su-27KU** or **Su-27KM-2**. By the time the prototype was rolled out, the slimmed down carrier programme had removed the need for a dedicated trainer, and the aircraft was redesigned as a fighter-bomber under the new designation Su-27IB. It first flew on 13 April 1990. The aircraft combined canard foreplanes with a new forward fuselage accommodating a side-by-side two-seat cockpit, with a titanium armoured cockpit, armoured glass, and three large CRT displays. The broad, flat, 'duck-nose' led to the Su-27IB's unofficial '**Platypus**' nickname, and accommodated a new Leninetz B-004 multi-function radar with a fixed phased array antenna. The intakes were redesigned for higher low-level speeds.

The prototype was followed by four aircraft built to the planned production standard, with twin-wheel main undercarriage bogies, and a raised, thickened tailsting housing a rearward-looking tail warning radar. The first of these productionised Su-27IBs (designated **Su-34**s by the OKB) flew on

The Sukhoi Su-32FN is a long-range maritime attack aircraft developed from the original Su-27IB. It exists only as a single demonstrator aircraft.

Sukhoi has developed several versions of the original two-seat Su-27IB which are all largely identical. These include the Su-32FN and the Su-34.

18 December 1993. For long range missions the aircraft had a lavatory and a galley, with room for the crew to stand upright or lie prone between the seats, A retractable IFR probe was also provided, together with ejection seats incorporating a 'back massage' function.

Development of the Su-27IB has been slow, due to funding and technical problems, and the planned in-service date of 1998 slipped by virtually unnoticed. There is still an aspiration for the Su-27IB to replace all Russian air forces' Su-24s (although not by 2005 as once announced). The programme is progressing slowly, and has not been cancelled. Production Su-27IBs are expected to use more powerful 175-kN (39,240-lb) Saturn AL-41F engines.

The aircraft was marketed as a dedicated maritime attack aircraft under the designation **Su-32FN** (using the third pre-production Su-27IB as a demonstrator), and as a multi-role export aircraft as the **Su-32MF**.

The basic side-by-side Su-27IB airframe now forms the basis of the **Su-33UB** (or **Su-27KUB**) carrier trainer, an **Su-30-2** long range interceptor, and as yet undesignated recce and EW variants. The prototype Su-27KUB trainer made its maiden flight on 29 April 1999.

Specification: Sukhoi Su-27IB
Powerplant: Two 130.43-kN (29,320-lb) Lyul'ka AL-31FM (AL-35F) turbofans
Dimensions: wing span 14.70 m (48 ft 2¾ in); length 23.335 m (76 ft 6¾ in) excluding probe; height 6.5 m (21 ft 4 in)
Weights: maximum take-off 45100 kg (99,428 lb)
Performance: maximum level speed 'clean' at 11000 m (36,090 ft) 1,900 kmh (1,180 mph) and at sea level 1,400 kmh (870 mph); service ceiling 19800 m (65,000 ft); combat radius 1,113 km (691 miles) on a hi-hi-hi mission
Armament: One 30-mm GSh-30-1 cannon, maximum ordnance 8000 kg (17,636 lb)

Sukhoi Su-35 'Flanker'

Russia
Super-manoeuvrable combat aircraft

The **Su-27M 'Flanker'** was designed to meet the same Frontal Aviation requirement that spawned the MiG-29M, for a multi-role tactical fighter to replace existing first-generation MiG-29s. Based on the existing Su-27 airframe, the Su-27M had a higher proportion of carbon fibre composites and aluminium-lithium alloys in its airframe and had minor airframe improvements, including a re-profiled forward fuselage and (on most aircraft) twin nosewheels and taller, square-topped tailfins with integral fuel tanks.

More obviously, the aircraft had canard fore-planes and a new quadruplex digital FBW control system (though the early prototypes retained the original analogue system). Canards were first used on the proof-of-concept **T-10-24** (first flown during 1982) and on the navalised, carrierborne Su-27K (later re-designated Su-33). The carrierborne 'Flanker' also featured folding wings and tailplanes, strengthened undercarriage and an arrester hook, but retained the original FBW control system and weapons system of the basic Su-27. The new Su-27M, by contrast, had new multi-role avionics, an advanced glass cockpit, new defensive systems and an N011 Zhuk radar. The first of six prototypes made its maiden flight on 28 June 1988.

The aircraft was re-designated as the **Su-35** by the Design Bureau in the early 1990s. Although the type was once expected to enter service from 1995. Despite marketing it to a number of potential

The key to the Su-37's performance is its thrust-vectoring AL-37FU engines, that give it a truly unique combat manoeuvring capability

customers Sukhoi has received no orders for the Su-35. Attention has now largely switched to Su-27 upgrades, and to the thrust-vectoring **Su-37**.

The first Su-37 was the penultimate aircraft of six planned pre-production Su-27Ms, modified before delivery with a pair of thrust-vectoring Saturn/Lyulka AL-31FU engines, and a revised flight control system, with a sidestick controller and new throttle/nozzle control lever. It first flew (with nozzles locked) on 2 April 1996, and was joined by a second aircraft in mid-1998.

The decision was soon taken to abandon the non-thrust vectoring Su-35 and to concentrate on the Su-37, whose planned production version may have used the designation **Su-37MR**. The new variant was to feature further improved avionics, including a new N011M radar with a fixed phased array antenna. The Su-37MR was expected to enter service with the two-dimensional thrust-vectoring, AL-37FP engine, or the AL-37FU. A three-dimensional thrust-vectoring AL-37PP engine is reportedly under development.

This is one of Sukhoi's Su-35 demonstrator aircraft, produced in the early 1990s. The Su-35 has since been overtaken by the even more advanced Su-37.

Specification: Sukhoi Su-37
Powerplant: two 142.2-kN (31,970-lb) thrust-vectoring Saturn/Lyulka AL-37FU turbofans
Dimensions: wing span 15.16 m (49 ft 9 in); length 22.185 m (72 ft 9½ in) excluding probe; height 6.36 m (20 ft 10¼ in)
Weights: empty 17000 kg (37,479 lb); maximum take-off 34000 kg (74,957 lb)
Performance: maximum level speed 'clean' at sea level 1400 kmh (870 miles); maximum rate of climb at sea level 13800 m (45,275 ft) per minute; service ceiling 18800 m (61,680 ft); range 3300 km (2,050 miles) on a hi-hi-hi interception mission with four AAMs
Armament: GSh-30-1 cannon with 150 rounds; maximum ordnance 8,200 kg (18,077 lb)

Transall C.160

The Franco-German **Transall C.160** was originally conceived as a Nord Noratlas replacement and was one of the first successful joint European aerospace ventures. Of similar configuration to the C-130 Hercules, albeit rather smaller and powered by a pair of Rolls Royce Tynes, the Transall is robust, reliable and enjoys excellent performance characteristics. Initial procurement comprised 50 **C.160F** aircraft for France and 110 **C.160D** aircraft for West Germany. The first of three prototypes made its maiden flight on 25 February 1963. Production-configured C.160s were delivered from 1967-72. Exports comprised nine **C.160Z**s for South Africa (now retired) and 20 **C.160T**s (former Luftwaffe C.160Ds) for Turkey.

The production line was reopened in France in the late 1970s. The Armée de l'Air ordered 29 **C.160NG (Nouvelle Génération)** aircraft which introduced additional fuel capacity, improved avionics and an IFR probe above the cockpit. Maximum payload is 16000 kg (35,275 lb), while 93 troops or 88 paratroops can be accommodated. Ten aircraft were completed with a hose-and-drum air-to-air tanking system in the port undercarriage sponson for refuelling tactical aircraft, and five more have provision for this feature so that they can be rapidly

France has converted some C.160NGs to act has supplemental air-to-air tankers. These Transalls carry a HDU in a modified undercarriage fairing.

The C.160G is the only tactical transport aircraft in service with the Luftwaffe. They will be replaced by the Airbus A400M airlifter now under development.

re-roled as tankers. France's 77 C.160s serve in the transport role with four transport squadrons, various test units and overseas detachments. The French Transall fleet underwent an upgrade to **C.160 Rénové** standards from 1993, gaining a multi-screen EFIS cockpit, a HUD and a new integrated defensive suite.

France operates six NG-standard aircraft that have been assigned to two forms of special duties. Two have been converted to **C.160 GABRIEL (C.160G)** Elint and jamming configuration and these entered service with EE54 'Dunkerque' in 1988. They are distinguished by wingtip pods with blade antennas, five fuselage blade antennas, a blister fairing on each side of the rear fuselage and a retractable ventral dome. Both retain IFR probes and HDUs.

Four C.160NGs were were converted to **C.160H ASTARTE** standards, being adapted to carry TACAMO VLF radio transmission equipment (also used by the US Navy's Boeing E-6A). This takes the form of a long trailing-wire aerial which enables underwater communication with the ballistic missile-armed nuclear submarines of the Force Océanique Stratégique. The ASTARTE entered service in January 1988.

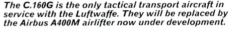

Specification: Transall C.160F/G
Powerplant: two 4548-kW (6,100-hp) Rolls-Royce Tyne RTy.20 Mk 22 turboprops
Dimensions: wing span 40.00 m (131 ft 3 in); length 32.40 m (106 ft 3½ in); height 11.65 m (38 ft 5 in)
Weights: empty equipped 28758 kg (63,400 lb); maximum take-off 49100 kg (108,245 lb); maximum payload 16000 kg (35,273 lb)
Performance: maximum level speed 536 kmh (333 mph); maximum rate of climb at sea level 440 m (1,444 ft) per minute; service ceiling 8500 m (27,885 ft); take-off distance to 10.7 m (35 ft) 1100 m (3,609 ft); landing distance from 15 m (50 ft) 640 m (2,100 ft); range 4500 km (2,796 miles) with an 8000-kg (17,637-lb) load

Tupolev Tu-22M 'Backfire'

Development of the **Tu-22M** began in 1962, concurrently with the variable-geometry Su-17 programme (with which it shared a very similar wing planform). The first of about nine **Tu-22M-0** prototypes made its maiden flight on 30 August 1969. Nine pre-production **Tu-22M-1**s were used for test and evaluation, and the first of 211 production **Tu-22M-2 'Backfire-B'** bombers made its first flight in 1975. This introduced a longer-span wing, a redesigned forward fuselage for four crew and a revised undercarriage, retracting inwards. The tail armament was increased to two remotely-controlled NR-23 23-mm cannons, controlled by the new 'Fan Tail' radar.

Initially, Tu-22Ms were usually seen carrying a single AS-4 'Kitchen' ASM on the centreline, semi-recessed, but today a more usual load seems to be two underwing missiles. In the later **Tu-22M-3 'Backfire-C'**, these bays can accommodate the rotary launchers for the RKV-500B (AS-16 'Kick-back') short-range attack missile, used mainly for defence suppression, with two more of these missiles under each wing. Defensive armament is reduced to a single cannon.

The new variant also introduced completely new wedge-type engine intakes, a recontoured upturned nose possibly housing a new attack radar and TFR. 'Backfire-C' is believed to have entered service during 1985, and 268 were built at Kazan. A **Tu-245** upgrade configuration is planned, with new

The final production version of the Tu-22M was the Tu-22M3 'Backfire-C' which introduced the improved NK-25 engine and superior weapons.

radar and avionics. A handful of **Tu-22MP** EW/escort jammers were produced but are not believed to have entered service, although 12 **Tu-22MR** recce aircraft with Shompol SLAR are in service with the AV-MF. Production continued at a rate of 30 per year until 1992, when about 497 had been completed.

With its wings fully swept back (to 65°), the Tu-22M is capable of a Mach 2 dash at high altitude, and of speeds up to Mach 0.9 at low level. Unrefuelled combat radius of the Tu-22M-2 'Backfire-B' is quoted as 4000 km (2,485 miles), and the radius of action of 'Backfire-C' may be even better. The Tu-22M continues to play a vital role in the Russian air forces (with 68 in use), and with Russian naval aviation (82 in service), and between 54 and 70 more are in service in the Ukraine. The Tu-22M-3 has been offered for export on several occasions, with customers such as Iran, Libya and Syria all expressing an interest. India is understood to have agreed a leasing deal with Russia for the supply of Tu-22M3s.

The 'Backfire' gives Russia an important theatre heavy-bombing and strike capability, in addition to its maritime attack role.

Specification: Tupolev Tu-22M-2 'Backfire-B'
Powerplant: two 196.13-kN (44,092-lb) KKBM (Kuznetsov) NK-22 turbofans
Dimensions: wing span 34.30 m (112 ft 6½ in) spread and 23.40 m (76 ft 9¼ in) swept; length 39.60 m (129 ft 11 in); height 10.80 m (35 ft 5¼ in)
Weights: basic empty 54000 kg (119,048 lb); maximum take-off 130000 kg (286,596 lb)
Performance: maximum level speed 2125 kmh (1,320 mph); service ceiling 18000 m (59,055 ft); ferry range 12000 km (7,457 miles); combat radius 2,159 nm (4000 km; 2,486 miles)
Armament: one GSh-23 23-mm cannon in tail turret; normal load 12000 kg (26,455 lb)

Tupolev Tu-95, Tu-142 'Bear'

The first **Tu-95/1** prototype of Tupolev's extraordinary **'Bear'** made its maiden flight on 12 November 1952. The swept-wing bomber had unheard of performance for a turboprop-powered aircraft. All of the early variants have now been retired, including the original **Tu-95** and **Tu-95M** **'Bear-A'** free-fall nuclear bombers (some of them converted as **Tu-95U** trainers). Various missile-carrying variants have also been retired, including the **Tu-95K-20**, and the refuelling-probe equipped **Tu-95KD 'Bear-B'**, and the **Tu-95KM 'Bear-C'** with an ECM tailcone. These variants had a broad under-nose radome housing 'Crown Drum' guidance radar and carried AS-3 'Kangaroo' missiles. The **Tu-95K-22 'Bear-G'** was externally similar but had a new 'Down Beat' radar and K-22 (NATO AS-4 'Kitchen') missiles. The AV-MF's **Tu-95RT 'Bear-D'** mid-course missile guidance/maritime radar recce platform has also been withdrawn, along with the long-range reconnaissance **Tu-95R 'Bear-Es'**.

The dedicated maritime reconnaissance/ASW **Tu-142 'Bear-F'** incorporated several significant improvements, including a strengthened wing, a redesigned undercarriage, a fuselage plug, uprated NK-12MV engines and redesigned weapons bays. Four sub-variants had detail differences, but most

The 'Bear-F' is the most up-to-date of the 'Bear' maritime reconnaissance variants and it uses the modernised and improved Tu-142 airframe.

For many years the Tu-95R was the most commonly encountered version of the 'Bear', as it routinely shadowed Western naval forces.

had a new cockpit with a raised roofline, and featured a new ventral radome housing a maritime search radar. About 55 **'Bear-Fs'** remain in AV-MF (Russian naval aviation) service.

The sole export customer was the Indian Navy, which received eight **Tu-142M**s. The **Tu-142M** **'Bear-F'** also formed the basis of the **Tu-142MR** **'Bear-J'** communications relay variant, which had an underfuselage trailing wire antenna pod but no search radar. A total of 24 of these aircraft are in service.

The 'Bear' production line re-opened in 1983 to build 33 **Tu-95MS-6 'Bear-H'** strategic bombers. This version was developed specifically to carry the new RK-55 (AS-15 'Kent') cruise missile. This was based on a shortened version of the Tu-142 airframe, but with a deeper, shorter radome and a new weapons bay accommodating a rotary launcher for six RK-55 missiles. Some 56 later aircraft (known as **Tu-95MS-16**s) carry an additional 10 RK-55s on underwing pylons, but these pylons were removed to comply with the provisions of the SALT and START treaties. The Tu-95MS remains in service with Kazakhstan (six aircraft) and Russia (68 deployed, 64 declared as missile carriers), but Ukraine's aircraft are being scrapped.

Specification: Tupolev Tu-142M 'Bear-F Mod 3'
Powerplant: four 11033-kW (14,795-hp) KKBM (Kuznetsov) NK-12MV turboprops
Dimensions: wing span 51.10 m (167 ft 7¾ in); length 47.50 m (155 ft 10 in) excluding IFR probe and 49.50 m (162 ft 4.8 in) including IFR probe; height 12.12 m (39 ft 9.2 in)
Weights: empty equipped 86000 kg (189,594 lb); maximum take-off 185000 kg (407,848 lb)
Performance: maximum level speed 925 kmh (575 mph); climb to 5000 m (16,405 ft) in 13 minutes; service ceiling 12000 m (39,370 ft); combat radius 6400 km (3,977 miles)
Armament: twin NR-23 23-mm cannon in tail turret; maximum ordnance 11340 kg (25,000 lb)

Tupolev Tu-160 'Blackjack'

Long-range bomber, cruise missile carrier

The **Tu-160 'Blackjack'** is the world's largest bomber, and is the heaviest combat aircraft ever built. The Tu-160 was heavily influenced by the Rockwell B-1A, designed to penetrate at high level, relying on performance and a highly sophisticated ECM suite to get through hostile defences. The B-1A was cancelled, and then subsequently resurrected as the B-1B, relying on low-level subsonic flight and reduced RCS to penetrate. The Tu-160 remains committed to both low-level transonic penetration and high-level supersonic penetration, however. The aircraft is a dedicated cruise missile carrier, with two tandem fuselage weapons bays each containing a rotary carousel for six RK-55 (AS-15 'Kent') cruise missiles (with 200-kT warhead and a range in excess of 3000 km), 12 Kh-15P (AS-16 'Kickback') 'SRAMskis' or free-fall bombs

The Tu-160's variable-geometry wing and full-span leading-edge slats and trailing-edge double-slotted flaps confer a useful combination of benign low-speed handling and high supersonic speed. Its cockpit is equipped with fighter-type control columns and conventional analog instrument displays, with no MFDs, CRTs and no HUD. The long pointed radome houses a TFR, with a fairing below for the forward-looking TV camera used for visual weapon aiming. A retractable IFR probe endows intercontinental range.

The development programme of the Tu-160 was extremely protracted. Following a first flight on 19

The Tu-160 clearly shares a common design 'inspiration' with the Rockwell B-1, but it is a far larger aircraft – built in far fewer numbers.

December 1981, series production eventually began at Kazan in 1986 and continued until termination in January 1992. One incomplete aircraft was later finished and delivered in 2000. Even after the aircraft entered service, problems continued to severely restrict operations. These included a shortage of basic flying equipment, problems with the aircraft's K-36A ejection seats and poor reliability of engines and systems.

Between 32 and 39 Tu-160s have been built, including prototypes, about four of which are now derelict at Zhukhovskii. Nineteen Tu-160s were delivered to the 184th Heavy Bomber Regiment at Priluki from 1987. These were left under Ukrainian command after the break-up of the USSR, but eight were later transferred back to Russian control and the remainder were scrapped (or, in the case of three aircraft, demilitarised as commercial satellite launch platforms). Six newer aircraft went to Engels, which had been intended to be the first Tu-160 base, where they were joined by the eight ex-Ukrainian aircraft in 2001.

The small numbers of Tu-160s available to the Russian air force restricts the bomber's effectiveness, but it is still a formidable warplane.

Specification: Tupolev Tu-160 'Blackjack-A'
Powerplant: four 245.16-kN (55,115-lb) SSPE Trud (Kuznetsov) NK-321 turbojets
Dimensions: wing span 55.70 m (182 ft 9 in) spread and 35.60 m (116 ft 9.75 in) swept; length 54.10 m (177 ft 6 in); height 13.10 m (43 ft 0 in)
Weights: empty equipped 118000 kg (260,140 lb); maximum take-off 275000 kg (606,261 lb)
Performance: maximum level speed 'clean' at 11000 m (36,090 ft) 2000 kmh (1,243 mph); range 14000 km (8,699 miles)
Armament: maximum ordnance load about 16330 kg (36,000 lb) in two tandem fuselage weapons bays.

Westland Lynx

Anti-tank, battlefield utility, naval ASW and ASuV helicopter

Launched under the Anglo-French helicopter agreement of February 1967, the Westland **Lynx** is an extremely versatile and agile helicopter with digital flight controls and a four-bladed semi-rigid main rotor. The first prototype flew on 21 March 1971. The production **Lynx HAS.Mk 2** undertook a range of shipboard missions including ASW, SAR, ASV search and strike, reconnaissance, troop transport, and VertRep duties. The **HAS.Mk 3** introduced Gem 41-1 turboshafts, and subsequent upgrades included the **HAS.Mk 3S** with secure speech facility, the **HAS.Mk 3ICE** for use aboard the Antarctic survey vessel *Endurance*, the **HAS.Mk 3CTS** with a new central tactical system and the **HAS.Mk 3GM** with improved cooling, IR jammers and ALQ-167 ECM pods. Foreign customers for the first-generation naval Lynx were Argentina, Brazil, Denmark, France, Germany, the Netherlands, Nigeria and Norway.

The second-generation Lynx introduced new composite rotor blades with swept 'BERP' high-speed tips, which were fitted to new-build **Super Lynx**es delivered to Brazil, South Korea and Portugal. These aircraft also had a new 360° undernose radar and some had provision for a nose-mounted FLIR. The new rotor was also a feature of

The German navy's newest Mk 88 Super Lynxes are fitted with the Sea Spray 3000 radar, FLIR, AQS-18 dipping sonar and Sea Skua missiles.

The Lynx HAS.Mk 3 is the Royal Navy's primary light anti-submarine and shipboard anti-surface helicopter. It is being replaced by the HMA.Mk 8.

the Royal Navy **Lynx HAS.Mk 8**, produced by conversion of surviving HAS.Mk 3s. This variant also introduced an undernose radome, a nose-mounted thermal imager turret, a rear-mounted MAD, Orange Crop ESM and a Yellow Veil ECM jamming pod.

The Army Lynx had a skid undercarriage, and was ordered by the UK Army Air Corps as the **Lynx AH.Mk 1**. The only export customer was the Qatar Police. Able to carry 12 troops or 907 kg (2,000 lb) of internal freight, most AAC Lynxes were modified with roof-mounted sights and provision for eight TOW anti-tank missiles. Most were subsequently converted to **Lynx AH.Mk 7** standards (also produced in small numbers as a new-build aircraft), with a reverse-direction tail rotor, uprated Gem 41 engines and a box-like IR exhaust shroud. The Lynx **AH.Mk 9** (offered for export as the **Battlefield Lynx**) incorporated all the AH.Mk 7 modifications and also introduced a new nosewheel undercarriage. The first new-build example flew on 20 July 1990.

Westland is now offering a **Super Lynx 200** configuration, with LHTEC CTS800-4N turboshafts, and a Super Lynx 300 with T800 engines, an EFIS cockpit, and advanced avionics. The latter version was ordered by Malaysia and South Africa.

Specification: Westland Lynx AH.Mk 7
Powerplant: two 846-kW (1,135-hp) Rolls-Royce Gem 42-1 turboshafts
Dimensions: main rotor diameter 12.80 m (42 ft); length overall, rotors turning 49 ft 9 in (15.16 m); height overall 12 ft (3.73 m) with rotors stationary
Weights: operating empty 3072 kg (6,772 lb) in the anti-tank role; maximum take-off 4876 kg (10,750 lb); maximum payload 3,000 lb (1361 kg)
Performance: maximum continuous cruising speed 256 kmh (159 mph); maximum rate of climb at sea level 756 m (2,480 ft) per minute; hovering ceiling 3230 m (10,600 ft); combat radius 46 km (29 miles) for a 2-hour patrol
Armament: 550 kg (1,210 lb) of ordnance

Westland Sea King

Four Sikorsky-built S-61s were shipped to Westland in 1966 as pattern aircraft for the Royal Navy's licence-produced **Sea King HAS.Mk 1**. Flying on 7 May 1969, it had British avionics and ASW systems, including search radar, sonar, Doppler and bathythermographic equipment, and AFCS. Weapons included Mk 44 torpedoes, Mk 11 depth charges or a WE177 nuclear depth bomb. The 56 RN HAS.Mk 1s were followed by 21 **HAS.Mk 2**s (and 37 conversions) with uprated engines, six-bladed tail rotors and intake deflector/filters. The withdrawal of HMS *Ark Royal* left the Royal Navy without shipborne AEW cover, and nine HAS.Mk 2s were converted to **Sea King AEW.Mk 2** standards, with a Searchwater radar with a retractable radome in an inflatable radome. Three similar AEW radar systems were sold to Spain for the conversion of three US-built Spanish navy SH-3H Sea Kings. The surviving AEW Sea Kings are now being upgraded to **AEW.Mk 7** standard, with a new pulse-Doppler multi-mode radar, new mission computer, JTIDS and IFF.

The Sea King **HAS.Mk 5** (85 produced, some 55 by conversion of HAS.Mk 2s) featured Sea Searcher radar, improved processing and Orange Crop ESM. The **HAS.Mk 6** has an integrated sonar processor, deep water dipping sonar, and Orange Reaper ESM. Five new-build HAS.Mk 6s followed the prototype (a converted HAS.Mk 5) and 69 conversion kits were supplied to RNAY Fleetlands.

The Royal Navy (and Royal Marines) rely on the Sea King HC.Mk 4, better known as the Commando, as its primary assault transport.

The similar **Advanced Sea King** was developed specifically for export, India buying 12 Sea Eagle-compatible **Sea King Mk 42B**s and six SAR-configured **Sea King Mk 42**Cs.

About half a dozen Royal Navy HAS.Mk 5s were stripped of ASW equipment for use in the SAR role as **HAR.Mk 5**s, while 19 dedicated Sea King **HAR.Mk 3** SAR aircraft were delivered to the RAF. Six more **HAR.Mk 3A**s were ordered in February 1992, equipped to an even higher standard, with a new radar, a new AFCS and improved nav systems and radios. ASW and SAR Sea Kings were exported to Australia, Belgium, Egypt, Germany, India, Norway, and Pakistan.

Development of an assault/tactical transport Sea King began in mid-1971, resulting in the **Westland Commando**. No interest was initially expressed by the UK, but Egypt and Qatar placed orders. RN interest began in 1978, as a replacement for the Wessex. Forty-one **Commando HC.Mk 4**s were procured for the RN. Two similar **Sea King Mk 4X**s were built for the RAE as test aircraft.

The Sea King HAS.Mk 6 is the Fleet Air Arm's primary anti-submarine helicopter. The Sea King is finally being replaced by the EH Industries Merlin.

Specification: Sea King HAS.Mk 6
Powerplant: two 1238-kW (1,660-hp) Rolls-Royce Gnome H.1400-1T turboshafts
Dimensions: main rotor diameter 18.90 m (62 ft); length overall, rotors turning 22.15 m (72 ft 8 in), fuselage 17.02 m (55 ft 10 in); height overall 5.13 m (16 ft 10 in) with rotors turning
Weights: empty equipped 7428 kg (16,377 lb); maximum take-off 9752 kg (21,500 lb)
Performance: maximum cruising speed 204 kmh (126 mph); maximum rate of climb at sea level 619 m (2,030 ft) per minute; range 1482 km (921 miles)
Armament: maximum ordnance 1134 kg (2,500 lb)